THE SHAKESPEARE SONNET ORDER

THE
SHAKESPEARE
SONNET ORDER: POEMS
AND GROUPS

BRENTS STIRLING

UNIVERSITY OF CALIFORNIA PRESS
BERKELEY AND LOS ANGELES

1968

University of California Press
Berkeley and Los Angeles, California

Cambridge University Press
London, England

Copyright © 1968, by
The Regents of the University of California

Library of Congress Catalog Card Number: 68–14332
Designed by Pamela F. Johnson
Printed in the United States of America

To "T. T." AND "MR. W. H."

T. T. (THOMAS THORPE) published the Sonnets in 1609, naming W. H. (identity unknown) as their "onlie begetter." Of Thorpe's publishing venture, the most favorable judgment we can make is that no one, least of all Shakespeare, appears to have authorized it. As for W. H.'s role, we can only guess whether he "begot" the Sonnets by inspiring them or by procuring them in manuscript for Thorpe's use. Beyond these uncertainties are the chances that Thorpe was guilty of piracy, W. H. of something close to theft.

Yet in raising these questions we sometimes forget to ask another: had it not been for T. T. and W. H., would there be any text of the Sonnets?

ACKNOWLEDGMENTS

PARTS of Chapter II have appeared as four published essays: "A Shakespeare Sonnet Group," *PMLA*, LXXV (1960), 340–349; "More Shakespeare Sonnet Groups," in *Essays on Shakespeare . . . in Honor of Hardin Craig* (Columbia, Mo., 1962), pp. 115–135; "Sonnets 109–126," *Centennial Review*, VIII (1964), 109–120; "Sonnets 127–154," in *Shakespeare 1564–1964* (Providence, R.I., 1964), pp. 134–153. I am grateful to publishers of these essays for permission to reprint them in substance. Although the presentation here may differ extensively, and the conclusions slightly, from those of earlier publication, I remain indebted to editors or readers of these journals and essay collections for valuable criticism. I wish to thank especially Professors Richard Hosley of the University of Arizona and Samuel Schoenbaum of Northwestern University.

And, as usual, for almost endless work on the manuscript as it went through one draft after another, my debt is to my wife, Alice Stirling.

 # CONTENTS

TABLE FOR LOCATING SONNETS IN THIS EDITION

Sonnets are listed here consecutively by their standard numbers,
those of the 1609 edition. A reader may find any sonnet by turning
to the page or pages opposite the sonnet's number.

# INTRODUCTION

ANYONE familiar with Hyder Rollins' commentary in the Variorum edition knows that rearrangement of Shakespeare's Sonnets is a disreputable calling. Rollins did not comment at length. Rather, by digest and quotation, he allowed rearrangers an opportunity to confound themselves; and with few exceptions, such as Tucker Brooke, they did so. As a result, tampering with the sonnet order, once a perennial enterprise, has all but disappeared. Why, then, resume the mischief? For one thing, because Thorpe's pirated or at least unauthorized 1609 text is a bad one. To rely on its sequence, except when the sonnet arrangement justifies itself, is a decision of convenience, of pragmatic 'necessity.' Since the Quarto—'Q' as most editors call it—is our only text, and since its doubtful sonnet order survives after more than a century of attempted revision, it remains 'virtually' authentic, supported by a defensive presumption in its favor. But a presumption of this kind, as Rollins plainly noted,[1] has nothing to do with authenticity, a fact that no amount of equivocation or reticence will change.

At the same time, Thorpe's Quarto has a kind of integrity. Its faults appear openly, and its sounder elements set a standard for correction. I base my editorial venture on principles derived from the 1609 text itself, which are fully explained in Chapter I. First, in example after example, Q gives us authentic 'runs' that establish a norm of cogency, a tight interconnection between sonnets, accurately though not too happily described as 'intensive linkage.' In many short runs—pairs, threes, fours, sixes—the sonnet order is plainly authentic. In many longer runs intensive linkage disappears and reappears, but a thematic logic remains, a logic implying that although the actual sonnet order may be in doubt, sonnet grouping based on close relevance is still evident. Yet these elements of coherent sequence are by no means continuous; in Q, as any reader knows, non sequitur—usually bland or dull, occasionally silly, sometimes surreal—continually interrupts, amuses, confounds.

Such observations about the 1609 text are not, of course, new or even controversial. But I suggest that we take them seriously, that we pay less respectful attention to norms of 'loose connection' in other sonnet sequences (which may or may not be in the right order) and attend more to Shakespeare's cogency where Q preserves it; that we entertain a simple question: did the poet who habitually linked sonnets in highly coherent though limited runs, lapse repeatedly, perversely, into incoherence? To avoid confusion of this question with one often asked rhetorically, I have been careful of its wording. It does not ask whether Shakespeare as a writer of sonnets simply dealt with a variety of subjects, changing from one to another; it asks instead whether he was prone to choose a subject, pursue it, lose it, find it, lose it again, and often complete it at some distant point—all the while maintaining a complex linkage that would serve to unite fragments closely, were their sequence not continually disturbed.

Chapter I allows a reader to answer this question with evidence from the text itself. If his answer happens to be that among other indignities Shakespeare endured in 1609, Thorpe's fragmentation of unified sonnet groups could not have been the least, then we are in substantial agreement.

Yet, in a traditional view of the matter, our troubles have just begun. To any rearranger it seems that the original sonnet order can be retrieved, especially since mere removal of intrusive elements from a series often restores connection. But here, whether aware of it or not, he meets the supposed impasse. A teasing loose affinity found at large among the Sonnets implies one restored order, then another, and another. Thus restoration, apparently so near at hand, becomes more remote with each easy solution. Here, then, is the familiar pons asinorum. The rearranger must perceive it and cross it. Whether I have done so remains, of course, to be seen. Toward the end of Chapter I, I adopt a principle based on the plainly authentic runs in Q, sequences in which interconnection turns out to be multiple: thematic, consecutively logical, and marked by recurring metaphor or phrase. Hence, under one standard established by Q itself, a misplaced or doubtfully placed sonnet may be relocated only if multiple linkage appears at the new point of connection. Such a condition, a strict one, at least makes selective relocation possible by eliminating the 'easy' alternatives.

Nor is this the only condition Q imposes. Movement of a sonnet usually involves in some way another sonnet or group of sonnets, and thus must be tested by its 'consequences.' Further, since Q was printed from a manuscript, any disorder we find in the 1609 text implies a manuscript form capable of disarrangement in a definite manner. So in addition to the standard of linkage involved, there are various other 'factors' present in any change of sequence. If all factors are independent of one another (not redundant) and if they all agree in supporting a given change of order, then perhaps they identify that order as the authentic sequence among several possibilities. Such is the 'multiple-factor' test which governs relocation of sonnets in this edition. It will scarcely solve all the problems, but by limiting the field of choice it can distinguish at least between responsible and irresponsible alternatives. Had a test of this kind been used consistently, revisers of the 1609 text would have established a very different history and tradition.

In Chapter I, I describe the problems one must meet, and give a reader the chance to sample a few typical attempts at solution. There he is referred to parts of Chapter II, the "Text and Commentary," where the Sonnets themselves appear with running discussion of their interconnection, whether it is new—part of a rearrangement—or old—simply a retention of the Q order. Thus after considering Chapter I, a reader can decide whether he wants to continue. If he does, Chapter II will spare him the hazard of reading commentary apart from the text, for there the Sonnets are printed with discussion, addressed to sequence, on adjacent pages. Using this commentary, a reader may turn it into a first-hand experience with the sonnets in question; and they are at hand for him to consider without forward or backward thumbing or the necessity of using two texts in order to bring separated fragments together for comparison.

Finally, after this experience with the primary evidence, with elements of the text itself, a reader will find in Chapter III, "Verification," several efforts to put qualitative judgment to an objective test. Naturally, subjective impressions must underlie any disposition of the Sonnets, but we can test these impressions to a degree that proves surprising. Without pretending to be scientific, we can invoke 'controls'—if we mean by 'control' the judging of a conclusion by all of its implications. Taken together, such implications can amount to a nonsubjective body of fact, a world of 'other' that reassures, verifies, simply because it is beautifully intractable.

After so describing what I have tried to do, perhaps I should let readers know what not to expect of this book. In the first place, there being no lack of good conventional editions, I make no attempt to reproduce the standard information they contain. To combine the revised text with a conventional text, and the evidence for revision with conventional notes, would serve no end but confusion. Since the problem of sequence is both extensive and demanding, I seldom comment on any other question. Naturally, if a sonnet's disputed meaning or the accuracy of Q's printing relates to the problem of order, I discuss the matter, but otherwise I assume easy access by most readers to the glossary and notes of the Variorum or some other source of general information. I attempt an accurately worded and punctuated printing of every line in the Sonnets, but I do not render original spelling or punctuation, or systematically note Q's misprints except, again, where such matters affect the question of sequence. When they do so, I believe that comparison, on the spot, of a modernized text with the original is the best procedure. Indiscriminate reproduction of an archaic text can fail to emphasize the very points at which it becomes useful. Moreover, if a reader wishes to check the original text at any point, or perhaps at all points, should not his reference be to an actual original or, at least, to a photographic reproduction?

An editor no less than a critic must take his poet's artistry into account, but there is no room here to deal with imagery, diction, rhythm or structure aside from discussing, adequately I hope, the very large part these matters play in establishing sequence. Most questions of sequence are substantially questions of artistry, but if an editor tries to establish a probable sonnet order running counter to Q's arrangement, his claims become public and controversial. Hence the internal evidence he uses, although certainly the evidence of poetry itself, must come from elements of the poem which are public or 'evidential' in nature. The matter will be argumentative, and the 'counters,' the currency of argument, must have some kind of publicly agreed-on value. Fortunately, our confinement here to tangible evidence is hardly more reductive than the limitation imposed by other critical or editorial approaches. Shakespeare took sonnet interconnection seriously enough to use the full range of his talent in achieving it. And within limits that talent is publicly verifiable.

No evidence, I believe, will ever reconstruct the Sonnets as one long Poem or several long poems. The testimony of Q strongly favors discrete groups composed of short poems having a remarkable internal coherence. But the discrete groups will not turn out to be long and many poems within them, while closely related, may have no fixed sequence. Certain singles, pairs, or threes, moreover, will show no sign of belonging within a group or at any set point in a larger series.

Thus, although the Sonnets can be praised for narrative art of short extent, they tell no definable continued story. And above all, in spite of some recent 'discoveries'[2] (shall we call them 'rousing'?)—discoveries hardly new in the history of interpretation—the Sonnets as yet have no demonstrable reference to 'true' or historical happenings. 'Demonstrable' is, of course, the key word. None of us really knows who "dear-my-love" was; whether the rival poet was Marlowe or Chapman; whether the first seventeen sonnets address the young man addressed in 18–126; or, for that matter, whether any character in a sonnet, including the "woman colored ill," is real or fictional. Nothing in this edition helps to answer such questions and nothing in it depends on any of them being answered. Unlike some readers, I should like to have a few of the answers, but I doubt whether they would alter either the question of critical interpretation or the essential problem of sequence.

Strangely enough, the question of sonnet order has become identified with these confused riddles of continuous narrative and journalistic biography. Apologists for the 1609 text never seem to consider the alternative—restoration of noncontinuous poems and groups based on internal evidence of the kind I describe. An editor with this limited aim is not interested in constructing from the 154 sonnets a comprehensive poem, or even the usual two comprehensive poems. So his efforts are at least immune from the traditional objection (Wolff's) restated not long ago by Nejgebauer that attempts at rearrangement "must fail, since it is impossible to see in [the Sonnets] any sort of complete and logical plot" (*Shakespeare Survey*, XV (1962), 13). Anyone who bases a restored sonnet order on norms of linkage and grouping actually found in the 1609 text can ignore this familiar and reductive warning because its assumptions have nothing to do with what he attempts. He may overestimate his evidence, but he knows it will never lead him to a "complete and logical plot."

Yet after discarding such grand possibilities, the stakes remain high. Rewarding his patience, a reader may find here some new poems by Shakespeare—new in that the 1609 text has kept them from being read. If half of the poems I have tried to restore are genuine and some of the others substantially so, I shall have done what I have wanted very much to do.

No one will be surprised at this extension of earlier studies, for a reviser of the sonnet order seldom retreats to prepared lines of defense. Remembering this, I look for a skeptical reception and will welcome it if based on a fresh reading of the text and an understanding that Q has no external authority governing sequence. I ask only that an old question be reopened experimentally, and above all that the experiment be addressed to Shakespeare's own lines.

I shall attempt one more disarming statement. I have friends who want their Sonnets 'in the original.' They have no illusions about the validity of Q's order; yet on the whole they find the disorder attractive, or at least not unattractive, and in any event prefer to have a firsthand experience with the text. Above all, they choose to make their own associations. Apparently they respond to emenders of the 1609 sonnet order as most of us respond to people who correct Shakespeare's grammar or clutter his plays with stage directions. To reply—truly—that such meddling hardly resembles improvement of a bad text, or to point out that certain sonnets are almost unreadable until Q's text is corrected, somehow fails to reach the point. Readers who 'like the Sonnets as they are, thank you,' can account very well for their views. Witness R. P. Blackmur, with whose motives at least I agree.

In "A Poetics for Infatuation," Blackmur hopes there will never be "by some chance of scholarship, any more authoritative order for Shakespeare's sonnets than that so dubiously supplied by the 1609 Quarto." He continues:

It is rather like Pascal's *Pensées*, or, even better, like the *order* of the Psalms. . . . No one can improve upon the accidentally established order we possess; but everyone can invite himself to feel the constant interflow of new relations, of new reticulations—as if the inner order were always on the move—in the sonnets, the *Pensées*, the Psalms. Thus the vitality of fresh disorder enters the composition and finds room there with every reading, with every use and every abuse we make of them. Each time we look at a set of things together but do not count them, the sum of the impression will be different, though the received and accountable numerical order remains the same. If we complain of other people's perceptions, it is because we feel there is greater vitality in our own; and so on; we had better persist with the received order as a warrant that all of us have at least that point in common.[3]

Those who know the text of Thorpe's Quarto and the circumstances of its publication will agree with Blackmur that the sonnet order is "dubiously supplied" and "accidentally established." Yet anyone who knows what rearrangers can do will share or at least understand his wish to keep the sonnets as Thorpe gave them to us—to set up the doubtful Quarto as a defense against public mischief and as a point of departure, or return, for innocent mischief that has the tact to remain private.

At the same time, should a better sonnet order by chance appear, it is hard to see how the state of affairs Blackmur cherishes would suffer. Surely a more authentic sequence would not invite more meddling, except by the obsessed who are scarcely restrained by the present text. And surely, if the sonnet order were somehow restored, the private adventure of finding "new relations," "new reticulations" would not languish since it is just the adventure we continually have with the most authentic of texts. The text of *Lear* is fixed in its sequence of scenes and episodes; yet, to adapt Blackmur's phrasing, 'in reading *Lear*, each time we look at a set of things together but do not count them, the sum of impressions will be different, though the received and accountable order remains the same.' The more certain the text, the more genuine our pleasure from such an experience with it: if we were not convinced that the order of scenes in Lear is authentic, our enjoyment of their shifting interrelations would be a little pointless. As Blackmur himself implies in his defense of Q's order, variety and change of perspective are significant or interesting only if fundamental patterns remain fixed. But they can remain so only in an authentic text; a bad one (the 1609 sonnet order), accepted for want of a better, actually inhibits the pleasure of sensing "new relations, new reticulations" in a series of poems, for if we do not adequately know what the poems are, any discovery of protean magic in them becomes partly a dull game of 'let's pretend.' When Shakespeare tells us that custom can never stale Cleopatra's variety, he relies on our understanding that there *is* a Cleopatra who is somehow the same—'customary'—from day to day. From that understanding comes the wonder of her change.

In attempting a better text for the Sonnets, one owes much more to ironical skeptics like Hyder Rollins than to one's predecessors, the true believers. With few exceptions—Tucker Brooke, for example—rearrangers have contributed less to a revised text than to a distrust of any and all revision, a prejudice they innocently and persistently invited. Perhaps such comment comes with bad grace from one who tries to succeed where they have failed, but it tells a simple truth. As an editor, Brooke [4] enhanced a tradition that most emenders of the text had done their unwitting best to discredit, and if I were reticent about the difference between their work and his I should be doing him little justice. In disclaiming 'the rearrangers,' I can only invoke again Rollins' caustic and, for the most part, accurate judgments in the matter. But no agreement on my part with Rollins can possibly identify him with the course I have taken; for though he had little faith in the 1609 text, he had none, I am sure, in the possibility of a better one. Yet, as a true skeptic, Rollins never appeared unwilling to listen, and it is hard to imagine him indifferent to proposals based on a new standard of evidence. Indifference is a role not of questioners but of those who question and no longer stay for the possible answer. They are the ones who confuse doubt with its opposite, the cutting off of inquiry. So I may say that while a modern editor's debt is surely to the skeptical tradition, he can best repay the obligation by doubting the doubters in their latter-day role of virtual certainty.

By means of digests and tables in the Variorum edition, Rollins lists all rearrangements prior to 1938.[5] Comparison of these with my tabular rearrangement on pages 40–41 will show that my disposition of sonnets occasionally duplicates or approximates part of an earlier rearrangement, and is sometimes wholly new.[6] But this question of novelty, or 'priority,' is hardly to the point. Whether someone else has grouped sonnets as I do in 'Poem 5,' or whether no one has grouped them as I do in 'IV C' is not, in itself, pertinent. In the elaborate history of rearrangement dozens of sonnet combinations have been tried and a great many remain untried. But the essential question remains the same: what is the evidence? what is its nature, its range, its variety? what are its implications (the issue faced in Chapter III)? Who relocates a sonnet, or suggests its relocation (as editors who retain the Q order sometimes do), is a minor question that only serves to introduce the large one—for what reason or reasons? Thus merely to list other rearrangements in this edition would contribute little or nothing. To list them with the wide variety of argument used in their support would now and then be to the point but would clutter the text hopelessly. Fortunately, such information appears in the Variorum, fully tabulated and fully digested. So I include it here only when it serves some special purpose of clarity or interest.

A few elements of format and usage need to be explained. Standard double quotation marks enclose any word or short passage taken verbatim from a text, that is, the actual words of a sonnet or the actual words of someone's commentary. Single quotation marks enclose lines of 'imaginary' comment or statement, words or phrases used colloquially, and words or phrases used ironically. The distinction is especially useful in the commentary where actual quotation from the sonnets needs to be distinguished clearly from other matter in quoted form.

Italics in a quoted passage are not in the original text unless I indicate otherwise. Since italics serve frequently to clarify parallel words or phrases in different sonnets, this understanding will avoid excess repetition of 'my italics.'

Although the sonnet order here varies frequently from Q's order, the sonnet numbers appearing in Q remain unchanged. In my printed text of the Sonnets these are enclosed in brackets. I try to avoid the confusion of Brooke's edition in which his renumbering of sonnets to suit a changed order led to a double system, arabic and roman, to distinguish Q's order from his own. Hence in Brooke's text many of the sonnets bear two numbers. Readers who know the Sonnets know most of them by their Q numbers (although we can be fairly sure that Shakespeare did not); hence a change in numbering, or double numbering, becomes equivalent in discussion to a cipher language. I assume that changing the sonnet order will be sufficiently irritating in some quarters, and have no impulse to compound this irritation by changing the familiar numerical guidelines. If a reader knows the number of a sonnet in Q and wishes to find it in this edition, reference to the table on page x will give him the place at which it appears.

Although sonnets must be accompanied by their Q numbers, it should be remembered that no number is part of a sonnet in the sense that a title is part of a poem. Unless this is understood, a statement that sonnets 100–101 introduce 63–68 may seem quite astonishing. Or a notation that 20 intervenes between 19 and 21 may be amusing. What one means, of course, is that the sonnets found in Q as 100–101 originally introduced the sonnets found in Q as 63–68; or that the sonnets Q prints as 19 and 21 were joined in manuscript until a sonnet Q prints as 20 parted them. To lose sight of the distinction, even unconsciously, can translate commentary, for a few unsteady moments, into a mad numerology. On the other hand, to insist on the distinction, to refer continually to 20 as 'the sonnet Q numbers as 20' will outdo Polonius in his mad devotion to explicit logic. Inevitably, a time comes when language literally absurd but easy to understand must prevail over pinpointed jargon.

Reference to sonnets by number and line is standardized thus: a notation of 4.1 means sonnet 4, line 1; a notation of 4.6–9, 14 means sonnet 4, lines 6 through 9, and line 14.

The only unfamiliar device will be one that designates regrouped sonnets. For example, restored poem C of Group II (I shall explain the meaning of 'poem' and 'Group' later) is composed of four sonnets, the first appearing in Q as 61, the next two as 27 and 28, and the last as 43. One might represent II C thus: 61, 27–28, 43. But this usage, with its commas, would be confusing in a sentence having other punctuation. Hence, a more simplified representation: 61 27–28 43, which means 61, followed by 27–28, followed by 43. Or, if another example is needed, the designation of II J as 33–35 40–42 indicates its content as 33 through 35, followed by 40 through 42.

Part of Chapter III considers hypothetical manuscripts having sonnets in their presumed original order inscribed on consecutive leaves. I indicate the leaf division with a slash mark. Thus

61/27–28/43 will mean an original sequence with sonnet 61 on the first leaf, 27–28 on the second, and 43 on an end leaf.

Several recurrent terms should be defined and qualified. 'Run-on' is used to describe any close continuity of thought or phrase proceeding from one sonnet to another. Yet, since no sonnet ends with an incomplete sentence, the term will never have the meaning it carries in the standard phrase 'run-on line.' For a special kind of run-on, I use Brooke's term 'syntactical link.' But again, this never implies that a sentence continues from one sonnet to another; instead, it means that the statement beginning a sonnet has immediate reference to a statement just made in the preceding sonnet.

Naturally, in any attempt to reestablish sequence, such a term as 'restored sonnet order' must appear frequently. I assume that no false assurance will be read into it. The term will always mean, of course, 'the sonnet order as I have tried to restore it.'

'The poet,' and 'the friend' or 'the young man' will appear often; variations like 'the fair youth' will not appear. Someday there may be a way of writing about the Sonnets without saying, 'Here the poet rebukes his friend for favoring another poet,' et cetera, et cetera. Needless to say, commentary in this edition will have to repeat the formula, although I have tried to avoid a fatuity that seems built into it. The most distressing aspect of this jargon of paraphrase is that banality largely absent in the actual lines becomes more oppressive with each repetition. Another difficulty is that the jargon can imply 'biographical' interpretation. As for this, one can only say what every trained reader knows—that a statement about 'the poet' is to be read as a statement about the speaker assumed in the poem. One tries actually using 'speaker,' but this too becomes jargon if repeated at any length.

For a reader about to begin the first chapter, there is a last reminder, and a suggestion. A book intended to revise the Shakespeare sonnet order must make a case—show a probability—and thus must offer full evidence, frequently evidence on 'both sides.' In many instances detail or statistical usage will be unavoidable, since the one matter of concern will be whether a conclusion is probably true or probably false. Hence complete statement, qualifying statement, and, above all, clear statement are the necessities. But these virtues of exposition, if they materialize, can be tiring, can place limits on any reader's patience.

May I suggest, then, not more than one or two restored poems at a time? To value a restored poem for the sonnets in it, and to judge its authenticity on the same occasion, is a rather full experience, especially since part of the evidence will lie outside the poem itself. And although the experience can bring pleasure—no matter what the judgment on authenticity—there are diminishing returns in repetition at any one sitting.

I. Standards of Coherence: What the 1609 Text Implies

THOMAS THORPE'S 1609 Quarto is a text lacking authority from the poet himself or from his legitimate representatives. Ultimately, if we are asked whether Shakespeare wrote the Sonnets and reply confidently that he did, we do not mean that Q vouches for them but that the lines printed in Q are Shakespearian, undeniably so. And when we say that certain sonnets are, or are not, in Shakespeare's order, we mean on the one hand that their order is 'right,' that it speaks for itself, or on the other that it is not right, that its coherence fails to meet Shakespearian standards—norms derived from sequences that *are* right.

The irony here is obvious enough. Q has no 'external' authority, but if we presume to affirm or deny its sonnet order at any point we must judge by standards derived from certain parts of the Q text. Such, of course, is what we have been doing all along, without great success. Is it worth trying once more?

This chapter—in fact, this book—rests on an assumption that Q's text is sufficiently intact to give us many sequences in the Shakespearian mode. Grant this, follow it through—which may be what we have not yet done—and there are possibilities. If a high order of sequential coherence appears again and again, we may assume tentatively that coherence is the norm, incoherence the aberration. Then, if the standard of coherence is unusually high, and if we allow it to control some test cases of restoration, the result should tell us whether we have made progress or have met the familiar impasse in a new form. At this point, should we happen to be on the right course, the 1609 text ought to supply evidence of a new kind. If Q is disarranged, a premise few deny, a sonnet causing incoherence in one sequence may furnish just the sort of coherence lacking in another sequence. Or two consecutive sonnets, apparently unrelated in Q's context, may have a surprising relation when kept consecutive and placed in a new context. Or adjacent sonnets in a miscellany, a hodgepodge, may explain their proximity to one another in Q by turning out to be disarranged fragments from a once-coherent group. Thus we may find that the Q order furnishes not only direct testimony of normal and abnormal sequence but verifies its direct evidence by circumstantial evidence, evidence of 'rational' disarrangement underlying what appears to be mere disorder.

In substance, my point in this chapter will be that the 1609 text has more to tell us than we have supposed. First, we may look into the matter of close or 'intensive' linkage. In doing so our concern will not be to discover a linkage between certain sonnets in their Q order—in most cases that is an old story. Instead, we need to know how they are linked—how closely and variously—and how far we can go in deriving from Q a norm, a standard of coherence.

INTENSIVE LINKAGE

On the following page is a table of units in Q, each containing from two to six sonnets. Within each unit the sonnet order, far from being merely plausible or 'justifiable,' is virtually certain; the connection between sonnets is cogent, multiple, self-justifying. Syntactical run-on from sonnet to sonnet occurs frequently, and where it is absent or doubtful a combination of other links establishes clear and immediate contact. Such concentrated linkage defines all units in the table and justifies the term 'intensive unit' as a distinguishing label. The close interconnection so represented does not extend from one unit to another; it is a relation of sonnets entirely within units (that is, in the table, between sonnets 1 and 2, or between 4, 5, and 6). Thus, although the connection between 87–90 and 91–93 may be 'fairly close,' it is not intensive. If it were, the two units would appear as one, 87–93. Opposite each unit in the table is the page in this edition on which the

SONNETS INTENSIVELY LINKED IN Q

	Intensive Unit	Page		Intensive Unit	Page
Sonnets	1–2	47	Sonnets	78–80	132–133
	4–6	48–49		82–86	134–136
	8–11	50–52		87–90	94–96
	12–13	52–53		91–93	98–99
	15–17	56–57		95–96	100–101
	25–26	61		97–99	152–153
	27–28	75–76		100–101	155
	29–31	64–65		102–103	145–146, 149–150
	33–35	112–113		107–108	174–175
	36–39	107–108		109–112	183–184
	40–42	113–114		113–114	68
	44–45	79		115–116	175–176
	46–47	70–71		117–121	185–187
	50–51	80		123–125	194–195
	53–55	168–169		131–134	205–206
	57–58	91		135–136	204
	63–65	156–157		139–140	210–211
	66–68	157–158		141–142	214–215
	69–70	99–100		147–152	215–218
	71–74	122–123		153–154	226

sonnets in question appear—usually with comment, closely following, on their affinity. If, for any reason, this comment is limited or absent, the intensive unit can easily be recognized without it. Few readers, I assume, will have the time or the will to consult text or commentary on every unit in the table. I ask only for a substantial sampling.

The table shows that, as they appear in Q, nearly three-fourths of Shakespeare's sonnets (114 of 154) are linked 'inviolably' with at least one other adjacent sonnet. And in almost all cases the actual sequence of sonnets within a unit is beyond challenge. But even where sequence may be questioned (should Q 97–99, for example, appear as 98, 99, 97?), the unit's integrity remains. Each of the forty units thus warrants its authenticity, and the units taken together establish Shakespeare's tendency to link sonnets tightly and unmistakably. That he did this invariably or over long sequences is not, of course, within the presumption.

NONINTENSIVE LINKAGE: CLOSE ASSOCIATION

Sonnets may be linked closely without being linked intensively. Besides the discrete 'tight' units listed in the table, there are in Q unbroken or virtually unbroken runs of sonnets that form 'homogeneous blocks.' Any such block may contain several intensive units, or a combination of intensive units and single sonnets. But all such elements—units or single sonnets—will express the same general theme. In Q, these elements may be out of their original order (exact sequence), and they may be fragments related but widely separated from their original context. Yet they will plainly show a thematic although nonintensive connection with one another, a homogeneous relationship. I list the homogeneous blocks in their Q order.

SONNETS 1–17. These, consecutive in Q, never depart from the so-called procreation theme, not present elsewhere in Shakespeare's collection. Sonnet 15 does not state the theme but it 'runs on' into 16 which restates it. Certain elements of the 1–17 block may be disarranged, but I can find no tangible evidence that this is so, or that anything is missing.

SONNETS 18–19. These are addressed to a single conventional theme but lack the intensive linkage found between certain other sonnets addressed to it (for example, 63–65).

SONNETS 33–42. Here three of the intensive units form a block. The common themes are alienation through a wrong or "trespass" (33–35, 40–42) and identity of poet and friend despite separation (36–39), despite alienation (40–42). Further, in the 36–39 unit, 36 may describe with double entendre the 'triangle' situation presented by 40–42.

SONNETS 43–52. In this block of ten the unifying theme is separation incidental to travel, and various kinds of 'psychic' communion that overcome physical absence. Sonnet 49 is not concerned with these matters, but its theme of feared alienation suggests an association with the reference to 'stealing' in the last three lines of 48. The 48–49 relationship must be called 'loose.'

SONNETS 62–68. Although not clearly linked with 63–65, an intensive unit, 62 shares a prominent note with 63—the aging poet (see 63.1–2). For close association between the themes of 63–65 and 67–68, see page 163.

SONNETS 76, 78–80, 82–86. Here nine sonnets form the familiar 'rival poet' series. If it were not for non sequitur induced by 77 and 81, the whole of 76–86 could be called an intensive unit. The two disruptive sonnets are so out of line with the theme found elsewhere in 76–86 that we may question their authentic presence in the group, or at least the order of their placement.

SONNETS 87–96. Forming this block of ten in Q are two distinct sequences, 87–90 and 91–96. But they are related; the theme of feared alienation developed in 87–90 is restated in a new context at the end of 91 and continues through 92 and 93. Sonnet 94 appears to be out of order between 93 and 95–96, but there is no doubt of its relationship to other sonnets in the series (see pages 102–106).

SONNETS 97–108. The poet's muteness, the failure of his Muse "To speak of that which gives thee all thy might" (100.1–2), is a prominent theme in these sonnets (see 97.12–14, 98.5–7,

100–101, 102–103). In 106.13–14 the poet's inadequacy to his subject (compare 103) is attributed to other poets as well. Closely associated with this note of muteness and abashed reticence is the poet's rededication, his resolve to write of his friend with the old zeal and the old simplicity that somehow have waned. All in all, the attachment between poet and friend appears as a long-standing one with a freshly assured future. A unifying motif is the cyclic procession of seasons (97–99, 102, 104).

SONNETS 122–126. These sonnets have an obvious unity as elements in a 'concluding statement,' a quality they retain whether or not my special interpretation (pages 196–199) is accepted.

SONNETS 127–154. Like the first seventeen sonnets in Q, these, the last twenty-eight, are distinctive in theme. They concern the poet's actual or fictional relations with a woman, or perhaps more than one woman; and where the poet's friend, the "man right fair," appears, he does so only to add a triangular scope to the situation. Among sonnets prior in Q to this last group, only 40–42 and possibly 36 mention such an involvement, and they are distinct from 127–154 by being addressed not to the woman but to the man. Sonnets 153 and 154 are often set apart from the rest, but they denote "my mistress' eyes" (153.14), as do 127 (lines 9–10) and 130 (line 1), which are in turn related on that score to 131–132. Also concerned with the woman's eyes are 139–140, to which 138 appears to serve as an introduction. Sonnets 128 and 145 may be independent 'singles,' but they fit the dominant poet-mistress theme. Some sonnets of the last group speak pleasantly of the woman, some satirically, and others with bitterness or revulsion. But whatever the differences in tone, an opposition of fair and foul or fair and black intermittently appears, along with a note of 'perjury.' Although lacking in specific reference to sensuality, sonnet 146 seems cognate with 129 and fits perfectly into the general context.

The structure (1–14 succeeded and concluded by 15–17) is cumulative (see pages 45, 57). It may be, of course, that in their impressive coherence the first seventeen sonnets deceive us by presenting not a Shakespearian norm but an aberration. Yet, to decide at this stage that they present either would beg the question; it is much more in order to consider their close unity as a possible norm, and to be experimentally skeptical, if not suspicious, of sequences in Q that depart from it.

The most extensive homogeneous block, one of twenty-eight sonnets, runs from 127 through 154. Its subject matter, unique in Q and consistent, has already been described. But when the group is measured, not just by the standard of 1–17 but by a standard it prescribes within certain segments for itself, the sequence appears faulty. Sonnets 130–136, 138–140, 141–142, 147–152—eighteen of twenty-eight in the block—when set apart from the others and read as they come in the Q order, measure up nicely to the level of coherence set by the first homogeneous block, 1–17. And nothing seriously incoherent emerges if we allow 153–154 to retain its position as a humorously pathetic statement at the end of the series, a poem separate from 147–152 but still addressed to a common theme, the poet and the woman. Hence, when taken in their relative Q order, twenty of the last twenty-eight sonnets fulfill a coherent plan. But the remaining eight are disruptive enough to throw the whole series into apparent confusion. The stern and monolithic 129, for example, is a howler in the pretty context furnished by 128 and 130. The crisis introduced by 137 casually disappears with 138–140, is resumed in detail at 141–142, goes underground again, and then emerges unmistakably at 147–148. With 147–152 it is developed pointedly and, this time, with a continuity quite surprising after the earlier fragmentation. In the interruption between 141–142 and 147–148, incoherence is compounded after 144, clearly a 'beginning' sonnet, introduces a story already told in 133–136. The next sonnet, 145, has nothing to do with this story and nothing to do with the memorable 146, which follows not just inconsequentially but with a resounding non sequitur that recalls 128, 129.

Thus in a block of twenty-eight sonnets, twenty would set a
standard of coherence equal to that of 1-17 if it were not for eight
that interrupt purposeful sequence in just the wrong places. We
have been told often enough, of course, that loose or incoherent
sequence was the invariable way of sonneteers, including Shakespeare. Proponents of this notion eagerly assume the validity of
texts that 'confirm' it, and seem unaware of Rollins' statement
(Variorum, page 75) that printers habitually rearranged poems.
And after asserting the theory, they rarely face up to embarrassing applications. I cannot recall an apologist of the 'loose association' school willing to use the incongruous parts of 127-154 as
examples of common practice. No poet capable of writing sonnet
129 would have placed it in the context of 128 and 130; and the
fact that he may have written the three sonnets consecutively as
independent poems will not justify their appearance in an undif-
ferentiated series. For the Q order, by presenting so many sonnets
in clearly related sequence, invites the reading of *any* sonnet as
related to adjacent sonnets. No poet capable of writing 146 would
have placed it after 145, or before 147 where it becomes a deliverance from the crisis of 147 before that crisis is stated. No poet
who could set forth, and presumably value, the cogent ties within
147-152 would have allowed equivalent (often identical) ties
joining this series with 137 and 141-142 to be broken by 138-140
and the miscellany running from 143 through 146. In isolation,
these statements may seem dogmatic and incautious. I hope they
will not seem so after a reasonably close reading of the sonnets in
question and of the adjoining commentary (pages 214-225). My
premise is simply that a poet who shows himself again and again
to be a master of cogent sense will neither write continually
recurrent nonsense nor approve a text of his poems in which
independent sonnets are sure to be read as a nonsense series.

The least a modern editor can do is experiment with removal of
obvious nonsense and restoration of obvious sense. Significantly,
with sonnets 127-154 the first of these ventures substantially
accomplishes the second. Set aside 128, 129, 145, and 146. Perhaps
129 and 146 can be joined and relocated, but for the present let

them stand in this miscellany of four independent sonnets, all
related to the general group. Recognize 138–140 for what it is, an
independent poem within the main group, and give it, tentatively,
an indeterminate position. Link sonnets 143–144 with the unique
situation they introduce—that of 131–136. With these minor adjustments, the confusion of 127–154 disappears. With the removal
of 128–129, sonnets 127 and 130 come together, pairing beautifully. With the setting-off of 138–140, the relocation of 143–144,
and the removal of 145–146, sonnets 137, 141–142, and 147–152
come together as a strongly unified series. Merely indicate clear
division points between one 'poem' and another, and the mini-
mally edited 127–154 now shows a coherence formerly apparent
only within fragments. Such editing, scarcely meddlesome when
the text is pirated or dubious, does little but relocate certain
discrete or fragmentary elements by putting them in a 'miscellany.' That done, intensively related elements become adjacent
largely by virtue of their Q order. And at this stage the process is
experimental.

Minimal and tentative editing within 127–154 transforms a
block of sonnets in Q from a merely homogeneous block (fragments sharing a general theme) into a series dominated by intensive linkage. With this, 127–154 attains a coherence not far below
the standard set by 1–17. But in subject matter and occasion
sonnets 1–17 and 127–154 are distinct from the large assortment in
between, and for that reason may yield a standard of coherence
untypical of the whole collection. Such a possibility needs checking; we may scout it by examining the Q series 71–86. Reference
to the text of these sonnets and the running commentary (pages
122–126, 132–142) will show intensive linkage within 71–74, a
change of subject in 75, an irrelevancy at 77, and another at 81.
After 81 the intensive unit 82–86 resumes and concludes the
'story' begun by 76 and 78–80. Again we find sequences memorable for clear, pertinent development interrupted in a manner not
only confusing but dull. And we are told again that this is 'loose
structure'—sonneteer's logic, that Shakespeare apparently ap-
proved of it, and that one learns to like it. But once more we find,

as we did with 127–154, that a very few sonnets induce confusion in a series of many. Here, except for three disruptive fragments, the series would be a model of coherence: two compatible sequences (71–74; and 76 , 78–80 , 82–86), each impressively organized and tightly joined. Under the circumstances, Q's sonnet order may well be faulty; and, if so, there should be additional clues. In looking for them, one naturally suspects that the interfering sonnets may belong somewhere else. I began with 81, not hopefully since 81 with its bestowal of immortality in eternal verse is a sonnet that may fit 'appropriately' into a dozen combinations and hence, demonstrably, into none. Nevertheless, one of the combinations, 32 and 81, began to emit signals. When these two are paired (see the "Text and Commentary," pages 127–130), 81 continues from 32 a specific note rarely found in the Sonnets, the friend as survivor after the poet's death; and the word "survive" in 32.1 and 81.2 appears nowhere else. Sonnet 32, moreover, is one of a dozen or so found neither in an intensive unit nor a homogeneous block. Since it stands as an isolated single between 29–31 and 33–35, its combination with 81 would remove it from no meaningful context.

Although the ties between 32 and 81 are impressive, they are hardly sufficient to rule out accidental affinity. Fortuitous connection between separated sonnets is hardly ever so pointed, but the fact that it can be so is something learned early in the game. Hence I had decided that removal of the troublesome 81 by pairing it with 32 was against the rules, when the obvious—long overdue—materialized. The affinity between 32 and 81 is one aspect of an elaborate affinity between 32 and 76–86, sonnets on the rival poet. Cumulative parallels of theme, subtheme, and language (pages 128–129) are pointed enough, I think, to leave no doubt about the isolated 32 belonging to the rival poet series. And if 32 belongs there, then 81—which in Q seems clearly out of place in the series—has strong ties with a sonnet originally found in it. Hence 81, no longer a puzzling intrusion, appears to belong at least in the context that Q provides.

Nor is this all, for 32 paired with 81 immediately shows obvious ties with 71–74, the short series just preceding 76–86 (page 131). As they stand in Q, the units 71–74 and 76–86 are 'compatible' yet unrelated, but when the paired 32 and 81 are placed as a bridge between them, the two units or poems become parts of a continuous and developing statement.

Except, of course, that two irrelevant sonnets, 75 and 77, remain to interrupt sequence. But the removal of 77 appears mandatory. Written to accompany the gift of a notebook, it urges the recipient to fill blank pages, "vacant leaves," with reflections on mutability and fugitive Time. It thus has no ties with sonnets on the rival poet, and no more connection with 71–74 than with a good many similar sonnets. Shakespeare could have presented the notebook and sonnet 77 to his friend along with 71–74 and the rival poet series, but if he did he could not have meant it to cancel the obvious link between 76 and 78–80. Had the second quarto *Hamlet* been printed with casual verses of birthday greeting to Burbage in the midst of Hamlet's first soliloquy, a modern editor would put the interesting verses in an appendix along with remarks about the devotion of compositors to their copy. But when something quite like this occurs in the 1609 text of the Sonnets—a clearly suspect publishing venture—editors perpetuate the anomaly, often without comment on the mangled sequence. The intrusion of 77 between 76 and 78–80 is plain evidence of disorder in the Q text.

At the point of interruption in the text by 77, there is also the incoherence caused by 75. This sonnet, in long simile form beginning "So are you to my thoughts as food to life," seems to call for a clear antecedent statement, but no such statement appears in the preceding 71–74. Brooke provided the antecedent by moving 76 to a position before 75, a questionable solution in view of the immediate link between 76 and 78–80. I believe that multiple evidence (pages 84–90) combines 75 with 48, 52, and 56 to form a remarkable 'pair of pairs' in the mode of 71–74, but I ask no one to consider such a venturesome notion at this stage of discussion. For the present we may simply put 75 aside as a 'single' that may or may not have something to do with the rival poet series.

The only conclusion I ask a reader to draw at this point is that there are signs, far too pertinent and various to ignore, of the Q series 71–86 having once been as clearly unified throughout as it now is within certain segments. Since there are signs of a similar original unity, although one less strict, within the series 127–154, and since in sonnets 1–17 Q presents an extended series with its original unity apparently intact, we now have three sizable portions of the 1609 text—representing its beginning, middle, and end—that imply something about Shakespeare's mode of composition. What they imply is that Shakespearian sonnet groups at once longer and more closely unified than any coherent series now found in Q (save 1–17) may have been typical.

There is no warrant from the evidence that such groups once combined to form a single grand poem or, above all, to tell a continued story. Nor does the evidence favoring longer and more cogent groups imply that there were no self-sufficient short pieces, including some isolated single sonnets. But it does suggest an original norm of coherence much more dominant than it now is in Q.

At minimum, the evidence we have considered justifies an 'attitude' or bias, subject, of course, to ultimate rejection or acceptance based wholly on its results. It can be stated thus: when we judge Q for authentic sequence, (1) any interruption of a strongly coherent pattern (such as that of 76, 78–80, 82–86 by 77 and 81; or that of 137, 141–142, 147–152 by intervening sonnets) is to be viewed seriously as a possible corruption of the text, and (2) multiple affinity between separated sonnets (even those so widely separated as 32 and 76–86) is not to be taken lightly. Just this and nothing more.

The traditional assumption in dealing with Q is quite different. It runs this way: (1) random sequence—even contradiction that breaks a cogent, immediate pattern—scarcely implies a disarranged text because it apparently was usual with sonneteers, and (2) although the text of Q may be disordered, there are so many contradictory ways of 'restoring' order that none may be trusted. Stemming from praiseworthy motives of skepticism, these tra-

ditional premises have hardened into dogma. And both of them
are finally either untenable or irrelevant. The first premise can
beg the question by assuming that certain 'representative' texts
disorderly in sequence are authentic, when we just don't know. It
is sure to evade the question in judging Shakespeare's work by an
externally derived standard, thus running counter to Q's own
internal testimony, the provocative evidence we have been considering. The second premise—that contradictory attempts to
restore the Shakespeare text cancel one another—properly invali-
dates many 'plausible' rearrangements, to say nothing of a myriad
based on revelation, fictionalized biography, or parallel platitudes.
Its main effect is to chasten enthusiasts who try to recombine
sonnets on a basis of simple likeness unsupported by other factors,
a venture so appallingly fruitful that success guarantees its failure.
The paradox is nicely described in Shakespeare's own phrase, "a
famine where abundance lies."

Appearance of these words in the very first sonnet thus
amounts to ironical prophecy. They should be memorized by
anyone who sets out to reorder the 1609 text, for there is no
better reminder of the difficulty to be met. For more than a
century the impasse has brought such equal embarrassment to
responsible and irresponsible ventures that many now see it as
denying demonstration to any solution, even one that should
happen to be right. Hyder Rollins, a consistent and therefore an
unusual skeptic,[1] took pains to say that a text like the 1609 Quarto
gains no validity whatever from continued failure to amend it.
But he scarcely doubted that the record of failure would persist,
if only because of the built-in hazard: it is not that possibilities are
lacking but that they abound; one rearranger vies with another
and, except for contenders who may be mad, the competition will
be about equal. Restoration of the text will fail from sheer opportunity.

So runs the traditional caveat. My statements about it may seem
inconsistent; I introduced it as a conventional but finally irrelevant warning, and I have ended by calling it essential. But such is
its double nature. Any satisfactory rearrangement of the Sonnets

must dispose of competing alternatives, and the famine-in-abundance principle remains essential because it can identify and reject alternatives by the dozen. Yet its ultimate effect is not to preclude demonstration of all rearrangements, spurious or genuine, but rather to demand a wholly new standard of proof, and, incidentally, to imply what the standard must be. Once this is understood, the traditional warning may lose relevance simply because the new kind of internal evidence it requires may avoid the old fallacies it exposed.

RESTORED COHERENCE: THE STANDARD OF EVIDENCE
IMPLIED BY Q

Nothing is unusual about this new standard of evidence save its tardy application to the text of Shakespeare's Sonnets. Nor is there anything recondite about it. If effective revision of the sonnet order in Q seems defeated by too many plausible options, why not try a procedure that validly limits the range of choice? Why not take our cue from combinations that survive in Q and are obviously authentic—the 'intensive units.' Almost any of these chosen at random from the table on page 17 shows a linkage between sonnets based on no single or general factor, such as parallel theme, but on multiple and highly tangible relationships—often those of immediate run-on, repetition of sharply defined motif or idea, echo of phrase, recurrence of image or metaphor. Within many intensive units, such as 50–51 or 57–58, linkage is at once pointed and varied enough to establish a unique relationship. Now, hypothetically, had either of these two units been split and scattered in a disarranged manuscript lying behind Q, a strong case could be made for its restoration unless, of course, the sonnet order—admittedly disturbed in our assumed case—continued to make very good sense at the new, the spurious points of contact. Barring this, we should have indications of vacant sequence or non sequitur, plus all the multiple ties between the hypothetically displaced sonnets—a tissue of links so various and yet so consistent that no accidental affinity, of the kind that unrelated sonnets can show, would be likely to match it.

The first requirement, then, of a restored sonnet order that can hold its own against competing alternatives, the "famine where abundance lies," is that if a sonnet appears to be misplaced or isolated in Q, its assignment to a new position should rest on multiple linkage. The new relationship, in other words, should be of the kind found in Q's plainly authentic units. Ideally the new linkage should correspond to that between 50 and 51, or 57 and 58 (the two examples just considered), and, if it does so, there is very little chance of a rival alternative appearing. But the standard set by 50–51 or 57–58 may be high even among the intensive units preserved in Q; if it alone is to govern restoration of the text, the result may be artifically limited. On the other hand, if we use a standard of restored linkage below that of 50–51 or 57–58, we are likely to have competing alternatives again—unless supplementary evidence is available to justify one choice over another.

Fortunately, such evidence appears with regularity; we have already encountered it in the instance of 32 and 81. Affinity between these two sonnets is striking but hardly of the kind found between 50 and 51 or 57 and 58. Yet, as described earlier, the 32 81 relation belongs to a series of relations, all of them cumulative. Here they are, summarized for clear reference. Three elements—71–74, 81, and 76–86 (less 81)—are found together in Q but appear unrelated. A fourth element, 32, turns out to be a catalyst. Sonnet 32 not only appears displaced in Q but has strong and quite independent links with 71–74, with 81, and with 76–86. When 32, the catalyst, is paired with 81, and the two placed between 71–74 and 76–80 82–86, then the series from 76 on becomes newly coherent (no longer disrupted by 81) and the entire series becomes related (with 32 81 as a transitional 'bridge'). Still, 75 and 77 remain to break continuity. But 77 is clearly an isolated 'occasional' piece. As for 75, anomalous in its Q position, I now invite attention to its multiple connection with three other singles isolated in Q: 48, 52, and 56—all of which, independently of links with 75, are themselves multiply related (see 'poem E' of Group II, pages 84–90).

In this illustration every relationship supported by independent evidence is a separate factor. And among the relationships are some telling ones that may escape notice: sonnets 71–74 and 76–86 are already adjacent in Q; sonnet 32 is stranded in the 1609 text between 29–31 and 33 ff.; sonnets 48, 52, 56 (of II E) come together 'automatically' when intervening discrete elements are removed. And there are factors within factors: 32, for example, has about a dozen separate but cumulative ties with the 76–86 series, all of them independent of its ties with 81 or 71–74. To 'count' these relationships not only would amount to pedantry but would oversimplify their interaction in pointing to a conclusion: the existence, prior to Q's disarrangement, of a sonnet series substantially like the one set forth (page 41) as Group III.

We now have at least a working principle. If sonnets appear to be misplaced in Q, there is a good chance of restoring the original text, or something close to it, if independent factors combine to imply a given result, and if they are sufficient in number and variety to minimize the role of chance or coincidence. Chance, including accidental affinity between sonnets, can scarcely explain the combined factors just described as underlying a restoration of Group III; and, to understate matters, no alternative competing with this restored group—an alternative differing in essentials [2] and yet based on a similar array of factors—is likely to appear.

Such is the multiple-factor test controlling various attempts in this edition to restore original sequence. Since any validity the edition may have depends on the test's validity as a working principle, I shall give two more examples of its application. From his experience with them, a reader can decide whether he wants to go further, on the chance that actual Shakespearian poems are being restored, or whether he has had enough of what strikes him as 'just another rearrangement.'

First, we may consider 'poems' H, I, and J of Group II. This attempt at restoration brings together sonnets from three distinct parts of the 1609 edition. In terms of Q numbers, the series runs:

H   91–93 69–70 95–96 94
I   36–39
J   33–35 40–42

Restoration of the sequence is supported by at least nine factors. Although each is established independently of any other, the factors join with increasing consistency to imply a single result, a cumulative effect hardly measurable, again, by mere counting. Hence I number the factors not to emphasize quantity but to make cross-reference possible. Should a reader want to check the evidence behind each factor, he may do so by using the "Text and Commentary," pages 98–118. Yet I suggest that, aside from occasional sampling, he postpone this necessity—that he consider the statement below not as a body of actual evidence but as something less demanding: a description of the *kinds* of evidence to be found in later discussion. Here, now, are the various factors supporting restored poems H, I, J of Group II.

(1) Sonnets 69–70 of H (see the tabulation above) are antithetical to 66–68 (page 303), and without relation to 71–74. Hence they can be placed elsewhere without disruption of a coherent sequence.

(2) When 69–70 are placed directly after 91–93 the relationship established is not loose but remarkably pointed and exact.

(3) Placed in this position, 69–70 also show an immediate and independent affinity for 95–96.

(4) The relocation of 69–70 between 93 and 95–96 displaces 94 from its Q position. But this displacement is supported by evidence that 94 offers serious confusion as a sonnet following 93 and equally serious confusion as a sonnet leading into 95 (thus we actually have two factors here).

(5) Displacement of 94 by 69–70 is supported further by evidence that 94 was designed to serve as an end sonnet, an 'envoy,' immediately after 95–96.

(6) Strong evidence links 36–39 of poem I with 91–93 and 95–96 of H. This evidence is independent of that linking 69–70 with H; yet in both recombinations couplet echo dominates in the scheme: we find striking parallels of couplet statement in 93 69–70, and actual repetition of couplets in 96 and 36. Thus, two independent steps in the restoration of H-I indicate couplet echo as a unifying element running through the

series. And we find couplet echo as a unifying note in four other poems of this restored group—A, B, C, and F (pages 68, 70, 75, 91).

(7) When, on the basis of evidence mentioned in (6), 36–39 are moved to a position directly following poem H (see again 'H I J,' page 32), two triads separated in Q, 33–35 and 40–42, 'come together'—are left without intervening sonnets. Internal evidence then justifies this result: the two triads form a remarkably unified poem (J), formerly obscured by the presence of 36–39.

(8) But this poem does have a connection with 36–39 (I), and thus must accompany I when I is joined with H. Far from creating difficulties, such a result fits consistently into the developing pattern: when J is moved with I into proximity with H, then J shows—quite independently—links with H that match those already noted between I and H.

(9) Among these links between J and H is one between 35 of J and 70 of H (page 117). So here we return to the starting point, 69–70. There, in factors (2) and (3), we found clear ties between 69–70 and sonnets of the 91–96 series; then, in factors (6) and (8), we found elements of 33–42 also linked with the 91–96 series. Now we find that 70 and 35, each thus related to 91–96, are also related, one to the other. The significance? If we note of three fragments widely separated in Q (33–35, 69–70, and 91–96) that the first two link closely with the third, it does not follow that the first two will link closely with one another. They may, in fact, be incompatible. But here we find a close affinity between them—one more independent factor implying an original conjunction of all three fragments.

For a 'tenth factor' to follow analysis of the nine just listed, may I suggest a reading of the three restored poems in series, without piecemeal reference to independent factors? 'Authenticity' is a whole quality that exceeds the sum of nine parts.

As one more sample of the multiple-factor test in operation, consider restored poem C of Group IV. In terms of Q numbers this poem runs:

$$100–101$$
$$63–68$$
$$19$$
$$21$$
$$105$$

At minimum, seven factors imply the restored sequence. Again, a reader may check them for evidence against the "Text and Commentary" (pages 155–167), or he may choose—wisely, I think—to postpone close verification until he encounters the whole of Group IV in due course. In either event, the factors as I describe them below are meant, as in earlier examples, not to introduce actual evidence but to indicate the kind of evidence Q will provide. As before, no factor depends for existence upon another but all join to imply the restored poem. Thus (1) and (2) in the list below point to isolated, objective facts. With the addition of (3), (4), and (5) these isolated facts steadily take on a meaning they lacked by themselves. When (6) is added, the growing hypothesis passes a test that could have denied its validity. And with (7) we discover a consistency in Q's seeming disorder that supports not just poem C but the larger group or series containing it. Now, the factors behind IV C:

(1) Q has preserved an authentic sequence, 63–68. Throughout the sequence Shakespeare refers to his friend only in the third person and, moreover, with a uniform epithet, "my love." Since the six sonnets are unified in other respects, we know that Shakespeare wrote a series in which this distinctive and continuing mode of address was meant to add rhetorical unity to a unity of subject or theme.

(2) Of the first 126 sonnets, eight agree with 63–68 in referring to the friend only in the third person. Surprisingly enough, five of these agree with 63–68 in combining such

reference with "my love" as the epithet. The five sonnets are 19, 21, 100–101, and 105. Hence, with 63–68, they form a unique class.

(3) Besides double agreement with 63–68 in mode of reference and epithet, the five sonnets listed in (2) show a remarkable affinity with 63–68 in theme and subtheme.

(4) The five sonnets also contain distinctive imagery and diction (not counting the epithet) that connect them with 63–68 and, moreover, with one another.

(5) Thus eleven sonnets (63–68 and the five just described) show multiple parallels of theme and style. Now, when placed in the order 100–101, 63–68, 19, 21, 105, the eleven sonnets, so closely unified in other ways, form a poem both conventional and impressive in structure. Sonnets 100–101 invoke the Muse and introduce 63–65 and 66–68, two triads. The transition from 101 to 63 is marked by last-line–first-line phrasal echo. Sonnet 19 brings the two triads pointedly together by echoing the specific theme of 66–68 and reintroducing that of 63–65. Then with something close to run-on, 21 follows 19 to set up impious comparisons that 105 will reject as "idolatry." Sonnet 105, in a perfect summation, brings all the related strands together.

(6) The five sonnets (100–101, 19, 21, 105) in multiple agreement with 63–68 all show signs of misplacement; all appear at points in Q where sequence becomes incoherent or doubtful. Sonnets 100–101, for example, are clearly designed to introduce a developed series, but nothing follows them with pertinence. Further, the 63–68 'nucleus' is not tied to 62 or 69: sonnet 62 requires no direct connection with 63–65, and the relation between 66–68 and 69–70 is antithetical.

(7) Finally, although scattered, elements of the restored poem C are found within three distinct 'runs' of Q: 18–23, 53–68, and 96–108. Sonnets 19 and 21 are in the first run or concentration; 63–68 in the second; 100–101 and 105 in the third. The three concentrations in Q contain the disparate fragments of other poems that unite with poem C to form restored Group IV, a unified series.

Could accident have produced such a collection of independent and varied circumstances, all of them pointing in a single direction? These circumstances, factors, are difficult to explain except by concluding that sonnets 63–68 form the nucleus, surviving in Q, of a poem that also included 19, 21, 100–101, and 105.

If, after sampling the instances chosen from Groups II, III, and IV, a reader chooses to go further, he will find the multiple-factor test yielding added results of equal interest. This implies one of two possibilities: either the test 'works' because the variety of cross-checking it entails can separate authentic from merely plausible rearrangements, or it just seems to work because Shakespeare's sonnets have such random affinity for one another that spurious recombinations will appear authentic even under severe checks or controls.

If the latter alternative holds we have a famine-where-abundance-lies far in excess of previous estimates, and nothing short of a newly discovered manuscript will ever solve the problem that Q presents. But there are several counts against this dire alternative. First, its premise—that 'most' of the Sonnets, having elements in common, are therefore interchangeable in various combinations—ignores exceptions. Combined experimentally, many sonnets prove incompatible and a good many more lack any connection. In the second place, the old premise of random affinity between sonnets is clearly based on loose or simple connection, not on cogent, manifold linkage, the kind of affinity our standard of evidence requires. Finally, if the disturbing premise were true, the conclusion drawn would have to be false: were there actually indiscriminate ties between sonnets, no spurious rearrangement of the full 1609 text could ever appear authentic under the multiple-factor test. For if a close but accidental affinity between sonnets were truly present on a large scale, there could be very few signs in Q (perhaps none) of a disturbed or interrupted text; and it is with these signs that the multiple-factor test begins. Under the test, a primary factor required to justify relocation of a sonnet is that it defies good sense in its Q position, or at least has no tangible connection with other sonnets at that point. In a very few cases I allow exceptional evidence for rearrangement to override a loose affinity found in the 1609 text (see page 147), and when I do this I warn the reader. In general, only when a sonnet is disruptive or equivocally placed does the multiple-factor test allow its relocation on the basis of additional factors. Witness, for example, the relocation of 32, 77, 81, 94, or 100–101 in the illustrations we have considered.

If the multiple-factor test eliminates rearrangements not based initially on signs of misplacement in Q, it eliminates a large number. And it rejects many more because it calls for truly diversified signs of connection in order to reorder sonnets that, like 32 or 100–101, pass the primary test of dislocation. Such diversity of connection—'multiple linkage'—is the norm established by Q's obviously authentic 'runs.' Finally, the multiple factor test seeks to verify all subjective judgements by their objective consequences. Of this, more in the last chapter.

With these selective standards, the famine-where-abundance-lies can be abated. Certainly we shall still have problems of difficult choice, but they should not be numerous and some will disappear with added evidence. Where an alternative persists we can either present or note it, as I have done in the case of poem B in Group V (page 208). We can do little more than hope for a wholly restored text, but we may not have to put up much longer with perversities of the 1609 edition.

✺II.✺ THE EMENDED SONNET ORDER: TEXT AND COMMENTARY

IN this presentation of text and commentary, the Sonnets appear in a restored order and grouping supported, I believe, by internal evidence of content and style, and other factors inherent in Q's arrangement. Since my efforts depend on a standard of linkage drawn from authentic parts of the 1609 text, I undertake to justify the sonnet order whether it is revised or not. Commentary supporting the order appears with each unit of the text—each independent poem, group, or poem within a group. Sonnets retain their Q numbers (in brackets), and any sonnet may be located in its restored position by referring to its Q number in the table on page x.

Again, may I note that the term 'restored order' is not meant to suggest a lifting of the veil or a light cast on darkness? Although modesty has its place, one cannot begin devising variant phrases such as 'the attempted revision' or 'the suggested restoration'; if one tries, he soon finds himself without variants and without readers.

As regrouped here, the Sonnets divide into six 'independent poems' and five 'groups.' In turn, the groups divide into separate but related poems. On the following pages the emended sonnet order appears in tabular form with arabic numbers designating the independent poems ('Poem 2') and roman numbers the groups ('Group II'). Letters are used to indicate constituent poems within groups ('Group I: A, B'). I should gladly do without this 'apparatus' because of the impression it gives of undue classification, subclassification, or arbitrary sequence. But the numbers and letters are necessary for reference in discussion, which would be utterly clumsy, if not impossible, without them.

THE EMENDED SONNET ORDER

(in terms of Q numbers [a])

Group 1	Poem 1	Poem 2	Poem 3	Group II	Poem 4
A 1–14	20	25–26	29–31	A 113–114	77
B 15–17				B 24	
				46–47	
				C 61	
				27–28	
				43	
				D 44–45	
				50–51	
				E 48	
				75	
				56	
				52	
				F 57–58	
				G 49	
				87–90	
				H 91–93	
				69–70	
				95–96	
				94	
				I 36–39	
				J 33–35	
				40–42	
				?[K; see page 191]	

[a] As explained on page 11, these numbers—used here for identification—became attached to sonnets on the occasion of Q's publication.

THE EMENDED SONNET ORDER
(in terms of Q numbers [a])

Group III	Group IV	Poem 5	Poem 6	Group V
A 71–74	A 62	109–112	122–126	A 127
	22–23	117–121		130
B 32	102–104			
81				B 144
	B 97–99			143
C 76				135–136
78–80	C 100–101			131–134
	63–68			
D 82–86	19			C 138 (?)
	21			139–140
	105			
				D 137
	D 53–55			141–142
				147–152
	E 18			
				E 129
	F 106			146
	59–60			
	107–108			F 153–154
	115–116			
				G 128 (?)
				145 (?)

I must explain what this regrouping of the Sonnets is supposed to mean and what it is not supposed to mean. It implies that
Shakespeare intended many sonnets to form groups; this is no
more than Q itself implies. But the sequential numbering of poems
and groups does not imply—necessarily—either a development
from one poem or group to another, or a close interaction. In the
restored text I attempt, the Sonnets as a whole—the entire content
of Q—do not become a continuing long poem, or a series of
related poems all meant to be read together, or a collection of
separate poems arranged in the time order of composition. Nor
could the Sonnets have been any of these things as they appeared
in 1609, whatever the publisher of Q may have thought he was
printing.

Still, Q frequently gives the impression of a 'right' order, even
of groups having no close connection. Hence, except where internal evidence calls pointedly for rearrangement, I have left the Q
order undisturbed. And since Q is a miscellany, the regrouped
sonnet order remains a miscellany, although the groups and poems
by themselves have a strong internal unity. Group I appears to be
intact in Q but it is not related in any true sense to other poems or
groups of the collection. Nor is there reliable evidence, internal or
external, fixing it as the earliest group or proving that Shakespeare
addressed it to the same young man who evoked sonnets 18
through 126. Some sonnets of Group V share a theme with poem
J of Group II (the poet-friend-woman triangle); hence the two
groups—although their elements are widely separated in Q—may
be contemporaneous. But there are no signs of any other connection between them. Group V, like Group I, stands by itself.
Group II contains themes of separation and alienation; Group III
also contains them, but in another context. Group IV celebrates
renewal and rededication of the friendship; poems 5 and 6 follow,
the first depicting a 'return' and renewed allegiance, the second
expressing renewed devotion with a clear note of finality. Yet we
have no assurance of a continuous narrative or 'plot' (whether
true or imagined) in this sequence. The 'return' celebrated in
Poem 5 seems to resolve the alienation expressed in Group II

(estrangement by mutual guilt) and to lack reference to the alienation set forth in Group III (estrangement induced by the rival poet). If I were sure of this, I should place Poem 5 after Group II. But the evidence is insufficient, in the face of Q's uncertain placement, to connect any of the reconciliation poems, as a sequel, with either of the 'alienation' groups. Nor is such evidence likely to materialize from reliable identification, if it ever comes, of the young man and the rival poet. This is to say, in effect, that biographical reconstruction, long a favorite among rearrangers, is one of the least likely means of emending the Q order.

None of these observations, I trust, will be taken to mean that the groups and independent poems I have tried to restore are in no way related. All sonnets in them were written, of course, by the same poet at work in a single medium. And they are addressed, with permutations, to common themes and subjects. But so far as I can tell, the independent poems and the groups remain discrete; where they interrelate, they belong together not like chapters in a novel or parts of a long poem, but more like Shakespeare's three plays on the reign of Henry VI. Poems 2 and 3, and Group II appear to represent earlier phases of the poet-friend relation; Groups III and IV, with Poem 5, appear to represent later phases; and Poem 6 is 'terminal.'

In this very loose time scheme the restored sonnet order agrees fairly well with Q. So long as the loose chronology ('early' and 'late') is undisturbed, the shifting of a discrete element like Group III from its position in Q may scarcely amount to rearrangement. For in Group III we may have a series not even tied sequentially to others as *2 Henry VI* is tied to *1 Henry VI*. There may be no more actual rearrangement in this case than in an anthology that happens to 'violate' the Folio order of history plays by its placement of *King John*.

But *within* restored groups optional placement of elements becomes far more restricted. Occasionally there may be leeway, just as often none at all. For example, the subject of poems A and B of Group V requires their placement in the same group and their proximity with one another, but it does not require that the order be A B rather than B A, or that the two poems be joined. On the other hand, the body of evidence relating poems G, H, and I of Group II virtually prescribes their appearance together in the specified order. In short, all poems of a group belong in the group, but whether they require the tabular sequence I have given them depends on the nature of each case. Commentary will make clear whether the tabular order of poems in the groups is necessary, likely, or optional.

Finally, within individual poems themselves there can be little hedging in the matter of exact sequence. I must, and do, take a stand that the sonnets of poem H in Group II or of C in Group IV should not only appear together but should follow the tabular order. Naturally I may be wrong, but I cannot accept one clear implication of the many-sided evidence and doubt another. Where alternatives do arise, I note them if they are interesting or important.

GROUP I
A 1–14   B 15–17

IN Chapter I, I state the case for presuming that most of Shakespeare's sonnets originally formed coherent groups of coherent 'poems.' Each of the disarranged groups I have tried to restore appears in Q as two or more fragments, one of them, at least, substantial enough to vouch for a unifying plan. But in sonnets 1–17, Q presents an intact group. There are no intrusions and no convincing signs of internal disarrangement. All sonnets of the group join to express a theme found nowhere else in the 1609 collection: the first fourteen urge a young man to father children that he may save his rare qualities from Time's ruin; the last three, 15–17, offer the poet's verse as a defense against Time only to question it as a means of preservation and to reassert fatherhood as Time's adversary.

Thus, Group I in its 1609 order never departs from the central theme, 'procreation,' at any stage. And the two poems, A and B, are clearly joined in the right sequence, for although 15, the opening sonnet of B, at first seems discontinuous, its departure from A has a purpose: to deviate momentarily, thus allowing for a climactic return in 16–17 to the original theme.

I distinguish poem A from poem B to mark the transition in 15 to a new note, the inability of verse to confer immortality. But this setting off of 1–14 from 15–17 is not meant to be arbitrary. An ideal rendering of the text would avoid the labels, A-B, and point to a break merely by extending the normal spacing between 14 and 15. Yet, by the same token, an ideal text would also avoid numbers—these, too, are labels—and use spacing as its only means of separating groups, poems, or individual sonnets. Unfortunately, however, we cannot talk or write of the Sonnets without using numbers. No more can we discuss groups or lesser combina-

tions without some kind of numerical and alphabetical designation. Hence the 'apparatus.' Just as we are able to refer in *Mac-
beth* to 'I.ii,' so we are able here to refer in the Sonnets to 'Group
I, poem B' (I B). Should anyone prefer to read A-B as a single
poem he may do so, of course. When such a close relationship
between poems of a group exists, the ensuing text and commentary should make the connection sufficiently clear.

Whether two poems or one, the first seventeen sonnets appear
in Q as a model of group unity that serves to question other
sequences marked by apparent disorder and incoherence. Coherence in Group I is so obvious that no further comment on the
consistent theme, procreation, is needed. Hence I shall stress the
close linkage between sonnets furnished by highly specific sub-
themes, syntactical connection ('run-on'), and pointed echo of
image and phrase. This commentary will appear immediately
after the text of each poem. Such an arrangement, to be followed
throughout, allows a reader to experience the text on his own
terms apart from, or as a test of, the analysis of sonnet interconnection.

I A

1–14

[1]

From fairest creatures we desire increase,
That thereby beauty's rose might never die,
But as the riper should by time decease,
His tender heir might bear his memory;
5   But thou, contracted to thine own bright eyes,
Feed'st thy light's flame with self-substantial fuel,
Making a famine where abundance lies,
Thyself thy foe, to thy sweet self too cruel.
Thou that art now the world's fresh ornament
10 And only herald to the gaudy spring,
Within thine own bud buriest thy content
And, tender churl, mak'st waste in niggarding.
    Pity the world, or else this glutton be,
    To eat the world's due, by the grave and thee.

[2]

When forty winters shall besiege thy brow
And dig deep trenches in thy beauty's field,
Thy youth's proud livery, so gazed on now,
Will be a tottered weed of small worth held:
5   Then being asked where all thy beauty lies,
Where all the treasure of thy lusty days,
To say within thine own deep-sunken eyes,
Were an all-eating shame and thriftless praise.
How much more praise deserved thy beauty's use,
10 If thou couldst answer, 'This fair child of mine
Shall sum my count and make my old excuse,'
Proving his beauty by succession thine.
    This were to be new made when thou art old,
    And see thy blood warm when thou feel'st it cold.

[3]

    Look in thy glass and tell the face thou viewest
    Now is the time that face should form another,
    Whose fresh repair if now thou not renewest,
    Thou dost beguile the world, unbless some mother.
5   For where is she so fair whose uneared womb
    Disdains the tillage of thy husbandry?
    Or who is he so fond will be the tomb
    Of his self-love, to stop posterity?
    Thou art thy mother's glass, and she in thee
10 Calls back the lovely April of her prime:
    So thou through windows of thine age shalt see,
    Despite of wrinkles, this thy golden time.
      But if thou live rememb'red not to be,
      Die single, and thine image dies with thee.

[4]

    Unthrifty loveliness, why dost thou spend
    Upon thyself thy beauty's legacy?
    Nature's bequest gives nothing, but doth lend,
    And being frank, she lends to those are free.
5   Then, beauteous niggard, why dost thou abuse
    The bounteous largess given thee to give?
    Profitless usurer, why dost thou use
    So great a sum of sums, yet canst not live?
    For having traffic with thyself alone,
10 Thou of thyself thy sweet self dost deceive.
    Then how, when Nature calls thee to be gone,
    What acceptable audit canst thou leave?
      Thy unused beauty must be tombed with thee,
      Which used, lives th' executor to be.

[5]

    Those hours that with gentle work did frame
    The lovely gaze where every eye doth dwell,
    Will play the tyrants to the very same
    And that unfair which fairly doth excel:
5 For never-resting time leads summer on
    To hideous winter and confounds him there,
    Sap checked with frost and lusty leaves quite gone,
    Beauty o'ersnowed and bareness everywhere.
    Then were not summer's distillation left
10 A liquid prisoner pent in walls of glass,
    Beauty's effect with beauty were bereft,
    Nor it, nor no remembrance what it was;
      But flowers distilled, though they with winter meet,
      Leese but their show; their substance still lives sweet.

[6]

    Then let not winter's ragged hand deface
    In thee thy summer ere thou be distilled:
    Make sweet some vial; treasure thou some place
    With beauty's treasure, ere it be self-killed.
5 That use is not forbidden usury
    Which happies those that pay the willing loan;
    That's for thyself to breed another thee,
    Or ten times happier, be it ten for one;
    Ten times thyself were happier than thou art,
10 If ten of thine ten times refigured thee.
    Then what could death do, if thou shouldst depart,
    Leaving thee living in posterity?
      Be not self-willed, for thou art much too fair
      To be death's conquest and make worms thine heir.

[7]

    Lo, in the orient when the gracious light
    Lifts up his burning head, each under eye
    Doth homage to his new-appearing sight,
    Serving with looks his sacred majesty;
5 And having climbed the steep-up heavenly hill,
    Resembling strong youth in his middle age,
    Yet mortal looks adore his beauty still,
    Attending on his golden pilgrimage;
    But when from highmost pitch, with weary car,
10 Like feeble age he reeleth from the day,
    The eyes, 'fore duteous, now converted are
    From his low tract, and look another way:
      So thou, thyself out-going in thy noon,
      Unlooked on diest, unless thou get a son.

[8]

    Music to hear, why hear'st thou music sadly?
    Sweets with sweets war not, joy delights in joy.
    Why lov'st thou that which thou receiv'st not gladly,
    Or else receiv'st with pleasure thine annoy?
5 If the true concord of well tunèd sounds,
    By unions married, do offend thine ear,
    They do but sweetly chide thee, who confounds
    In singleness the parts that thou shouldst bear.
    Mark how one string, sweet husband to another,
10 Strikes each in each by mutual ordering,
    Resembling sire and child and happy mother,
    Who all in one, one pleasing note do sing:
      Whose speechless song, being many, seeming one,
      Sings this to thee, 'Thou single wilt prove none.'

[9]

    Is it for fear to wet a widow's eye
    That thou consum'st thyself in single life?
    Ah, if thou issueless shalt hap to die,
    The world will wail thee like a makeless wife;
5 The world will be thy widow and still weep
    That thou no form of thee hast left behind,
    When every private widow well may keep
    By children's eyes her husband's shape in mind.
    Look what an unthrift in the world doth spend
10 Shifts but his place, for still the world enjoys it;
    But beauty's waste hath in the world an end,
    And kept unused, the user so destroys it.
       No love toward others in that bosom sits
       That on himself such murd'rous shame commits.

[10]

    For shame, deny that thou bear'st love to any,
    Who for thyself art so unprovident.
    Grant, if thou wilt, thou art beloved of many,
    But that thou none lov'st is most evident;
5 For thou art so possessed with murd'rous hate
    That 'gainst thyself thou stick'st not to conspire,
    Seeking that beauteous roof to ruinate
    Which to repair should be thy chief desire.
    O change thy thought, that I may change my mind.
10 Shall hate be fairer lodged than gentle love?
    Be as thy presence is, gracious and kind,
    Or to thyself at least kind-hearted prove:
       Make thee another self for love of me,
       That beauty still may live in thine or thee.

[11]

    As fast as thou shalt wane, so fast thou grow'st
    In one of thine, from that which thou departest;
    And that fresh blood which youngly thou bestow'st
    Thou mayst call thine when thou from youth convertest.
5   Herein lives wisdom, beauty and increase;
    Without this, folly, age and cold decay:
    If all were minded so, the times should cease
    And threescore year would make the world away.
    Let those whom Nature hath not made for store,
10 Harsh, featureless and rude, barrenly perish:
    Look, whom she best endowed she gave the more,
    Which bounteous gift thou shouldst in bounty cherish:
      She carved thee for her seal, and meant thereby
      Thou shouldst print more, not let that copy die.

[12]

    When I do count the clock that tells the time,
    And see the brave day sunk in hideous night,
    When I behold the violet past prime,
    And sable curls all silvered o'er with white;
5   When lofty trees I see barren of leaves,
    Which erst from heat did canopy the herd,
    And summer's green all girded up in sheaves,
    Borne on the bier with white and bristly beard;
    Then of thy beauty do I question make,
10 That thou among the wastes of time must go,
    Since sweets and beauties do themselves forsake,
    And die as fast as they see others grow;
      And nothing 'gainst Time's scythe can make defence
      Save breed, to brave him when he takes thee hence.

[13]

    O that you were yourself; but love, you are
    No longer yours than you yourself here live;
    Against this coming end you should prepare,
    And your sweet semblance to some other give.
5 So should that beauty which you hold in lease
    Find no determination; then you were
    Yourself again after yourself's decease,
    When your sweet issue your sweet form should bear.
    Who lets so fair a house fall to decay,
10 Which husbandry in honor might uphold
    Against the stormy gusts of winter's day
    And barren rage of death's eternal cold?
      O none but unthrifts; dear my love, you know
      You had a father; let your son say so.

[14]

    Not from the stars do I my judgement pluck,
    And yet methinks I have astronomy,
    But not to tell of good or evil luck,
    Of plagues, of dearths, or season's quality;
5 Nor can I fortune to brief minutes tell,
    Pointing to each his thunder, rain and wind,
    Or say with princes if it shall go well
    By oft predict that I in heaven find;
    But from thine eyes my knowledge I derive,
10 And, constant stars, in them I read such art
    As truth and beauty shall together thrive
    If from thyself to store thou wouldst convert;
      Or else of thee this I prognosticate:
      Thy end is truth's and beauty's doom and date.

I A
1–14

IN the development of theme through sonnets 1 and 2 several
links appear: "thine own bright eyes" (1.5) appropriately becomes "thine own deep-sunken eyes" (2.7); the "glutton" metaphor (1.13–14) finds its echo in "all-eating shame" (2.8). Similar
links occur in the transitions from "rose" and "bud" (1.2, 11) to
"weed" (2.4), and from "gaudy spring" (1.10) to "forty winters"
(2.1).

"Unthrifty" (4.1) recalls "thriftless" (2.8); "niggard" (4.5)
echoes "niggarding" (1.12). The usury-use note, expanded in 4,
has its likely beginning in the "beauty's use" figure of 2.9; in any
event the metaphor of commerce, "acceptable audit" (4.12), is
strongly reminiscent of 2.9–12, lines having as their center the key
phrase, "sum my count."

In 5.9–14 and 6.1–4 appears the first clear run-on between
sonnets: a 'then' clause (6.1) proceeding directly from the last
line of sonnet 5 completes the expanded "distillation" metaphor
and its adjuncts of "summer," "winter," "glass," "vial," "beauty."
In 6, the usury-use note, last found in 4, develops pointedly.

Although it continues the primary theme, 'procreation,' sonnet
7 has no other close relation to adjacent sonnets. It stands impressively as a divider between the strongly consecutive series 4–6 and
the equally continuous 8–11.

In 8–11 four sonnets of a typically cogent series are joined by
phrasal echo. "Singleness" and "single" (8.8, 14) are heard
immediately in the next sonnet: "single life" (9.2). "Murd'rous
shame" (9.14) recurs directly in "For shame" (10.1) and
"murd'rous hate" (10.5). Similar linkage between the end of one
sonnet and the beginning of another appears in "Make thee another self . . . That beauty still may live in *thine* or thee"
(10.13–14), which is carried immediately into "thou grow'st In

one of thine" (11.1–2) and echoed again in "Thou mayst call thine" (11.4).

Also linking 8 and 9 is an expansion of "sire and child and happy mother" (8.9–12) into the note of widowhood and orphaned children (9.1–8). The remaining lines of 9 (9–14) reassert the usury-use metaphor of sonnets 2, 4 and 6; and the appearance of "unthrift" (9.9) makes this continuity even more pointed (see 2.8 and 4.1).

The last four lines of 12 lead to 13. "*Sweets* and *beauties* do *themselves* forsake, And *die* . . ." is particularized in 13.1–2, "O that you were *yourself;* but love, you are No longer yours than you *yourself* here *live*," and also in the "*sweet* semblance" and "*beauty*" of 13.4–6. Besides, "*this* coming end" (13.3) has its antecedent in 12.13–14.

Sonnet 14 ends the first 'poem' with a prophecy that unless the young man fathers a child his death will be "truth's and beauty's doom and date." There are two echoes here of previous sonnets: "thine eyes," line 9 (see 1.5 and 2.7), and "to *store* thou wouldst *convert*," line 12 (see 11.9, 4).

IB

15–17

[15]

When I consider every thing that grows
Holds in perfection but a little moment,
That this huge stage presenteth nought but shows
Whereon the stars in secret influence comment;
5   When I perceive that men as plants increase,
Cheerèd and checked even by the selfsame sky,
Vaunt in their youthful sap, at height decrease,
And wear their brave state out of memory;
Then the conceit of this inconstant stay
10 Sets you most rich in youth before my sight,
Where wasteful Time debateth with Decay,
To change your day of youth to sullied night;
    And all in war with Time for love of you,
    As he takes from you, I engraft you new.

[16]

But wherefore do not you a mightier way
Make war upon this bloody tyrant Time?
And fortify yourself in your decay
With means more blessèd than my barren rhyme?
5   Now stand you on the top of happy hours,
And many maiden gardens yet unset,
With virtuous wish would bear your living flowers
Much liker than your painted counterfeit:
So should the lines of life that life repair,
10 Which this (Time's pencil or my pupil pen)
Neither in inward worth nor outward fair
Can make you live yourself in eyes of men.
    To give away yourself keeps yourself still,
    And you must live drawn by your own sweet skill.

[17]

Who will believe my verse in time to come,
If it were filled with your most high deserts?
Though yet, heaven knows it is but as a tomb
Which hides your life and shows not half your parts.
5   If I could write the beauty of your eyes
And in fresh numbers number all your graces,
The age to come would say 'This poet lies;
Such heavenly touches ne'er touched earthly faces.'
So should my papers, yellowed with their age,
10   Be scorned, like old men of less truth than tongue,
And your true rights be termed a poet's rage
And stretchèd meter of an antique song;
    But were some child of yours alive that time,
    You should live twice, in it and in my rhyme.

I B
15–17

SONNET 15 is the first to promise the young man immortality in
the poet's verse. But as noted before, this new theme is actually a
device for returning to the old one. In 15 the poet introduces his
verse as Time's adversary so that he may renounce it in 16–17 and
reintroduce procreation as the essence of survival, the "mightier
way" of warring on Time. He dramatizes the reversal by run-on,
by an unexpected reference back to 15 in the opening line of 16.
    The new note of sonnets 15–17 is enhanced by their agreement
in a new mode of address, "you" instead of "thou." All earlier
sonnets save 13 use the "thou" form, and it is 13 that 15–17 echo
with deliberate play on "yourself." Compare 13.1–8 and 16.12–14.
This echo and the final reassertion of procreation as a theme join

15–17 closely with the earlier series. Poems A and B seem distinct, but they are plainly meant to be read together.

I must repeat that I stress details of intensive linkage in Group I not to 'prove' that sonnets 1–17 belong together but to present them as a model of the coherence found in an authentic Shakespearian series. As pointed out in Chapter I, the very recognition of fragmented groups and poems, to say nothing of their restoration, depends on standards set by clearly authentic sequences.

 # POEM **I**

[20]

> A woman's face with Nature's own hand painted
> Hast thou, the master-mistress of my passion,
> A woman's gentle heart but not acquainted
> With shifting change, as is false women's fashion,
> 5 An eye more bright than theirs, less false in rolling,
> Gilding the object whereupon it gazeth,
> A man in hue, all hues in his controlling,
> Which steals men's eyes and women's souls amazeth.
> And for a woman wert thou first created,
> 10 Till Nature as she wrought thee fell a-doting,
> And by addition me of thee defeated
> By adding one thing to my purpose nothing.
> > But since she pricked thee out for women's pleasure,
> > Mine be thy love and thy love's use their treasure.

POEM **I**

20

ALTHOUGH this pleasantly outrageous tour de force makes a clear statement, there has been no lack of explication, some of it by critics whose education or experience has not been equal to the subject.

In structure the sonnet is nearly perfect. The first eight lines suggest a routine compliment; the third quatrain then takes an unusual direction, posing a riddle with just enough ambiguity to set the answer in motion. Then the couplet with its pun on 'prick' simultaneously reveals the drift of previous lines and moves to a conclusion.

Without question, sonnet 20 belongs by itself, although the ending may refer lightly to the 'procreation' sonnets of Group I. Note lines 13–14: "pleasure, . . . thy love's use their treasure"; and compare sonnet 6, lines 3–6: "treasure," "use," "usury," "happies." These parallels suggest little more than composition at about the same time, which can justify Q's placement of 20 shortly after 1–17.

POEM 2
25–26

[25]

Let those who are in favor with their stars
Of public honor and proud titles boast,
Whilst I, whom fortune of such triumph bars,
Unlooked for joy in that I honor most.
5 Great princes' favorites their fair leaves spread
But as the marigold at the sun's eye,
And in themselves their pride lies burièd,
For at a frown they in their glory die.
The painful warrior famousèd for worth,
10 After a thousand victories once foiled,
Is from the book of honor rasèd [forth],
And all the rest forgot for which he toiled.
    Then happy I that love and am beloved
    Where I may not remove nor be removed.

[26]

Lord of my love, to whom in vassalage
Thy merit hath my duty strongly knit,
To thee I send this written ambassage
To witness duty, not to show my wit:
5 Duty so great, which wit so poor as mine
May make seem bare in wanting words to show it,
But that I hope some good conceit of thine
In thy soul's thought, all naked will bestow it,
Till whatsoever star that guides my moving
10 Points on me graciously with fair aspect,
And puts apparel on my tottered loving
To show me worthy of thy sweet respect.
    Then may I dare to boast how I do love thee;
    Till then not show my head where thou mayst prove me.

POEM 2
25–26

IN describing a love both mutual and secure, sonnet 25 suggests a link with the serene, confident poems containing 107–108, 115–116, and 122–126. Its relation to 116 is provocative, for the couplet, ". . . I that love and am beloved Where I may not *remove* or be *removed*," squares uniquely with two lines of 116 (2–4) declaring that love is not love if it alters with change, "Or bends with the *remover* to *remove*." And the possible link between 25 and 115–116 becomes doubly interesting when we note that 24 is closely related to 113–114 (page 69). Two unrelated sonnets adjacent in Q (24 and 25) may thus link respectively with two unrelated pairs adjacent in Q (113–114 and 115–116).

But if 25 is reminiscent of 115–116, its companion, sonnet 26, is not; for 26, running counter to 115–116, plainly implies an early or 'trial' period in the poet-patron relationship. Hence, if 25 is to be joined with 116, it must be parted from 26—no light undertaking since the two sonnets, together in Q, are joined by something very close, at least, to a last-line–first-line run-on. Love's inviolable allegiance, declared at the end of 25, directly anticipates the opening of 26; the lover who "may not remove nor be removed" (25.13–14) is bound "in vassalage" to the "Lord" of his love (26.1–2). Pertinent also is the "boast" motif governing both the opening of 25 (the first quatrain) and the ending of 26 (the couplet). Further, in 25.1–2 and 26.9–12, there are parallel allusions to status or worth controlled by the stars. One rule of the game has to be that sonnets found together in Q, and so linked, must remain together.

Finally 25, like 26, is quite compatible with the earlier sonnets. Its couplet taken alone may express more intimacy and confidence than are becoming in an 'unestablished' poet, but not when the sentiment is qualified as it is by 26. Sonnets 1–17, moreover, clearly imply the mutual respect of two friends, and to judge from 29–31—especially the couplet of 29—the poet of the earlier sonnets had no doubt of his friend's affection.

I leave 25–26 together, substantially in their Q position between sonnets 1–17 and the series containing 29–31 followed by other sonnets expressing fervent allegiance. But we cannot tell whether the two sonnets concluded the first seventeen, introduced 29–31, stood by themselves, or accompanied a "written ambassage" unrelated to any group of sonnets. A responsible guess would be that the first quatrain of 25 and the last six lines of 26 reveal a close relationship with sonnet 29.

I retain Q's reading, "famousèd for worth," at 25.9 and emend line 11, substituting "rasèd forth" for "rasèd quite." One of the two lines is misprinted, and the usual emendation at line 9, "famousèd for fight," replaces a phrase that rings true with one that rings false. The emendation of line 11, not original with me, has no bearing on the meaning or placement of Poem 2.

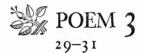

POEM 3
29–31

[29]

   When in disgrace with fortune and men's eyes,
   I all alone beweep my outcast state,
   And trouble deaf heaven with my bootless cries,
   And look upon myself and curse my fate,
5 Wishing me like to one more rich in hope,
   Featured like him, like him with friends possessed,
   Desiring this man's art and that man's scope,
   With what I most enjoy contented least;
   Yet in these thoughts myself almost despising,
10 Haply I think on thee, and then my state,
   Like to the lark at break of day arising
   From sullen earth, sings hymns at heaven's gate;
     For thy sweet love rememb'red such wealth brings
     That then I scorn to change my state with kings.

[30]

   When to the sessions of sweet silent thought
   I summon up remembrance of things past,
   I sigh the lack of many a thing I sought,
   And with old woes new wail my dear time's waste;
5 Then can I drown an eye, unused to flow,
   For precious friends hid in death's dateless night,
   And weep afresh love's long since canceled woe,
   And moan th' expense of many a vanished sight;
   Then can I grieve at grievances foregone,
10 And heavily from woe to woe tell o'er
   The sad account of fore-bemoanèd moan,
   Which I new pay as if not paid before.
     But if the while I think on thee, dear friend,
     All losses are restored and sorrows end.

[31]

Thy bosom is endearèd with all hearts,
Which I by lacking have supposèd dead,
And there reigns love and all love's loving parts,
And all those friends which I thought burièd.
5 How many a holy and obsequious tear
Hath dear religious love stol'n from mine eye,
As interest of the dead, which now appear
But things removed that hidden in thee lie.
Thou art the grave where buried love doth live,
10 Hung with the trophies of my lovers gone,
Who all their parts of me to thee did give;
That due of many now is thine alone.
    Their images I loved I view in thee,
    And thou, all they, hast all the all of me.

POEM 3
29–31

IN 29, deservedly one of the best known of the Sonnets, the poet
surmounts envy and self-contempt—"in these thoughts myself
almost despising"—by turning in second thought to his friend:
"Haply I think on thee. . . ." In 30, "sweet silent thought" turns
from the present woes of 29 to "old woes," to a "remembrance of
things past." And again in the couplet, thoughts of misfortune are
transcended in thoughts of friendship: "But if the while I think
on thee. . . ." In the second quatrain of 30 we hear of the poet's
"precious friends hid in death's dateless night," and the way opens
for 31 which attends (line 4) upon "all those friends which I
thought burièd," friends which the "dear friend" of the present
now embodies: "Their images I loved I view in thee."

In structure this triad is remarkably like 97–99: the first two
sonnets run parallel in theme; the third and concluding sonnet
develops a specific motif introduced by the second. Here again is
a model of Shakespearian coherence preserved in Q.

# GROUP II

A 113–114 B 24 46–47 C 61 27–28 43
D 44–45 50–51 E 48 75 56 52 F 57–58 G 49
87–90 H 91–93 69–70 95–96 94 I 36–39
J 33–35 40–42 [K 109–112 117–121]?

IN this group the poet alludes continually to separation from his
friend. At first the separation amounts to simple absence; then
with poem E a note of feared alienation enters to accompany
absence, and from F through J it becomes dominant. Most of the
poems resolve separation and alienation into their opposite, 'oneness' ("my friend and I are one"—42.13); and in this respect E, I,
J are definitive.

The absence theme of poems A through E develops into the
friend's presence-in-absence as he becomes an image or "picture"
in the poet's eye, mind, heart; a "shadow" in the poet's dreams; a
"treasure" in the poet's breast. The two commune by "nimble
thought." Transition from the opening poems to the ensuing
alienation series occurs in 48, the first sonnet of E, which continues in its first line the poet's journey away from his friend
and then introduces the fear of estrangement. This theme,
progressively intensified, leads to I and J, the two concluding
poems that accept division or separation as ultimate but translate
it into a kind of union.

More extended commentary to follow will show a close relation between elements of this group, a relation Q itself supports
by presenting fragments of the poems substantially in the restored
order. Thus, after 24, a fragment of B, comes 27–28, a fragment
of C. After 43, another fragment of C, appear 44–45, the opening
sonnets of D. Fragments of E—48, 52, 56—follow in Q and are
succeeded by 57–58, F intact. Then we find that 49 links cogently
with 87–90 to form poem G which continues the alienation theme

with a pointed echo of F. From 87, the second sonnet of G, the restored sonnet order substantially follows the Q order through 96 to complete poem H. A remarkable link between 96 of H and 36 of I then brings us back to sonnets that form I and J, disarranged but 'clustered' in Q as 33–42.

Sonnets 109–112 117–121 appear in this edition as an independent series, 'Poem 5,' retained finally in its Q relationship with 122–126. But these sonnets of Poem 5 have interesting claims to a position in the present group as a terminal poem (see pages 190–193). Hence, although I have allowed Q's placement of the sonnets to decide a matter of doubt, I list them conjecturally as K in the tabular order of Group II, above.

 II A

113–114

[113]

    Since I left you mine eye is in my mind,
    And that which governs me to go about
    Doth part his function and is partly blind,
    Seems seeing, but effectually is out;
5   For it no form delivers to the heart
    Of bird, of flower, or shape which it doth latch:
    Of his quick objects hath the mind no part,
    Nor his own vision holds what it doth catch;
    For if it see the rud'st or gentlest sight,
10 The most sweet favor or deformed'st creature,
    The mountain or the sea, the day or night,
    The crow or dove, it shapes them to your feature:
      Incapable of more, replete with you,
      My most true mind thus maketh mine eye untrue.

[114]

    Or whether doth my mind, being crowned with you,
    Drink up the monarch's plague, this flattery?
    Or whether shall I say mine eye saith true,
    And that your love taught it this alchemy,
5   To make of monsters and things indigest
    Such cherubins as your sweet self resemble,
    Creating every bad a perfect best,
    As fast as objects to his beams assemble?
    O 'tis the first; 'tis flattery in my seeing,
10 And my great mind most kingly drinks it up;
    Mine eye well knows what with his gust is 'greeing,
    And to his palate doth prepare the cup.
      If it be poisoned, 'tis the lesser sin
      That mine eye loves it and doth first begin.

II A
113–114

THE misplacement of this pair in Q is obvious from its disruption of close continuity between 109–112 117–121 (pages 187–190), and from an inconsistency between the poet's absence as represented in 113 and in 109–110, 119. In the latter sonnets the poet writes vividly of a past absence and of his return from it, while in 113.1, and lines that follow, his absence is current and continuing.

The reference to absence at the beginning of 113, the theme of eye and mind (or heart), and the uniquely contrived manner, combine to relate 113–114 to poem B, 24 46–47. Sonnets 46 (lines 9–10) and 47 (lines 7–8) both duplicate 113's equation of mind and heart (lines 1–5). Although poems A and B do not necessarily interconnect, it is hard to believe that they are unrelated in point of time or occasion. Placement of 113–114 at the beginning of Group II secures their unique relationship with poem B and at the same time allows for interplay between 46–47 (ending B) and following sonnets.

In Q, 113.14 reads "maketh mine untrue." The emendation here is widely accepted, and in any event has no bearing on the question of rearrangement.

 **II B**

24 46–47

[24]

Mine eye hath played the painter and hath stelled
Thy beauty's form in table of my heart;
My body is the frame wherein 'tis held,
And perspective it is best painter's art.
5 For through the painter must you see his skill
To find where your true image pictured lies,
Which in my bosom's shop is hanging still,
That hath his windows glazèd with thine eyes.
Now see what good turns eyes for eyes have done:
10 Mine eyes have drawn thy shape, and thine for me
Are windows to my breast, wherethrough the sun
Delights to peep, to gaze therein on thee;
    Yet eyes this cunning want to grace their art,
    They draw but what they see, know not the heart.

[46]

Mine eye and heart are at a mortal war,
How to divide the conquest of thy sight;
Mine eye my heart thy picture's sight would bar,
My heart mine eye the freedom of that right.
5 My heart doth plead that thou in him dost lie,
A closet never pierced with crystal eyes,
But the defendant doth that plea deny,
And says in him thy fair appearance lies.
To 'cide this title is impanelèd
10 A quest of thoughts, all tenants to the heart,
And by their verdict is determinèd
The clear eye's moiety and the dear heart's part:
    As thus, mine eye's due is thy outward part,
    And my heart's right thy inward love of heart.

[47]

    Betwixt mine eye and heart a league is took,
    And each doth good turns now unto the other:
    When that mine eye is famished for a look,
    Or heart in love with sighs himself doth smother,
5   With my love's picture then my eye doth feast
    And to the painted banquet bids my heart;
    Another time mine eye is my heart's guest
    And in his thoughts of love doth share a part.
    So either by thy picture or my love,
10 Thyself away art present still with me;
    For thou not farther than my thoughts canst move,
    And I am still with them and they with thee;
      Or if they sleep, thy picture in my sight
      Awakes my heart to heart's and eye's delight.

II B
24 46–47

ALTHOUGH the three sonnets of this restored poem spin out a
derived conceit, they have the unmistakable style that can lend
character to a banal subject. And significantly, for our purposes,
they show another Shakespearian quality: close, multiple linkage.
Beyond this they display a typical feature of the 1609 text:
authentic linkage preserved at one point (46–47) and lost at
another (the separation and isolation of 24). As a poem the three
sonnets lack substance, but the editorial problem they raise and its
solution are representative. If fragmentation of this poem can be
established in Q, then we may be sure that much better poems
have been disturbed in a similar manner.

    The most casual regard for subject matter (eye, heart, and the
cherished picture), or for continuity (47 as a completion of 46)

leaves no doubt that Q presents two of the sonnets in their original order. Moreover, if we note the theme of absence (47.10–12), with the allied theme of presence-in-absence through the friend's image held in the poet's eye and frustrating distance spanned by the poet's "thoughts" (47.5–14), we can understand why Q happens to place 46–47 close to 43, 44–45, 48, 50–51, and 52. All of these sonnets express such notions in one way or another and apparently belong together in a group which Q preserves in a fragmentary state.

Since 24 has no ties with 23 or 25, and since there is nothing in 46–47 having immediate reference to 44–45, the way opens for possible restoration of the order 24 46–47. Although many rearrangers observe the affinity between these sonnets, a fair number hesitate to bring all three together. Brooke, for example, kept 24 apart, believing that it discourses on a metaphorical picture while 46–47 refer to an actual portrait. Certainly the picture in 24 is metaphorical, but there is no assurance that the picture in 46–47 is 'real'; key lines, in fact, seem to place it as the figment of eye and heart depicted in 24 (see 46.5–8, passim). I suspect that traditional reluctance to join 24 with the other two sonnets amounts to little more than reverence for the Q text in the face of many signs indicating disarrangement.

Sonnets 24, 46, and 47 present the same subject, and do so elaborately. This obvious fact does not, of course, require that they be brought together. But if we venture beyond the obvious or, more precisely, venture a bit further into it, little doubt may remain that the sonnets were originally joined. Some of the best evidence concerns structure. In 46–47 Shakespeare shows clearly that he is working with parallel opening lines and parallel concluding couplets: "Mine eye and heart" of 46.1 is echoed by the identical phrase in 47.1. And in each sonnet the first two lines present a relation between eye and heart that succeeding lines develop. Then, as we encounter the couplets, we find that the last two lines of 46 and the last two of 47 do precisely the same thing; they state epigrammatically a division of domain or function between eye and heart—what the eye has or does that complements what the heart has or does ("they" in 47.13 means the heart's thoughts; see 47.7–8).

This rhetorical design, used so effectively to link 46 and 47, extends unmistakably to, or from, 24. First, the two opening lines: in a context of 46.1–2 and 47.1–2, note the parallel "Mine eye" in 24.1, and note that 24.1–2 also states in a 'topic sentence' the relation between eye and heart that ensuing lines develop. Now the couplet of 24: it likewise follows the scheme of 46–47 by distinguishing in epigram the eye's role from the heart's role.

Further evidence for linkage appears in the first quatrain of 46. Lines 1 and 2 declare that eye and heart, having made a "conquest of thy sight," are now warring over the spoils. But thus far no one reading 46 by itself can tell what the statement means. Then from line 3 it appears that the prize of conquest is a picture, but the information scarcely comes as developing explanation; implicit in this line is the poet's assumption that we have already recognized the "conquest" by eye and heart in line 2 as a picture, so that mere mention of "thy picture's sight" in line 3 will continue an established association. Yet, if 46 is read as an opening sonnet, line 3 has no clear meaning or, at best, too many possible meanings (what picture?). But if we allow 24 to precede 46 the reference becomes perfectly clear; with 24 in mind, the first two lines of 46 immediately denote the picture and its entire history without help from 46.3. Beyond explaining the sudden reference to a picture in 46, sonnet 24 supplies a basis, heretofore lacking, for understanding the picture as a conquest. In 24, the first 'chapter' of the story, we learn of the eye's triumph in catching "Thy beauty's form" and lodging it (in true perspective) within the poet's "bosom"—delineated in the tablet of his heart. Hence reference in 46 to the picture, a tour de force, as a conquest. Hence reference to the "war" between eye and heart to "divide" the spoils of conquest, the picture. The eye captured it; the heart holds it. With this explained by 24, sonnets 46–47 can now proceed clearly.

Someone is sure to object that a metaphor of 46, the heart as a "closet never pierced with crystal eyes," contradicts a metaphor of 24, "my bosom's shop" that "hath his windows glazèd with thine eyes . . . wherethrough the sun Delights to peep" (lines 7–12). But the friend's eyes as windows to the poet's bosom (24) are not the equivalent of prying eyes that try to pierce the poet's heart (46.6). Besides, the metaphor of 46 is part of the heart's allegation, which the "defendant" eye denies (46.7). Who is to say the defendant is wrong although the verdict of a hung jury, "tenants to the heart" (46.10), may be against him? If this pedantry fails to answer a somewhat pedantic objection, my final refuge (perhaps it should have been the first) is in the truism that Shakespeare's metaphors often shift. And the two main metaphors of sonnet 24 itself provide a shining example.

 II C

61 27–28 43

[61]

    Is it thy will thy image should keep open
    My heavy eyelids to the weary night?
    Dost thou desire my slumbers should be broken,
    While shadows like to thee do mock my sight?
5   Is it thy spirit that thou send'st from thee
    So far from home into my deeds to pry,
    To find out shames and idle hours in me,
    The scope and tenure of thy jealousy?
    O no, thy love though much is not so great:
10 It is my love that keeps mine eye awake,
    Mine own true love that doth my rest defeat,
    To play the watchman ever for thy sake:
      For thee watch I whilst thou dost wake elsewhere,
      From me far off, with others all too near.

[27]

    Weary with toil I haste me to my bed,
    The dear repose for limbs with travel tired;
    But then begins a journey in my head
    To work my mind, when body's work's expired:
5   For then my thoughts, from far where I abide,
    Intend a zealous pilgrimage to thee,
    And keep my drooping eyelids open wide,
    Looking on darkness which the blind do see;
    Save that my soul's imaginary sight
10 Presents thy shadow to my sightless view,
    Which like a jewel hung in ghastly night,
    Makes black night beauteous and her old face new.
      Lo thus by day my limbs, by night my mind,
      For thee and for myself no quiet find.

[28]

How can I then return in happy plight,
That am debarred the benefit of rest?—
When day's oppression is not eased by night,
But day by night and night by day oppressed;
5 And each, though enemies to either's reign,
Do in consent shake hands to torture me,
The one by toil, the other to complain
How far I toil, still farther off from thee.
I tell the day to please him thou art bright,
10 And dost him grace when clouds do blot the heaven;
So flatter I the swart-complexioned night,
When sparkling stars twire not thou gild'st the even.
    But day doth daily draw my sorrows longer,
    And night doth nightly make grief's strength seem stronger.

[43]

When most I wink then do mine eyes best see,
For all the day they view things unrespected;
But when I sleep, in dreams they look on thee,
And darkly bright, are bright in dark directed.
5 Then thou whose shadow shadows doth make bright,
How would thy shadow's form form happy show
To the clear day with thy much clearer light,
When to unseeing eyes thy shade shines so.
How would, I say, mine eyes be blessèd made
10 By looking on thee in the living day,
When in dead night thy fair imperfect shade
Through heavy sleep on sightless eyes doth stay.
    All days are nights to see till I see thee,
    And nights bright days when dreams do show thee me.

II C
61 27–28 43

IN its Q position 61 is opposed in subject and tone to 60 and 62. Although the position of 25 and 26 suggests that they could be dedicatory sonnets in a series that includes 27–28, there is nothing in either pair that requires immediate proximity of the other. Nor is there any clear relationship between 27–28 and 29–31. An obvious change of subject occurs in the Q transition between 40–42 and 43; hence separation of these sonnets breaks no continuity. With 43 as the end of poem C and 44 as the beginning of D, the Q order 43–44 is unchanged.

Sonnets 61, 27–28, and 43 have a theme in common: absence, nocturnal wakefulness or vivid dreams, and a haunting of the poet by his friend's "shadow" or image. The three elements of this multiple theme are not present here just in aggregate; all of them appear in each sonnet of the restored poem.

Thematic parallels are supported by pointed echo of phrase and image: "keep open My heavy eyelids" (61.1–2) and "drooping eyelids open wide" (27.7); "doth my rest defeat" (61.11) and "debarred the benefit of rest" (28.2); "*shadows* like to thee do mock my *sight*" (61.4), "thy *shadow* to my *sightless view*" (27.10), "thy . . . *shade* . . . on *sightless eyes*" (43.11–12), and "to *unseeing eyes* thy *shade* shines so" (43.8; note also the play on "shadow" in 43.5–6). Nor is the absence theme merely generalized; it is the absence of increasing physical distance expressed with parallel phrasing: "far from home" (61.6), "from far where I abide" (27.5), "still farther off from thee" (28.8).

In addition to strong thematic and verbal unity the four sonnets show a remarkable structural affinity. Sonnet 61 (1–8) establishes the night vigil by asking whether the loving friend sends his "spirit" in jealousy to visit the poet and disturb his sleep. The question is then answered, but not completely, in the remainder of 61: the poet's love alone disturbs his rest. Sonnet 27 immediately augments this answer by matching the alternative rejected in 61—a "spirit" emanating from friend to poet—with one that nicely balances it—"thoughts" emanating (in a "pilgrimage") from poet to friend. Then, after elaborating the night watch, sonnet 27 in its couplet introduces the day-night opposition that will sustain the rest of the poem. The whole of 28 is taken up with this motif in an obvious run-on from 27. Finally, in lines 5–14 sonnet 43 carries the day-night antithesis to a resolution of "shadow" into substance, or coming reality. If the shadow has made the night beautiful (27) and gilded the evening (28), how much more brightly and happily will the "shadow's form" (the actual object casting the shadow or semblance) appear in the "clear day" (43). But all this is mere paraphrase. For the essential development, in terms of "day"–"night," that augments the pain of absence and ends in a promise of deliverance, read the restored poem, noting successively the matched couplets ending 27, 28, and 43. All three play on day–night, and the couplet of 43 fulfills, completes, those of 27 and 28. The parallel, cumulative design speaks for itself. Compare it with the design enhanced by echoing couplets in 46–47 and 69–70 (pages 72 and 104).

These unifying elements of theme, diction, and structure are more than enough to outweigh a literalist's objection that 61, 27, and 28 describe a poet open-eyed and cursed with insomnia, while 43 describes one who "winks," who is sound asleep. 'Contradictions' like this are not uncommon in the Sonnets (see again the 'inconsistently' shifting metaphor within a single sonnet, 24). In any event, it is the *eye* that wakes during the broken slumber of the earlier sonnets (61.1–4, 10; 27.7–10), and it is still the eye that sees so piercingly while the poet sleeps in 43.

II D

44–45 50–51

[44]

If the dull substance of my flesh were thought,
Injurious distance should not stop my way;
For then despite of space I would be brought,
From limits far remote where thou dost stay.
5 No matter then although my foot did stand
Upon the farthest earth removed from thee,
For nimble thought can jump both sea and land
As soon as think the place where he would be.
But ah, thought kills me that I am not thought,
10 To leap large lengths of miles when thou art gone,
But that, so much of earth and water wrought,
I must attend time's leisure with my moan,
    Receiving nought by elements so slow
    But heavy tears, badges of either's woe.

[45]

The other two, slight air and purging fire,
Are both with thee, wherever I abide;
The first my thought, the other my desire,
These present-absent with swift motion slide.
5 For when these quicker elements are gone
In tender embassy of love to thee,
My life, being made of four, with two alone
Sinks down to death, oppressed with melancholy,
Until life's composition be recured
10 By those swift messengers returned from thee,
Who even but now come back again assured
Of thy fair health, recounting it to me:
    This told, I joy, but then no longer glad,
    I send them back again and straight grow sad.

[50]

How heavy do I journey on the way,
When what I seek, my weary travel's end,
Doth teach that ease and that repose to say,
'Thus far the miles are measured from thy friend.'
5   The beast that bears me, tired with my woe,
Plods dully on to bear that weight in me,
As if by some instinct the wretch did know
His rider loved not speed, being made from thee;
The bloody spur cannot provoke him on
10 That sometimes anger thrusts into his hide,
Which heavily he answers with a groan,
More sharp to me than spurring to his side;
    For that same groan doth put this in my mind,
    My grief lies onward and my joy behind.

[51]

Thus can my love excuse the slow offence
Of my dull bearer when from thee I speed:
From where thou art why should I haste me thence?
Till I return, of posting is no need.
5   O what excuse will my poor beast then find
When swift extremity can seem but slow?
Then should I spur though mounted on the wind,
In wingèd speed no motion shall I know;
Then can no horse with my desire keep pace;
10 Therefore desire, of perfect'st love being made,
Shall neigh—no dull flesh in his fiery race;
But love, for love, thus shall excuse my jade—
    Since from thee going he went wilful-slow,
    Towards thee I'll run and give him leave to go.

II D
44–45 50–51

THIS poem follows directly after 43; hence the Q order 43–44 is unchanged. Restoration here calls for a change in the Q sequence simply by removal of 46–49 from a position between 44–45 and 50–51. Although 46–49 belong in the same group with the poem thus formed by their removal, no internal evidence requires that they follow immediately after 44–45 or that they precede 50–51. The evidence points, in fact, to a relocation of 46–47 in poem B, of 48 in E, and of 49 in G. See the commentary, above and below.

A number of editors, including Pooler,[1] have seen a relationship between 44–45 and 50–51. But mere similarity of theme will not justify a change in the sonnet order. If it is to override Q, the case for revision must bring together sonnets that demand immediate sequence on several counts.

Sonnets 44–45 50–51 appropriately follow poem C in which the journeying speaker's "thoughts" are pilgrims seeking his absent friend (27), a spanning of distance by fantasy and dream that gives way to a vision of physical reunion: "All days are nights to see till I see thee" (43.13). This visitation by thoughts that can only sharpen a desire for actual meeting now finds expression in 44: "If the dull substance of my flesh were thought, Injurious distance" could not "stop my way." Yet "thought kills me that I am not thought" whose nimbleness "can jump both sea and land"; instead "[I am] so much of earth and water wrought" that "I must attend time's leisure . . . , Receiving naught by elements so slow But heavy tears. . . ." Linked syntactically with 44, sonnet 45 proceeds from the "slow" elements of earth and water to "The other two, slight air and purging fire." "The first," air, is the poet's "thought"; "the other," fire, is his "desire." When these "quicker elements" depart in an "embassy of love," the poet's "life," made of four elements and thus left "with two alone,"

borders on death until air and fire return to recount the youth's
"fair health." "This told," the poet is joyful but "straight grow[s]
sad" as he sends air and fire back in a new embassy.

Thus, the first two sonnets. If, tentatively at this point, we
remove 46–49 from the Q order, we find that 50 and 51 continue
the theme, imagery, and phrasing of 44–45 with a directness that
compels recognition. "How *heavy* do I journey on the way"
(50.1); the tired beast plods "to *bear that weight* in me" (50.5–6).
Compare these lines with 44.13–14, "heavy tears," and with
45.7–8, "My life . . . Sinks down." Note "on the way" (50.1) and
"stop my way" (44.2); "Thus far the miles are measured" (50.4)
and "To leap large lengths of miles" (44.10). The "dull substance" of the poet's flesh (44.1), heavy and spiritless, now becomes imaged in his "dull bearer" (51.2), the "beast" of 50.5–6
that "Plods dully on" (Q reads "duly"), answering "heavily" the
spur on the poet's reluctant course away from his friend. On this
outward journey love can excuse the plodding, but what excuse
will the poor beast find on the journey homeward, when speed
itself will "seem but slow"? "Then should I spur though mounted
on the wind" (51.7). Compare the air-borne motion here with the
thought-air equation of 45.1–3 which stems from the "nimble
thought" that can "jump both sea and land" (44.7). And now,
51.9–11: "Then can no horse with my desire keep pace; Therefore *desire* . . . Shall neigh—no *dull flesh* in his *fiery* race." Recall
again the "dull substance of my flesh" (44.1) and the equation of
"desire" and "fire" (45.1–3). Finally, note the slow-go, slow-woe
rhymes in the couplets of 51 and 44, and compare the parallel
grief-joy antitheses in the couplets of 50 and 45.

This array of echo links between 44–45 and 50–51 is inseparable
from an identity of theme and measured progress of thought
running from one pair through the other. All elements combine
to yield a continuity that no attentive reader, I should say, could
regard as accidental. They reproduce, moreover, just the sort of
straight-line development, enhanced by incremental repetition
and variation, that we find in sonnets 1–17 and other authentic
sequences preserved in Q.

What can be the editorial reason for retaining sonnets 46–49 in the midst of such a closely joined series? This is the Q order, but remember that Q has no authority prescribing arrangement except where the sequence is self-justifying. Sonnets 46–47 do speak of absence and bodiless visitation in absence, but in an elaborately new context which, in Q, smothers that of 44–45 50–51. At first glance, sonnet 48 has a fair claim for retention: in it the poet travels, and the opening line closely resembles the opening line of 50. Yet, as in 49, the dominant note of 48 is alienation, a subject not even present by implication in the concentrated poem before us. As noted, sonnets 46–49 will be found related to this poem, and the relationship will be preserved. But in Q there is no relationship save one in which elements of several poems cancel one another.

Thus the prime case against keeping sonnets 46–49 in their Q order is that their presence spoils a designed and elaborate interplay between 44–45 and 50–51. Four sonnets intervening between 45 and 50 cancel the thematic unity, thought development, and echo linkage we have observed, and any poet would know this to be their effect. For that matter, even one intervening sonnet introducing a new note (48 if allowed to stand) would be disruptive. Believers in the 'loose association' theory as a governing principle in Shakespeare's Sonnets are sure to object that 44–45 and 50–51 are companion pieces 'characteristically' separated by 46–49. But here they encounter difficulties beyond those already noted. There is remarkably strong evidence that 46 and 47 belong with 24, that 48 is part of a series that includes 52, and that 49 belongs with 87–90 (see poems II B, II E, II G). Further, if we take seriously the placement in Q of 44 with 45 and 50 with 51, the loose association principle becomes a shaky one. Unifying detail within each of these authentic pairs is matched by unifying detail relating one pair to the other. Did the poet who linked sonnets so carefully in the two pairs expect a cogent pair of pairs to function with four irrelevantly discursive sonnets between them? The loose associationist will doubtless answer that 'irrelevantly' begs the question. But I suspect that had Q appeared with 46–47 squarely between 44 and 45—thus destroying a syntactical link—he would find the sequence somehow appropriate.

 II E

4⁸ 75 56 52

[48]

How careful was I when I took my way,
Each trifle under truest bars to thrust,
That to my use it might unusèd stay
From hands of falsehood, in sure wards of trust.
5 But thou to whom my jewels trifles are,
Most worthy comfort, now my greatest grief,
Thou, best of dearest and mine only care,
Art left the prey of every vulgar thief.
Thee have I not locked up in any chest,
10 Save where thou art not though I feel thou art,
Within the gentle closure of my breast,
From whence at pleasure thou mayst come and part;
    And even thence thou wilt be stol'n, I fear,
    For truth proves thievish for a prize so dear.

[75]

So are you to my thoughts as food to life,
Or as sweet-seasoned showers are to the ground,
And for the peace of you I hold such strife
As 'twixt a miser and his wealth is found;
5 Now proud as an enjoyer, and anon
Doubting the filching age will steal his treasure,
Now counting best to be with you alone,
Then bettered that the world may see my pleasure;
Sometime all full with feasting on your sight,
10 And by and by clean starvèd for a look,
Possessing or pursuing no delight,
Save what is had or must from you be took.
    Thus do I pine and surfeit day by day,
    Or gluttoning on all, or all away.

[56]

    Sweet love, renew thy force; be it not said
    Thy edge should blunter be than appetite,
    Which but today by feeding is allayed,
    Tomorrow sharp'ned in his former might:
5   So love, be thou; although today thou fill
    Thy hungry eyes even till they wink with fulness,
    Tomorrow see again, and do not kill
    The spirit of love with a perpetual dulness.
    Let this sad int'rim like the ocean be
10 Which parts the shore where two contracted new
    Come daily to the banks, that when they see
    Return of love, more blest may be the view;
       Or call it winter, which being full of care,
       Makes summer's welcome thrice more wished, more rare.

[52]

    So am I as the rich whose blessèd key
    Can bring him to his sweet up-lockèd treasure,
    The which he will not every hour survey,
    For blunting the fine point of seldom pleasure.
5   Therefore are feasts so solemn and so rare,
    Since seldom coming, in the long year set
    Like stones of worth, they thinly placèd are,
    Or captain jewels in the carcanet.
    So is the time that keeps you as my chest,
10 Or as the wardrobe which the robe doth hide,
    To make some special instant special blest
    By new unfolding his imprisoned pride.
       Blessèd are you whose worthiness gives scope,
       Being had to triumph, being lacked to hope.

II E
48 75 56 52

AS noted, sonnet 48 is part of a Q series that obliterates all links between 44–45 and 50–51. For the doubtful position of 75 in Q see page 137. Sonnet 56 does not proceed from 53–55 and is opposite in tone to the petulance of 57–58. The Q order 51–52 is also suspect, for in 51 the speaker is an impatient man who will "run" toward reunion with his friend, while in 52 he holds himself in check, like a rich man who temperately refrains from surveying his treasure. Sonnet 52 has no more than a vague tie with the strongly unified series 53–55.

In this edition 48 no longer precedes 49, which is now joined with 87–90. But although the elaborate design connecting 49 with 87–90 (II G) has little or nothing to do with 48, one must grant that Q's order 48–49 makes sense; hence a separation of the two in restoring II E is no light matter. Still, if we allow 48 to accompany 49 in joining 87–90 we run counter to very strong evidence connecting 48 with 52. The 'treasure chest' theme linking these two neighboring sonnets outweighs the loose relation between 48 and 49.

But the problem is not easy. Although 48 and 52 seem immediately related, no reading of the two in sequence can avoid a clash in point of view (uneasy 'possessiveness' versus serene possession), a clash that does not resolve itself into successful paradox or antithesis. When read together the two sonnets fail to mesh. Could there have been transitional sonnets between them? If, experimentally, we remove the self-sufficient triad 53–55, we have 52 and 56 together, and find a singular relationship. In form, sonnet 52 is a long simile with the usual beginning, "So . . ."; and as a long simile it can follow 56 perfectly. Yet in Q it follows 51 with an effect typical of disarrangement: seeming relevancy ending in non sequitur.

Thus the poem that begins to take form is 48, 56, 52. But something is missing, something between 48 and 56. The reconstructed pair 56 52 and the yet unfulfilled 48 suggest an original poem of four stanzas made up of two balanced pairs (note, for example, Q 71–72, 73–74). And if the pairs are to balance precisely—and characteristically—a sonnet in long simile form should follow 48, just as 52, in our tentative restoration, follows 56. Is there such a sonnet among apparently misplaced singles in Q? The one meeting all specifications is 75: it is stranded irrelevantly between 71–74 and 76–86; it is an extended simile; it continues unmistakably the statement of 48; and, significantly, it leads directly into 56, thus linking the 'paired pairs.' Just as remarkably, moreover, 75 harks back to 46–47 of poem B.

Now, the detailed evidence. Sonnet 48 in its first line, similar in phrasing to the first line of 50, presents the travel-absence theme found in the opening poems of Group II. At line 9 it introduces the locked treasure chest, "where thou art not though I feel thou art," and ends with anxious fear that the treasure will be "stol'n"—"even thence"—from the "gentle closure of my breast."

With pointed relevance to the closing lines of 48—the chest and fear that its contents will be "stol'n"—sonnet 75 introduces a continuing metaphor, the miser who fears a "filching age will steal his treasure." Like the miser, the speaker wants at one moment to be alone with his wealth and at another to let the world know his "pleasure" in it. But this is not all. In 48.10–11 the treasure chest ("where . . . I feel thou art") is the speaker's breast, and the beginning of 75 runs, "So are you to my thoughts as food to life." The simile of 48 75 thus depends on immediate association of *breast* and *thoughts*. This association, it turns out, has been well established in poem B (24 46–47), and the play on "thoughts" in C–D has been emphatic. In 46.10 "thoughts" are "tenants to the heart" or breast (compare "my bosom's shop," 24.7); in 47.7–8 the heart has custody of "thoughts of love"; and in the remainder of 47 the conceit extends into a statement that lays a foundation for 48 75: the absent friend is always present

(47.10), "For thou not farther than my thoughts canst move
. . ." (47.11–12).

Thus far, the parallel heart-breast-thoughts note in 46–47 and
48 75 might be written off as commonplace. But fortunately, in
both 46–47 and 48 75 it becomes unique by combination with the
note of starving and feasting: compare 47.3–6 with 75.1 ("food")
and 75.9–10, 13–14; note also the association of feeding with
seeing in 47.3, 5 and 75.9, 10. Here the parallel is marked by
phrasal echo: "famished for a look" (47.3) and "clean starvèd for
a look" (75.10); the "eye's delight" (47.14) and the sight-feaster's
"delight" (75.9–11).

Thus multiple parallels not only relate the distant 75 to 48 but
place it in a context furnished by other sonnets of Group II. And
in doing so they answer a possible although literal objection that
75 (in lines 7–10) implies not absence but physical presence of the
poet's friend, and thus contradicts 48, 56, and 52, to which I
have linked it. Actually, in 48, 56, and 52, in 46–47, and indeed in
most poems of Group II, absence *is* presence by virtue of thought
and "imaginary" sense, which in one way or another bridge
"injurious distance." So, in 75 the poet either "alone" with his
friend or "feasting on [his] sight" suggests the friend's presence,
but no more vividly than do the images, dreams, or thoughts of
wholly imaginary communion in poems B, C, and D. And when
we recall that 48 speaks of the friend being stolen from a chest
that actually does not contain him, a stressing of imagination, of
fancy, in 75 ("So are you to my thoughts . . .") follows most
aptly. The long simile of 75, including the alternatives (lines 7–8)
of being "with you alone" or allowing "the world" to "see my
pleasure," thus has to do with events pictured in the poet's
thoughts, not with 'real' events requiring the friend's physical
presence.

The metaphor of seeing-as-feeding that relates 75 to earlier
poems of Group II simultaneously joins it with 56, which follows
impressively. In the last six lines of 75, climaxed by the couplet,
the metaphor develops to a point of dilemma—either "glutton-
ing" or starving. So ends 75; and 56, linked by immediate run-on,

now resolves the dilemma. Loves "edge" must not "blunter be than appetite" (56.2). If appetite, not surfeited as in 75.13, is but "allayed" by today's feeding (56.3), and thus "Tomorrow sharp'ned in his former might" (a cycle of normal hunger and normal feeding), so should it be with love—"So love, be thou . . ." (56.5 ff.). And, typically, this remarkable continuation of 75 by 56 is sustained by phrasal echo: "*full* with *feasting* on your *sight*" (75.9) and "*hungry eyes*" filled "till they wink with *fulness*" (56.5–6); pining and surfeiting "day by day" (75.13) and eyes fed "today"—hungry "tomorrow" (56.5, 7).

Just as 75 leads directly to 56, so 56 prepares the way for 52. In 56 the unified double metaphor—of appetite merely allayed today so it may be sharpened tomorrow, and of lovers who cherish separation so that reunion may be "blest" the more—justifies the "sad int'rim" (56.9) of parting between poet and friend. From this, cogently, the long simile of 52 moves: "So" is the poet (52.1–4) as the rich man who holds a key to his "up-lockèd treasure" but will not survey it "every hour"; so (52.5 ff.) are feasts made rare that they may be savored, "stones [jewels] of worth" "thinly placed" that they may show more beautifully. Here the feasts echo 75 and 56; the locked treasure chest (52.2, 9) and the jewels bring us full circle by restoring the metaphor of 48. Other specific echoes are "treasure," "pleasure" as rhymes (75.6, 8 and 52.2, 4); "Thy edge . . . blunter," "blunting the fine point" (56.2 and 52.4); "worthy," "worthiness" (48.6 and 52.13); and "blest," "blessed" (56.12 and 52.1, 13—functioning integrally with run-on between the two sonnets).

And reappearance of the treasure chest is much more than echo; it is a resolution by paradox in the final sonnet (52) of the predicament framed in the beginning sonnet (48). In 48 the imaginary locked chest ("gentle closure of my breast") serves precariously to safeguard a treasure during absence; in 52 the treasure chest *becomes* duration of the absence, which by withholding the treasure enhances its worth: "So is the time that keeps you as my chest." It is the wardrobe that hides the robe, "To make some special instant special blest By new unfolding his imprisoned pride." The relationship between 48 and 52, sonnets on the same theme but apparently antithetical in statement, is no longer a puzzle, for when 75 and 56 are placed between them, 48 and 52 take on a reciprocal meaning wholly lost in the disarranged Q sequence.

Before understanding the full range of these links, I had given Q's sonnet order benefit of the doubt by carrying 48–49 together into poem G (making it 48–49 87–90), and by placing 75 in III C as a long simile after 76 (Brooke's solution; see page 137). Such an arrangement, based on loose connection in the existing Q order (except, of course, that connection between 75 and 76 requires their transposition), reduces poem E of Group II to the single pair, 56 52. Should a reader prefer this solution as a conservative alternative to the one I offer, it is available. I feel strongly, however, that the evidence behind 48 75 56 52 far outweighs Q's doubtful testimony, and that to opt for Q under the circumstance would be more reckless than conservative.

II F

57–58

[57]

Being your slave, what should I do but tend
Upon the hours and times of your desire?
I have no precious time at all to spend,
Nor services to do, till you require.
5 Nor dare I chide the world-without-end hour
Whilst I, my sovereign, watch the clock for you,
Nor think the bitterness of absence sour
When you have bid your servant once adieu;
Nor dare I question with my jealous thought
10 Where you may be, or your affairs suppose,
But like a sad slave stay and think of nought
Save where you are how happy you make those.
  So true a fool is love that in your Will,
  Though you do any thing, he thinks no ill.

[58]

That god forbid, that made me first your slave,
I should in thought control your times of pleasure,
Or at your hand th' account of hours to crave,
Being your vassal bound to stay your leisure.
5 O let me suffer, being at your beck,
Th' imprisoned absence of your liberty;
And patience, tame to sufferance, bide each check,
Without accusing you of injury.
Be where you list, your charter is so strong
10 That you yourself may privilege your time
To what you will, to you it doth belong
Yourself to pardon of self-doing crime.
  I am to wait though waiting so be hell,
  Not blame your pleasure, be it ill or well.

II F
57–58

WHEN sonnets 53–55, a discrete triad, are linked with Group IV, the pair 57–58 follows poem E of II (48 75 56 52) by virtue of its Q position. With 56 52, poem E resolves momentarily the impatient anxiety of earlier Group II poems. Sonnets 57–58 (F) reintroduce it, intensify it, and thus lead effectively to the aggravated fear of alienation expressed in 49 87–90 (G). Absence, to which the speaker reconciles himself in 56 52, now becomes absence compounded by the friend's inattention and neglect. The transition is poignant. At the close of poem E (52.9 ff.), "the *time*" that separates poet and friend has become a means of enhancing communion by enforcing its rarity: "So is the time that keeps you as my [treasure] chest"; thus is the "special instant [of reunion] special blest." Now, in 57–58, the enhancement vanishes. But the metaphor, "time" = absence, conspicuously remains in a new context of anxiety and depression. I must "tend Upon the hours and times of your desire"; "I have no precious time at all to spend . . . till you require [appoint it]"; "Nor dare I chide the world-without-end hour Whilst I, my sovereign, watch the clock for you." These instances fill sonnet 57, and the time-absence equation continues throughout 58 (lines 2, 3, 10).

Sonnets 57–58 are worth noting as an example of the intensive, multiple linkage found in Shakespearian pairs. Besides the time-hour-clock terms for absence and alienation, note "slave" (57.1, 11; 58.1) and "vassal" (58.4). In both sonnets the slave-vassal echo is combined with parallel construction: "Being your slave" (57.1), "Being your vassal" (58.4), "being at your beck" (58.5). Parallel phrases appear at exactly parallel points of development: "times of your desire" (57.2) and "your times of pleasure" (58.2). Finally, there is the play on "Will" and "ill" begun in the couplet of 57 and expanded to an interplay of "will," "ill," "hell," "well" in 58.11–14. (I retain Q's capitalization of "Will" at 57.13, for to regularize the usage, as some editors do, disregards a likely pun on the poet's name.)

Pooler, thinking that "Being your slave" in the first line of 57 calls for a preceding statement of the speaker's slavery, found in 58, suggested that the two sonnets may be reversed. But no such antecedent is required; the first words of 57 can mean 'since I am your slave,' and the rest of the sonnet will follow clearly, as will the retrospective beginning of 58. Actually the two sonnets make perfect sense in either order, but if the Q arrangement is reversed the pair ends on a pathetic, helpless note found in the couplet of 57, and the effect changes materially. For in Q's order, ending with 58.9–14, the "slave" suddenly 'turns' to define his state with spirited petulance. The existing structure of 57–58 is thus dramatic, not anticlimactic, and no internal evidence suggests anything else as the poet's intention.

Sonnets 57 and 58 begin the theme of anxiety and recrimination, of feared alienation between poet and friend that will appear in closing poems of the current group. The next poem (49 87–90) not only continues the theme but echoes two defining elements of 57–58: the poet as ironical apologist, even 'advocate,' presenting his friend's case against himself, and his use, in this role, of language drawn from legal practice. Characteristic of the latter is 58.9, "Be where you list, your charter is so strong . . . ," which anticipates 87.3, "The charter of thy worth gives thee releasing."

 II G
49 87–90

[49]

Against that time, if ever that time come,
When I shall see thee frown on my defects,
Whenas thy love hath cast his utmost sum,
Called to that audit by advised respects;
5   Against that time when thou shalt strangely pass,
And scarcely greet me with that sun, thine eye,
When love converted from the thing it was
Shall reasons find of settled gravity—
Against that time do I ensconce me here
10   Within the knowledge of mine own desert,
And this my hand against myself uprear,
To guard the lawful reasons on thy part:
      To leave poor me thou hast the strength of laws,
      Since why to love I can allege no cause.

[87]

Farewell, thou art too dear for my possessing,
And like enough thou know'st thy estimate;
The charter of thy worth gives thee releasing;
My bonds in thee are all determinate.
5   For how do I hold thee but by thy granting,
And for that riches where is my deserving?
The cause of this fair gift in me is wanting,
And so my patent back again is swerving.
Thyself thou gav'st, thy own worth then not knowing,
10   Or me, to whom thou gav'st it, else mistaking;
So thy great gift, upon misprision growing,
Comes home again on better judgement making.
      Thus have I had thee, as a dream doth flatter,
      In sleep a king, but waking no such matter.

[88]

When thou shalt be disposed to set me light,
And place my merit in the eye of scorn,
Upon thy side against myself I'll fight,
And prove thee virtuous though thou art forsworn.
5 With mine own weakness being best acquainted,
Upon thy part I can set down a story
Of faults concealed, wherein I am attainted,
That thou in losing me shalt win much glory;
And I by this will be a gainer too,
10 For bending all my loving thoughts on thee,
The injuries that to myself I do,
Doing thee vantage, double-vantage me.
   Such is my love, to thee I so belong,
    That for thy right myself will bear all wrong.

[89]

Say that thou didst forsake me for some fault,
And I will comment upon that offence;
Speak of my lameness and I straight will halt,
Against thy reasons making no defence.
5 Thou canst not, love, disgrace me half so ill,
To set a form upon desirèd change,
As I'll myself disgrace, knowing thy will.
I will acquaintance strangle and look strange,
Be absent from thy walks, and in my tongue
10 Thy sweet belovèd name no more shall dwell,
Lest I, too much profane, should do it wrong,
And haply of our old acquaintance tell.
   For thee, against myself I'll vow debate,
    For I must ne'er love him whom thou dost hate.

[90]

Then hate me when thou wilt; if ever, now,
Now while the world is bent my deeds to cross,
Join with the spite of fortune, make me bow,
And do not drop in for an after-loss:
5   Ah do not, when my heart hath 'scaped this sorrow,
Come in the rearward of a conquered woe;
Give not a windy night a rainy morrow,
To linger out a purposed overthrow.
If thou wilt leave me, do not leave me last,
10 When other petty griefs have done their spite,
But in the onset come; so shall I taste
At first the very worst of fortune's might;
    And other strains of woe, which now seem woe,
    Compared with loss of thee will not seem so.

II G
49 87–90

SONNET 49 has no apparent ties with 50–51; on its separation
from 48 see pages 86–90. Although possibly related to the Q
sequence 76–86 (plainly a separate group), and clearly associated
with 91–93, the series 87–90 is discrete. Addition of 49 to 87–90 in
no way affects a relation of the series to other sonnets.

As a self-justifying sequence, 87–90 is typically Shakespearian.
Its two themes—a releasing of the friend from all allegiance, and
advocacy by the poet of the 'case' against himself—occur elsewhere, but here they appear elaborately and consistently as a legal
issue stated in legal terms. See for example "charter . . . releasing," "bonds," "hold," "granting" (87.3–5); "patent" (87.8);
"misprision" (87.11); "attainted" (88.7); and "defence" (89.4).
A clear logic of transition supports the unity of metaphor: 88

follows from 87, 89 pointedly develops the thought of 88, and 90, the end sonnet, not only climaxes the whole but proceeds from 89 with a syntactical link supported by verbal echo, "hate" (89.14 and 90.1).

This design understood, the relation of 49 to 87–90 becomes unique. First, 49 introduces alienation as a menacing possibility, meanwhile beginning the trend of legal imagery with "Called to that audit" (line 4) and "love converted"—compare the common-law term, 'conversion'—(line 7). Then in its last six lines, 49 introduces the poet as self-opposing advocate, "To guard the lawful reasons on thy part," and announces the legal theme of 87–90 in the plainest of terms: "To leave poor me thou hast the strength of laws, Since why to love I can allege no cause." Hence, directly from 49 the sudden "Farewell" of 87—in terms of charter, bond, grant, and patent—can now come as a dramatic turn both fitting and precise.

Sonnet 49 also anticipates phrasing of other sonnets in the 87–90 series. "To guard the lawful *reasons* on thy *part*" (line 12) finds an echo in 88.6, "Upon thy part," and in 89.4, "Against thy reasons making no defence." Likewise anticipated is some nonlegal phrasing. Compare "when thou shalt *strangely pass*, And scarcely greet me . . ." (49.5–6) with 89.8–9: "I will acquaintance strangle and look *strange*, Be absent from thy *walks*. . . ."

And in structure 49 builds with "*Against* that time" at the beginning of each quatrain to the punning turn "against myself" in line 11. In the vivid context so established, lines of 87–90 echo 49: "Upon thy side against myself I'll fight" (88.3), "Against thy reasons making no defence" (89.4), "For thee, against myself I'll vow debate" (89.13).

II H
91–93 69–70 95–96 94

[91]

    Some glory in their birth, some in their skill,
    Some in their wealth, some in their body's force,
    Some in their garments, though new-fangled ill,
    Some in their hawks and hounds, some in their horse;
5   And every humor hath his adjunct pleasure
    Wherein it finds a joy above the rest.
    But these particulars are not my measure;
    All these I better in one general best:
    Thy love is better than high birth to me,
10 Richer than wealth, prouder than garments' cost,
    Of more delight than hawks or horses be;
    And having thee, of all men's pride I boast—
      Wretched in this alone, that thou mayst take
      All this away and me most wretched make.

[92]

    But do thy worst to steal thyself away,
    For term of life thou art assurèd mine,
    And life no longer than thy love will stay,
    For it depends upon that love of thine.
5   Then need I not to fear the worst of wrongs,
    When in the least of them my life hath end;
    I see a better state to me belongs
    Than that which on thy humor doth depend:
    Thou canst not vex me with inconstant mind,
10 Since that my life on thy revolt doth lie;
    O what a happy title do I find,
    Happy to have thy love, happy to die.
      But what's so blessèd-fair that fears no blot?
      Thou mayst be false, and yet I know it not.

[93]

    So shall I live supposing thou art true,
    Like a deceived husband; so love's face
    May still seem love to me though altered new,
    Thy looks with me, thy heart in other place.
5 For there can live no hatred in thine eye;
    Therefore in that I cannot know thy change.
    In many's looks the false heart's history
    Is writ in moods and frowns and wrinkles strange,
    But heaven in thy creation did decree
10 That in thy face sweet love should ever dwell;
    Whate'er thy thoughts or thy heart's workings be,
    Thy looks should nothing thence but sweetness tell.
      How like Eve's apple doth thy beauty grow,
      If thy sweet virtue answer not thy show.

[69]

    Those parts of thee that the world's eye doth view
    Want nothing that the thought of hearts can mend;
    All tongues, the voice of souls, give thee that due,
    Utt'ring bare truth, even so as foes commend.
5 Thy outward thus with outward praise is crowned;
    But those same tongues that give thee so thine own,
    In other accents do this praise confound
    By seeing farther than the eye hath shown.
    They look into the beauty of thy mind,
10 And that, in guess, they measure by thy deeds;
    Then, churls, their thoughts although their eyes were kind,
    To thy fair flower add the rank smell of weeds.
      But why thy odor matcheth not thy show,
      The soil is this, that thou dost common grow.

[70]

 That thou art blamed shall not be thy defect,
 For slander's mark was ever yet the fair;
 The ornament of beauty is suspect,
 A crow that flies in heaven's sweetest air.
5 So thou be good, slander doth but approve
 Thy worth the greater, being wooed of time;
 For canker vice the sweetest buds doth love,
 And thou present'st a pure unstainèd prime.
 Thou hast passed by the ambush of young days,
10 Either not assailed, or victor being charged,
 Yet this thy praise cannot be so thy praise,
 To tie up envy evermore enlarged.
  If some suspect of ill masked not thy show,
  Then thou alone kingdoms of hearts shouldst owe.

[95]

 How sweet and lovely dost thou make the shame
 Which like a canker in the fragrant rose
 Doth spot the beauty of thy budding name;
 O in what sweets dost thou thy sins inclose.
5 That tongue that tells the story of thy days,
 Making lascivious comments on thy sport,
 Cannot dispraise but in a kind of praise;
 Naming thy name blesses an ill report.
 O what a mansion have those vices got
10 Which for their habitation chose out thee,
 Where beauty's veil doth cover every blot
 And all things turn to fair that eyes can see.
  Take heed, dear heart, of this large privilege;
  The hardest knife ill used doth lose his edge.

[96]

Some say thy fault is youth, some wantonness,
Some say thy grace is youth and gentle sport;
Both grace and faults are loved of more and less;
Thou mak'st faults graces that to thee resort.
5 As on the finger of a thronèd queen
The basest jewel will be well esteemed,
So are those errors that in thee are seen
To truths translated and for true things deemed.
How many lambs might the stern wolf betray,
10 If like a lamb he could his looks translate;
How many gazers mightst thou lead away,
If thou wouldst use the strength of all thy state.
    But do not so; I love thee in such sort,
    As thou being mine, mine is thy good report.

[94]

They that have power to hurt and will do none,
That do not do the thing they most do show,
Who moving others are themselves as stone,
Unmovèd, cold and to temptation slow—
5 They rightly do inherit heaven's graces
And husband nature's riches from expense;
They are the lords and owners of their faces,
Others but stewards of their excellence.
The summer's flower is to the summer sweet,
10 Though to itself it only live and die,
But if that flower with base infection meet,
The basest weed outbraves his dignity;
    For sweetest things turn sourest by their deeds;
    Lilies that fester smell far worse than weeds.

II H
91–93 69–70 95–96 94

ALTHOUGH it is plain that 91–93 begin a new poem, the correct placement in Q of these sonnets after 87–90 must be presumed. Not only does the couplet of 91 resume the note of feared alienation appearing in 87–89, but the first line of 92, ". . . do thy worst to steal thyself away," repeats the drastic wish, expressed in 90, for a clean and final break in the friendship.

The most casual reader of sonnets 91–93 will find in them a unity of theme and cleanly pointed transition that mark other authentic portions of Q. The couplet of 91 and the first two lines of 92 form a syntactical link augmented by verbal echo ("away"); likewise the couplet of 92 and the opening of 93 form another syntactical link (a 'so' clause), reinforced this time by antithesis ("Thou mayst be false" followed by "supposing thou art true").

So far clear sailing, but we now meet the crux. Following Q's order, not the restored order, read the couplet of 93 and the first five lines of 94. The seven lines appear to form a third syntactical link ("Eve's apple"—"temptation"), again with phrasal echo ("thy show"—"most do show"). It seems at first that 94 proceeds as surely from 93 as 93 proceeds from 92. Yet, with no overreading, this ostensible link in Q rings false.

True, it can be rationalized by commentary. The last ten lines of 93 make it clear that the friend's outward appearance can never disclose a possible treachery beneath; his only "*show*" can be a show of "sweetness." Then, the opening of 94 brings us to the forbearing souls who will not use their "power to hurt," who "do not do the thing they *most do show*." Now if "show" still means what it meant so plainly in 93, this power to hurt becomes, interestingly enough, a power to injure by sweetness and true love, the only qualities, according to 93, that can "show" in the young man's disarming countenance. But in 94 the power to hurt is the power to tempt. Hence an explication justifying Q's order will be that the young man's outward show of beauty and fidelity (93.5–12) becomes—potentially—Eve's apple (93.13–14) which represents, of course, power to hurt (94.1) by temptation (94.3–4), a power that those who are "lords and owners" of their natural endowments will not exercise (94.1–8).

So put, the logic is beyond reproach. But turn now from the standard explication to actual lines in the two sonnets. If they are supposed to convey this logic they misfire badly. Run-on from one sonnet to the other is controlled by the word "show" at the end of 93, immediately repeated at the beginning of 94. But in 93.14 "show" means, emphatically, the outward appearance (possibly false) of being *unable* to hurt (sweet, loving, loyal), while in 94.2 it suddenly means, emphatically, the outward appearance of being "most" able to hurt. A reader stops. He reexamines the end of 93 to see whether it says what he thinks it said. It does, and so does 94.1–2. He begins to muse on ambiguity, on paradox, on 'controlled dichotomy.' With all forward movement lost— movement that a run-on between sonnets is supposed to enhance—the experience now turns into static analysis which manages at length to bring in the 'evidence' of 94.3–4 and to solve the 'problem.'

What we have here is not ambiguity but quite unnecessary confusion that keeps a pleasurable ambiguity from arising. Either the Q text is faulty or Shakespeare mismanaged his lines. If there were no other internal evidence we should have to grant the poet's lapse and accept this crux as it stands. But it happens that sonnets 69–70, clearly at odds with adjacent sonnets in Q (page 303), have extraordinary claims to a position following 91–93, claims based, interestingly enough, on a cogent interplay of "show," the very element lacking cogency in Q's order, 93–94. Moreover, when 69–70 are placed after 91–93, the memorable 94 fits naturally and easily with 95–96 into a context that grants full play to its excellence.

In 93 the poet has implied his friend's possible falsity while declaring that, at least to him, it can never "show" in the friend's countenance. In line 11 the young man's "thoughts or . . . heart's workings" denote his 'inner self,'—potentially evil. The first two lines of 69 echo this with a pointed shift in connotation: "thought of hearts" here apparently means essential inner self (or selves),[2] potentially good ("mend" = improve). Sonnet 69 begins with the friend's outward beauty, the subject of 93, and refers to the universal praise it inspires. But unlike the speaker of 93, those who sound this praise "confound" it by "seeing farther than the eye hath shown" into the young man's mind which *they* measure by his deeds. Sonnet 70 then rings changes on this theme which leave no doubt that Q's pairing of 69 and 70 is authentic. Occasional commentary (see Hubler's edition) holds that 70 inconsistently depicts the youth's innocence after 69 has pointed to his misdeeds. But 70 does not do this. It follows the statement of 69 with a reminder: blame, slander, is inevitable but of no real consequence—if you remain "good" (lines 1–6). *So far* your reputation is intact, but you cannot expect lasting immunity from detraction (lines 9–12). And the fact is, you are suspected (the couplet, which in its sinister note parallels exactly the couplet of 69; see below).

Thus far, we have an association between 69–70 and 91–93 but little more. To break an equivocal Q sequence, 93–94, we need multiple, unequivocal evidence, and we have it in the couplets of 93, 69, and 70. When we recognize that couplet echoing couplet is a Shakespearian mode of linkage found in undoubted Q sequences, the parallel construction met with here cannot be laid to coincidence. Three sonnets perfectly unified in theme and consecutive development all end in lines having the key word "show." This, in fact, is weak understatement, for the sequence is *"answer not* thy show" (93), *"matcheth not* thy show" (69), *"masked not* thy show" (70). The couplet rhymes of 93 and 69 moreover, are grow-show and show-grow, respectively. Finally, the three couplets epitomize exactly a progressive logic that the three sonnets develop when read in sequence: 93 presents the disquieting possibility ("*If* thy sweet virtue answer not thy show"); 69 reveals the growing actuality and its explanation ("*why* thy odor matcheth not thy show"); and 70, warning of the consequences, ends with incentive for reform ("If some suspect of ill masked not thy show, *Then* . . .").

Now, what of sonnet 94? Unless the remarkable affinity of 93, 69, and 70 is accidental, 94 must be out of place; nothing would destroy the incisive 'build' or progression within 93 69–70 more surely than a sonnet like 94, climactic and 'final,' coming after 93. Here, then, is evidence confirming our earlier suspicion of Q's 93–94 order, which rested on quite different grounds. But should the order be 93 69–70 94–96? At first it seems so because 94–96 continue themes of 93 69–70—outward freshness, inner decay, reputation—with specific carry-over of image: "looks," "sweet," "bud," "flower," "weed," "canker," "vice," "ill"—an incomplete list that corroborates previous evidence (the couplets) for inserting 69–70 into the 91–96 series. But if we follow Q by retaining the 94–96 order we encounter a third and most emphatic sign of Q displacement, the incompatibility of 94 and 95. The most receptive reading of 94.13–14 followed by 95.1–3 cannot smooth over the nonsense of a festering-lily smell that in a trice, and with no change of context, becomes "sweet and lovely." This nonsequitur, and the sentimental anticlimax that 95–96 present as they follow—in Q—the icy sermon of 94, I leave to a reader's own judgment; but I must add that it will not do to talk of a 'dramatic shift in perspective,' for fatuity is never dramatic.

Where, then, does 94 belong? In idea and in imagery it clearly links with 91–93 69–70 95–96, and the one position left for it is the end of the series. Whatever emerges when we place it there should either unsettle or reinforce previous judgments. What appears? Not just an appropriate conclusion (in essence 94 is an 'envoy') but a perfect run-on between 96.9–14 and 94.1–5: temptation, betrayal by looks or *show* (the theme of both sonnets), plus "*strength* of all thy state" (96.12) echoed by "*power* to

hurt" (94.1). This appears, and more: in every sonnet of the
restored poem II H, the couplet serves to undercut suddenly an
illusion developed in previous lines—to dampen, to warn, to star-
tle with a terse afterthought, a casual but jolting reminder of
reality beneath nicety. In this unifying design the part played by
94 is climactic. Its couplet, far more decisive and disquieting than
the others, now caps not only a sonnet but the poem as a whole.
And its reference back to previous sonnets—to their opposition of
sweetness and corruption imaged in decaying "flower," "rank
smell," "odor," "weeds," "deeds"—is definitive.

II I
36–39

[36]
    Let me confess that we two must be twain,
    Although our undivided loves are one;
    So shall those blots that do with me remain,
    Without thy help by me be borne alone.
5 In our two loves there is but one respect,
    Though in our lives a separable spite,
    Which though it alter not love's sole effect,
    Yet doth it steal sweet hours from love's delight.
    I may not evermore acknowledge thee
10 Lest my bewailèd guilt should do thee shame,
    Nor thou with public kindness honor me
    Unless thou take that honor from thy name.
      But do not so; I love thee in such sort,
      As thou being mine, mine is thy good report.

[37]
    As a decrepit father takes delight
    To see his active child do deeds of youth,
    So I made lame by fortune's dearest spite,
    Take all my comfort of thy worth and truth;
5 For whether beauty, birth, or wealth, or wit,
    Or any of these all, or all, or more,
    Entitled in thy parts do crownèd sit,
    I make my love engrafted to this store;
    So then I am not lame, poor, nor despised
10 Whilst that this shadow doth such substance give
    That I in thy abundance am sufficed
    And by a part of all thy glory live.
      Look, what is best, that best I wish in thee;
      This wish I have; then ten times happy me.

[38]

How can my Muse want subject to invent
While thou dost breathe that pour'st into my verse
Thine own sweet argument, too excellent
For every vulgar paper to rehearse?
5 O give thyself the thanks if aught in me
Worthy perusal stand against thy sight,
For who's so dumb that cannot write to thee
When thou thyself dost give invention light?
Be thou the tenth Muse, ten times more in worth
10 Than those old nine which rhymers invocate;
And he that calls on thee let him bring forth
Eternal numbers to outlive long date.
    If my slight Muse do please these curious days,
    The pain be mine but thine shall be the praise.

[39]

O how thy worth with manners may I sing
When thou art all the better part of me?
What can mine own praise to mine own self bring,
And what is 't but mine own when I praise thee?
5 Even for this let us divided live,
And our dear love lose name of single one,
That by this separation I may give
That due to thee which thou deserv'st alone.
O absence, what a torment wouldst thou prove,
10 Were it not thy sour leisure gave sweet leave
To entertain the time with thoughts of love,
Which time and thoughts so sweetly doth deceive;
    And that thou teachest how to make one twain,
    By praising him here who doth hence remain.

II I
36–39

ALTHOUGH in Q these sonnets are disruptive and therefore out of place between 33–35 and 40–42 (pages 115–117), they are still related to the poem restored, J, when 33–35 and 40–42 are brought together. This relationship, described later, must continue in any revised sonnet order.

Misplacement in Q of 36–39 is also apparent from the immediate relation of 36 to 96 and other sonnets of poem H. Beginning with 91–93 and continued in 69–70 95–96 94, there is steady development of a theme, feared alienation associated with the young man's "shame" (95.1) or sin. This theme, still in a context of "shame" and now linked with the poet's own "bewailèd guilt," reappears in 36 (line 10) accompanied by extraordinary repetitions of phrase. By no means negligible as a connective is "blot," meaning sin or disgrace (92.13, 95.11—echoed by "blots," 36.3). The word does not appear with this meaning elsewhere in the Sonnets. But far outweighing other links is the common theme of oneness or identity expressed in both 96 and 36 with identical couplets: "But do not so; I love thee in such sort, As thou being mine, mine is thy good report."

Some editors have questioned this unique duplication of end lines. It can be laid, for example, to a scribe's error in copying. If that explains it, the two sonnets, 96 and 36, must once have been close together instead of widely separated as they are in Q—which is my conclusion although not the reasoning behind it. Or, if Q was set by formes, the duplication might be a compositor's error. Bibliographical evidence, however, shows this to be improbable if not impossible.[3] Still another explanation of the repeated lines is that a scribe or editor supplied a couplet missing in the manuscript by copying one from another sonnet. Although such theories are pure guesswork, they would have point if a textual crux were actually present—if the couplet in either 36 or 96 were at odds with the meaning or tone of preceding lines. But there is no such contradiction. Although context differs strongly in the two sonnets, the identical couplet functions in each case to make not just ordinary but impeccable sense. Hence accidental error or editorial meddling become unlikely assumptions, to say the least.

Accepting the repetition as it stands, Brooke read the couplet of 96 as a remote but meaningful reference to 36, written earlier. I have no doubt that one sonnet so echoes the other, but I doubt very much that Shakespeare expected couplet echo to be heard over a distance of sixty sonnets, Q's interval between the two. So I have given 96 and 36 a nearness allowing for interaction. Couplet echo can now be heard and, being heard, controls a sensitive development of thought and feeling. In 96 the poet begs his friend to avoid shame and scandal because "thou being mine, mine is thy good report." Yet this concern for another's report or reputation is colored by self-interest, the speaker's reputation. But in 36 the self-interest becomes self-effacement, self-exile: having confessed that the two must remain apart, "Lest my [own] bewailèd guilt should do thee shame," the speaker asks his friend never to acknowledge him in public—again because "thou being mine, mine is thy good report."

If 36 is restored to proximity with 96, then 37–39 must go with it, for in 36–39 Q preserves a characteristic series made up of two interlocking pairs (compare, again, 71–74). Both 36–37 and 38–39 reassert the oneness of poet and friend and at the same time paradoxically draw from it a necessity for separation: the first pair declares for separation in order to preserve the young man's reputation, which must also be the poet's; the second pair justifies separation as the only condition allowing the poet to praise his friend without praising himself—since the two, after all, are one. Sonnet 37 follows directly from the couplet of 36 as an amplifying simile and serves also to introduce 38 by presenting the friend as source of all that is "best" in the poet (in 38 the young man becomes the poet's "tenth Muse"). At 38.9, "ten times more in worth" appears a likely echo of "ten times happy me" (37.14). Sonnet 39 now follows as a development of 38: in addition to obvious continuity of idea, note its echo in line 1 of "worth" (38.9), which itself is an echo of 37.4. Finally, 39 ends the series of four by clear reference back to the opening lines of 36, which read: ". . . we two must be twain, Although our undivided loves are one." At line 5, sonnet 39 not only reaffirms this statement but repeats the very terms in which it appears. With 36.1–3 compare 39.5–6 ("divided," "love," "one") and 39.13–14 ("twain," plus the rhyme with "remain").

In 36–39 a half-serious, half-comic set of complications induced by identity is resolved in separation, division. In the next poem, 33–35 40–42, a half-serious, half-comic crisis of division will be resolved in identity.

 II J

33–35 40–42

[33]

    Full many a glorious morning have I seen
    Flatter the mountain tops with sovereign eye,
    Kissing with golden face the meadows green,
    Gilding pale streams with heavenly alchemy,
5   Anon permit the basest clouds to ride
    With ugly rack on his celestial face,
    And from the forlorn world his visage hide,
    Stealing unseen to west with this disgrace;
    Even so my sun one early morn did shine
10 With all-triumphant splendor on my brow;
    But out, alack, he was but one hour mine,
    The region cloud hath masked him from me now.
       Yet him for this my love no whit disdaineth;
       Suns of the world may stain when heaven's sun staineth.

[34]

    Why didst thou promise such a beauteous day,
    And make me travel forth without my cloak,
    To let base clouds o'ertake me in my way,
    Hiding thy brav'ry in their rotten smoke?
5   'Tis not enough that through the cloud thou break
    To dry the rain on my storm-beaten face,
    For no man well of such a salve can speak
    That heals the wound and cures not the disgrace.
    Nor can thy shame give physic to my grief;
10 Though thou repent yet I have still the loss:
    Th' offender's sorrow lends but weak relief
    To him that bears the strong offence's cross.
       Ah but those tears are pearl which thy love sheds,
       And they are rich and ransom all ill deeds.

[35]

    No more be grieved at that which thou hast done;
    Roses have thorns, and silver fountains mud;
    Clouds and eclipses stain both moon and sun,
    And loathsome canker lives in sweetest bud.
5 All men make faults, and even I in this,
    Authorizing thy trespass with compare,
    Myself corrupting, salving thy amiss,
    Excusing thy sins more than thy sins are;
    For to thy sensual fault I bring in sense—
10 Thy adverse party is thy advocate—
    And 'gainst myself a lawful plea commence.
    Such civil war is in my love and hate
       That I an accessary needs must be
       To that sweet thief which sourly robs from me.

[40]

    Take all my loves, my love, yea take them all;
    What hast thou then more than thou hadst before?
    No love, my love, that thou mayst true love call;
    All mine was thine before thou hadst this more.
5 Then if for my love thou my love receivest,
    I cannot blame thee for my love thou usest;
    But yet be blamed if thou thyself deceivest
    By wilful taste of what thyself refusest.
    I do forgive thy robb'ry, gentle thief,
10 Although thou steal thee all my poverty;
    And yet love knows it is a greater grief
    To bear love's wrong than hate's known injury.
       Lascivious grace in whom all ill well shows,
       Kill me with spites, yet we must not be foes.

[41]

    Those pretty wrongs that liberty commits
    When I am sometime absent from thy heart,
    Thy beauty and thy years full well befits,
    For still temptation follows where thou art.
5 Gentle thou art and therefore to be won,
    Beauteous thou art, therefore to be assailed;
    And when a woman woos, what woman's son
    Will sourly leave her till she have prevailed?
    Ay me, but yet thou mightst my seat forbear,
10 And chide thy beauty and thy straying youth,
    Who lead thee in their riot even there
    Where thou art forced to break a twofold truth:
      Hers, by thy beauty tempting her to thee,
      Thine, by thy beauty being false to me.

[42]

    That thou hast her it is not all my grief,
    And yet it may be said I loved her dearly;
    That she hath thee is of my wailing chief,
    A loss in love that touches me more nearly.
5 Loving offenders, thus I will excuse ye:
    Thou dost love her because thou know'st I love her,
    And for my sake even so doth she abuse me,
    Suff'ring my friend for my sake to approve her.
    If I lose thee my loss is my love's gain,
10 And losing her my friend hath found that loss;
    Both find each other and I lose both twain,
    And both for my sake lay on me this cross.
      But here's the joy: my friend and I are one;
      Sweet flattery, then she loves but me alone.

II J
33–35 40–42

PLACEMENT of 36–39 after poem H leaves 33–35 and 40–42 without intervening sonnets—brings them together. And if internal evidence shows that they belong together, it will verify the independent case for relocation of 36–39.

The continuity restored when 33–35 join with 40–42 is a prime example of intensive linkage distinguished from loose or 'associational' unity. Beginning the series, 33–34 introduce as a sun-obscuring cloud the young man's "stain," his transgression. He has repented; but, as the speaker complains (34.10 ff.), the "offender's sorrow lends but weak relief To him that bears the strong offence's cross." A quick afterthought in the couplet withdraws the complaint: "Ah but those tears are pearl which thy love sheds, And they are rich and ransom all ill deeds." Sonnet 35 immediately expands the note of forgiveness, echoing 33 and 34 with "Clouds" that "stain both moon and sun." "All men make faults," including the poet who corrupts himself by "salving" his friend's misdeed (a further echo—compare "salve," 34.7). Then in another resolving couplet (35.13–14) comes the first suggestion of what the young friend has done: "that sweet thief which sourly robs from me." Full disclosure of the robbery will begin at sonnet 40, but preparation for it comes in 35. There the poet undertakes to justify the wrong he has suffered; assuming a legal role, he declares himself both "Thy adverse party" and "thy advocate," who " 'gainst myself a lawful [legal] plea commence." Many readers will remember the elaborate tongue-in-cheek casuistry of 40–42 which concludes that since "my friend and I are one, . . . she loves but me alone." But how many have sensed the logic-chopping on oneness and mine-is-thine of sonnet 40, plus the mitigating defence of youth in 41, as completing a legal "plea" the poet avowedly "commences" on his friend's behalf in 35?

Besides fulfilling this plea—the advocate's case against himself (see 35.10)—sonnets 40–42 reveal the actual nature of the 'crime,' the robbery cryptically mentioned in 35 but not explained. And the reference back is unmistakable. The first lines of 40 follow directly from the last lines of 35 ("rob"–"take"). Line 9 of 40 stems from 35.14: "I do forgive thy robb'ry, gentle thief" clearly echoes "that sweet thief which sourly robs from me." In addition, the "loss"–"cross" note of 34.10–12 recurs with identical rhyme in the corresponding lines of sonnet 42. (In 34 Q plainly misprints "crosse" as "losse" in line 12.)

These links are impressive but they do not account fully for the close unity of 33–35 40–42 as a restored poem. So I suggest now a reading of the six sonnets followed by a reading of Q 33–42 as it stands. Then a question: could the poet whose standard of coherence marks each half of the restored poem have intended that the halves form anything but a coherent whole? Could he have failed to see that presence of 36–39 between the two triads would ruin their interaction and destroy the clarity of 36–39 as well? As a separate poem, sonnets 36–39 are related to 33–35 40–42. Yet it remains that their appearance in Q between 35 and 40 is a gross intrusion. For Pooler it was "not easy to believe" that 35 and 36 are connected and Brooke (page 27 of his edition) removed 36–39 from the Q sequence, finding the sincere regard they express for Shakespeare's friend incompatible with 33–35 and 40–42, which "deal so poignantly with his offense." Much more tenable grounds for rearrangement are those we have considered: the multiple linkage between two neighboring fragments and the elaborate digression in Q which keeps the linkage from functioning. If from caution an editor allows the 1609 text to stand here, he must accept the implication—a poet who could bring into full play the extraordinary logic of his art and at the same time wreck it, not through inadvertence but by laborious design. An editorial policy that implies such perversity in composition is hardly 'conservative.' Yet, there is a conservative course open here, a recognition that Shakespeare may have composed these sonnets in their Q order: first 33–35, then 36–39, and finally, as a continuation of

33–35, sonnets 40–42. But even if we grant this, what should govern an edition? Should a guess about the order of composition determine the sonnet order in deference to Q's shaky authority, or should we heed strong and varied evidence of the poet's unifying intent?

Internal evidence supporting the last four restored poems of Group II (G, H, I, J) is cumulative. Close ties between 91–93 69–70 95–96 94 (poem H) and 36–39 (poem I) bring these sonnets together. The new location thus given 36–39 leaves two triads, 33–35 and 40–42, with no sonnets between them. And we find the two triads clearly linked, forming poem J; hence relocation of the intervening 36–39 as poem I receives strong independent support. But we have noted before that I, although a distinct poem, is related to J.

Now, since I is closely linked with H and cognate with J, we place the sonnets of H, I, and J in a continuous series, bringing together widely separated elements of the Q order. What relation, if any, then appears between H and J? The question is critical: not to find some sort of affinity would be merely disappointing, but to find that H and J, now joined in the same series, are incompatible—a clear possibility—would be embarrassing.

But the affinity is there. Poem J continues the note of sensual guilt and alienation found in H, and accompanies this repetition of theme with sustained verbal echo. First, the two poems share a four-fold metaphor or 'cluster': "rose," "bud," "canker," "sweet." The cluster happens to be a commonplace found also in 54 and 99; yet here we find it concentrated in the first quatrains of 95 (H) and 35 (J) with metaphorical reference in both to guilt, to the friend's misdeeds, an association lacking in 54 and 99. Moreover, one line of the concentration in 35 runs, "And loathsome canker lives in sweetest bud" (35.4), phrasing parallel with a one-line concentration in another part of H (this time at 70.7): "For canker vice the sweetest buds doth love." And in this line of 70 the reference again, as might be expected, is to the young man's misbehavior.

A further cluster, one with no suggestion of the commonplace, appears in J at 40.13: "Lascivious grace in whom all ill well shows." Compare this with the passage in H running from 95.5 through 96.4 in which the play on "lascivious," "ill," and "grace" is prominent. And the "ill well shows" phrase of 40.13 in J (evil appears as grace) repeats both the imagery and the context of still another passage in H: "If some suspect of ill masked not thy show" (70.13). "Show," moreover—in this sense of denoting an equivocal outward appearance of the friend's inner nature—is the most decisive unifying element found in H (see again the couplets of 93, 69, 70 and the opening lines of 94). Its appearance linked in one line of J (40.13) with three other elements also associated in H is hard to accept as coincidence.

Three more details should be noticed: the play on "fault" in H (96.1–4) and in J (35.5–9); the denotation of "stain" in H (70.8: "unstainèd") and in J (33.14; 35.3); plus the special sense of "deeds," meaning misdeeds or sins, in H (69.10; 94.13) and in J (34.14).

At this point, without being redundant, one can say that the cumulative links between H and J are compounded. Poem H brings together two widely separated elements of Q, 69–70 and 91–96, and their affinity for one another is matched by an affinity for J that each shows quite independently.

A final cumulative element in the restoration of Group II is poem J's unexpected reference back to G. The greater part of G, 87–90, is already adjacent in Q to the greater part of H, 91–96. Having noted the affinity of J for H, we now discover that J also reasserts, in its own way, an essential element of G—the poet as advocate against himself 'defending' his friend in legal terms. See the case for restoring 49 to G (pages 96–97) and compare the legal 'pose' and the legal imagery found in 35, a key sonnet of J (page 113). Thus J, cognate with I, is necessarily carried along when I is linked with H; J then is found nicely related to H on independent grounds. Now on further independent grounds it ties in with G, whose link with H is not only independent but attested further by Q's own sonnet order. Pieces of the 1609 puzzle are falling together.

POEM 4
[77]

Thy glass will show thee how thy beauties wear,
Thy dial how thy precious minutes waste;
The vacant leaves thy mind's imprint will bear,
And of this book this learning mayst thou taste.
5 The wrinkles which thy glass will truly show
Of mouthèd graves will give thee memory;
Thou by thy dial's shady stealth mayst know
Time's thievish progress to eternity.
Look, what thy memory cannot contain
10 Commit to these waste blanks, and thou shalt find
Those children nursed, delivered from thy brain,
To take a new acquaintance of thy mind.
    These offices, so oft as thou wilt look,
    Shall profit thee and much enrich thy book.

POEM 4
77

OBVIOUSLY written to accompany the gift of a blank notebook (compare the "tables" of 122), this sonnet belongs to an occasion, not to a group of poems. I place it before sonnets of the 'rival poet' series only because Q prints it among them. Thus Shakespeare's presentation of the blank-leaf book and the sonnet recommending its use may have accompanied his presentation of some or all of the sonnets in Group III. But even if this guess should prove true it would not justify retention of 77 within the group itself, where it interrupts the continuity of 76 78–80.

119

GROUP III
A 71–74   B 32 81   C 76 78–80   D 82–86

GROUP III contains nine well-known sonnets on the 'rival poet' prefaced by 71–74, which precede them in Q. Removed from the series are 75 and 77, apparent intrusions. Added is 32, combined with 81 to form poem B which becomes a bridge joining 71–74 and the two remaining poems.

The consecutive order of poems A, C, and D is thus Q's order. The C-D sequence is confirmed by its implicit time scheme: alarmed anticipation in C of the rival poet's success, followed in D by a retrospective view of his piracy, his capture of "the prize" (see the commentary). Placement of restored poem B is justified by its function, already described, as a transition between A and C-D.

Earlier (pages 39, 42–43), I explained that the numbering of groups (I–V) and of independent poems (1–6) implies neither a hard and fast chronological order of composition, nor an integral order of development like that of chapters in a novel or autobiography. Although the five groups and six independent poems occasionally seem to refer to one another, the relationship is vague; each is discrete.

These remarks clearly describe the nature of Group III. It is almost certainly later than Group II and 'fits' nicely before Group IV and Poems 5 and 6, all of which seem to lead out of the silence, the constriction of the poet's art, as his rival (in the present group) abashes and confounds him. But there is no clear sign of Group III's original position. For all we actually know, Shakespeare could have written it after the "return" celebrated in Poem 5, or after the ensuing valedictory sonnets of Poem 6. As noted before, we have no proof that the Sonnets, even 18–126, form a single, coherent poem telling a continued story, although many interpreters have found in them a purposeful narrative with something like a beginning, middle, and end.

It may be, of course, that sonnets 18–126 if properly reordered do tell such a story. In its position between Groups II and IV, the rival poet series (III) appears to be a properly timed narrative episode. But I must say that the only basis for placing Group III directly after Group II is that in Q's presumed disarrangement fragments of III are found consistently with fragments of II and never with fragments of the other groups (see page 257). If the two groups mingled, they must have been together in manuscript at one time, but whether they came together by accident or were together from the outset is another matter. It is interesting that the evidence of manuscript mingling suggests for Group III a highly appropriate position in a narrative order. But to say this is interesting just about exhausts the implication.

III A
7 1–74

[7 1]

No longer mourn for me when I am dead
Than you shall hear the surly sullen bell
Give warning to the world that I am fled
From this vile world with vilest worms to dwell.
5 Nay, if you read this line remember not
The hand that writ it, for I love you so
That I in your sweet thoughts would be forgot
If thinking on me then should make you woe.
O if, I say, you look upon this verse
10 When I perhaps compounded am with clay,
Do not so much as my poor name rehearse,
But let your love even with my life decay;
        Lest the wise world should look into your moan,
        And mock you with me after I am gone.

[72]

O lest the world should task you to recite
What merit lived in me that you should love
After my death, dear love, forget me quite,
For you in me can nothing worthy prove;
5 Unless you would devise some virtuous lie,
To do more for me than mine own desert,
And hang more praise upon deceasèd I
Than niggard truth would willingly impart.
O lest your true love may seem false in this,
10 That you for love speak well of me untrue,
My name be buried where my body is,
And live no more to shame nor me nor you.
        For I am shamed by that which I bring forth,
        And so should you, to love things nothing worth.

[73]

That time of year thou mayst in me behold
When yellow leaves, or none, or few do hang
Upon those boughs which shake against the cold,
Bare ruined choirs where late the sweet birds sang.
5 In me thou see'st the twilight of such day
As after sunset fadeth in the west,
Which by and by black night doth take away,
Death's second self that seals up all in rest.
In me thou see'st the glowing of such fire
10 That on the ashes of his youth doth lie,
As the death bed whereon it must expire,
Consumed with that which it was nourished by.
   This thou perceiv'st, which makes thy love more strong,
   To love that well which thou must leave ere long.

[74]

But be contented when that fell arrest
Without all bail shall carry me away;
My life hath in this line some interest
Which for memorial still with thee shall stay.
5 When thou reviewest this thou dost review
The very part was consecrate to thee:
The earth can have but earth, which is his due;
My spirit is thine, the better part of me.
So then thou hast but lost the dregs of life,
10 The prey of worms, my body being dead,
The coward conquest of a wretch's knife,
Too base of thee to be rememberèd.
   The worth of that is that which it contains,
   And that is this, and this with thee remains.

III A
71–74

THIS memorable poem, intact in Q, consists of two sonnet pairs. In each pair opening lines of the second sonnet run on from concluding lines of the first; in 71–72 the run-on is enhanced by echoing phrases: "Lest the wise world" (71.13)—"O lest the world" (72.1). And in each sonnet of this pair a reference to the poet's "name" or reputation closes the third quatrain and prepares for the couplet.

Linkage within each pair is both forthright and subtle, but what of the connection between one pair and the other? Literal or casual reading of the four sonnets seems to raise an incompatibility between 71–72 and 73–74 that tempts some editors—Pooler, for example—to question the Q order. For although the theme of both pairs is the same, the first expresses the poet's shame at what he "bring[s] forth" and his wish to be forgotten, while the second offers his verse as his very "spirit" or essence for which he hopes to be remembered.

One way out of the supposed difficulty is to assume that in 71–72 the poet is ashamed of his plays, his earlier ones at least, while in 73–74 he is proud or at least unashamed of his verse, which becomes his true memorial. But the text, it seems to me, refuses to tolerate the reading: if Shakespeare's reference is to plays in the first pair, why did he specify "this line" (71.5) and continue with "remember not The hand that writ it"? Why did he write (71.9–11): "if . . . you look upon this verse . . . Do not so much as my poor name rehearse"? With the clear run-on from 71 through 72, these specifications of verse—"*this* line," "*this* verse"—become, at 72.13–14, antecedents of "that which I bring forth" and "things nothing worth," things that "shame" the poet. To imagine that the reference has changed is to deny normal function to the syntax. And if the dishonored "things nothing worth" in 71–72 are distinct from those of lasting worth in 73–74, why is the same designation, "this line," used at 71.5 and again at 74.3? At 74.3 "this line" is often read as a legal metaphor, 'this estate' or 'line of descent.' But the reading 'this line of verse' makes perfect sense in allowing lines 3–4 to say what the rest of the sonnet says; it is by far the simpler reading, directly anticipating line 5, and it echoes 71.5. Perhaps as typical double entendre, both meanings are intended. In any event the mode of reference is uniform throughout both pairs: "this line," "this verse" (71), "that which I bring forth" (72); and "this line," "When thou reviewest this," "And that is this, and this with thee remains" (all from 74).

Apparently the two pairs speak of the same subject, the poet's verse, but diverge pointedly in attitude. Yet there can be no doubt of their belonging together as Q prints them. So we are left with two possibilities: either the paired pairs lamely contradict one another or they express a nicely balanced opposition—'two ways of looking at my verse.' If the second alternative holds, we should find—without straining of text—the development in 71–72 of a point of view that in some way suggests its opposite, a view to emerge in 73–74 with relevant or 'dramatic' contrast. Now in 71 the poet asks that he be forgotten as author of his verse "Lest the wise world" mock both him and the friend who remembers. Quite literally, it is the mockers, the wise ones, who are to be feared, and if immediately following sonnets (76–86) are at all pertinent, the wise ones should be poets of the new age ("the time" in 76.3) and those who admire them. Sonnet 72 simply grants their case: "lest the world should task you to recite" my "merit," forget me; I tell you I have no merit; I am "shamed by that which I bring forth" (line 13), and so will you be shamed if you own to loving such "things" (line 14).

Thus in 71–72, the friend who would remember his poet with love and admiration is told not to, lest the wise, the knowing— right as usual—mock him. Sonnets 71–72 speak of a public world derisively hostile to private feeling. But this immediately suggests a private world of gentler judgment, and prepares us for 73–74.

Hence 73 starts all over again, echoing the formal statement of coming death found in the first quatrain of 71. With 74 we come to the private world where, in the terms of 72.1–2, no one ever will be "task[ed]" to recite a poet's merit, where (now in terms of 74 itself) poems are a poet's "spirit," his "better part," and through their consecration to a subject of worth (74.6, 13–14) establish their own merit.

Editorial and critical comment that finds conflict between 71–72 and 73–74 overlooks their reciprocal themes and their parallels of language, even to the extent of ignoring a final and rather obvious part of the process: interplay of the couplets ending each pair. As already noted, at 72.13–14 the wise world's judgment dominates for the moment as the poet owns to his shame for what he brings forth, adding "And so should you, to love things nothing worth." The couplet ending 73–74 aptly answers this simply by echoing "worth" and redefining it: away from the world, and between poet and friend, "The worth of that is that which it contains, And that is this, and this with thee remains." The "things nothing worth" (72.14) do have a worth after all, for (74.13–14) "the worth of that" (of anything) lies in what it contains (in this instance "my spirit"; note 74.5–8). "And that" (again, "my spirit") "is this" (my verse), "and this with thee remains."

III B

32 81

[32]

    If thou survive my well-contented day
    When that churl Death my bones with dust shall cover,
    And shalt by fortune once more resurvey
    These poor rude lines of thy deceasèd lover,
5   Compare them with the bett'ring of the time,
    And though they be outstripped by every pen,
    Reserve them for my love not for their rhyme,
    Exceeded by the height of happier men.
    O then vouchsafe me but this loving thought:
10 'Had my friend's Muse grown with this growing age,
    A dearer birth than this his love had brought,
    To march in ranks of better equipage;
       But since he died, and poets better prove,
       Theirs for their style I'll read, his for his love.'

[81]

    Or I shall live your epitaph to make,
    Or you survive when I in earth am rotten,
    From hence your memory death cannot take,
    Although in me each part will be forgotten.
5   Your name from hence immortal life shall have,
    Though I once gone to all the world must die;
    The earth can yield me but a common grave,
    When you entombèd in men's eyes shall lie.
    Your monument shall be my gentle verse,
10 Which eyes not yet created shall o'erread,
    And tongues to be your being shall rehearse
    When all the breathers of this world are dead:
       You still shall live—such virtue hath my pen—
       Where breath most breathes, even in the mouths of men.

III B
32 81

WE might 'justify' 32 in its Q order by noting that it refers to the
poet's approaching death after 31 has recalled the death of
friends; or we can surmise with Pooler that 32 is "a dedication of
the previous five sonnets, and perhaps others now out of place."
But such apologies for the 1609 text are made very doubtful by a
wholly new theme which 32 introduces: other poets with "style"
have "outstripped" the speaker's "poor rude lines." This departure in Q from the theme of preceding sonnets is matched by a
lack of tangible connection between 32 and sonnets which follow
it.

Although isolated in Q as a single sonnet, 32 becomes part of a
unique and detailed context when linked with 76–86, the 'rival
poet' series (for the text of 76–86, see pages 132–136). If we look
first to basic matters, we find 32 plainly expressing the theme of
76–86: a new and disquieting "age," or fashion, of versifying in
which the poet's ingenious competitors challenge his simplicity.
Sonnet 32 also voices a strong subtheme of the rival poet series,
the poet's expression of love in his verse, balanced against the
mere "style" of others (lines 7 and 14).

Beyond reproducing the themes of 76–86, sonnet 32 elaborately
echoes language of the series: "my sick Muse" (79.4), "My
tongue-tied Muse" (85.1), and "Had my friend's [the poet's]
Muse grown with this growing age . . ." (32.10); note also "my
rude ignorance" (78.14) and "These poor rude lines" (32.4). If
these parallels seem insufficient, note further: "Making his [the
rival's] style admirèd everywhere" (84.12), "In others' works
thou dost but mend the style" (78.11), and "Theirs [the rival
poets' lines] for their style I'll read . . ." (32.14). There is also
"reserve" (85.3 and 32.7); in both lines the reference is to poems
and the word means 'to preserve.' "Style" and "reserve" occur

nowhere else in the Sonnets. But none of these parallels matches a final one: "Why with *the time* [the new age of poetic fashion] do I not glance aside . . . ?" (76.3), "Some fresher stamp of *the time-bettering* days" (82.8), and "Compare them [my lines] with *the bett'ring* of the *time*" (32.5). Again, the compound usage in 82 and 32 appears in no other sonnet.

We now find another clue. As placed in Q, sonnet 81 speaks irrelevantly in the midst of sonnets on the rival poet, a series distinguished for coherent, developing statement. But if we allow 32 to introduce 81, a surprising change occurs. The two sonnets form a unified pair, and the pair, unlike 81 by itself, has relevance to the Q series. First, the evidence for pairing. Aside from 71–74, shortly to join the present group, 32 and 81 are unique in presenting an assumed situation, one in which the poet dies and his friend lives on, cherishing the poet's verse. Death with verse as a legacy to posterity is, of course, a frequent theme, but the friend himself as survivor and beneficiary of the poems is confined to 71–74 and the two present sonnets. Not only is the death-survival theme so limited, but in the Sonnets the word "survive" itself appears only in 32 and 81. Sonnet 32 begins "If thou survive my well-contented day," and asks the young man in that event to value the poet's lines not for their outmoded "style" but for the love they express. Compare the beginning of 81: "Or [whether] I shall live your epitaph to make, Or you survive. . . ." "Survive" echoes here with perfect relevance: 32 deals with a contingency, 'your' survival, and 81 enlarges this to include the alternative—whether I live on or you survive. But no matter who survives, "From hence your memory death cannot take" (81.3); "Your name from hence immortal life shall have" (81.5). These two lines further support a pairing of 32 and 81, for the repeated phrase "from hence" in 81 doubtless means 'from this verse.' (It could mean 'from the living world' in line 3, but that meaning is impossible in line 5, which restates and develops line 3; it could mean 'henceforth' in line 5, but such a reading is implausible in line 3, which anticipates line 5.) Yet when properly understood as 'from this verse,' the phrase

"From hence" in 81 is confusing without an immediate context. If it refers to "epitaph" in line 1, we have a muddle caused by line 2; if it refers to anything in 80, the prior sonnet in Q, equal confusion results. But if 81 is allowed to follow 32 (on the basis of independent evidence, above), the confusion clears. "From hence," from this verse, then refers directly to the subject 32 develops so elaborately—the poet's "lines."

When paired, 32 and 81 yield a coherent, continuing statement. Sonnet 32: if you survive me, compare my poor lines with the newer verse, and though they may be inferior, value them for the love they express. Now 81: whether I live to write your epitaph, or you survive me—as I had assumed (32)—this verse will give you immortality. *It* will be your epitaph, "Your monument" (line 9), "Which eyes not yet created shall o'erread."

Still there may be difficulty: is there a contradiction between the poet's "poor rude lines" (32.4), whose only virtue is the love they contain, and the immortal, life-perpetuating lines—"such virtue hath my pen"—of 81? The objection could be answered by pointing to Shakespeare's avowal, in the rival poet series and in 71–74, that love transcends rhetoric. But there is a better answer in sonnet 107, where in the space of four concluding lines the poet declares that he will "live in *this poor rhyme*, . . . And thou in *this* shall find thy monument, When tyrants' crests and tombs of brass are spent." Self-deprecation by a poet, or anyone else, is often a prelude to self-confident assertion. So in 32 81.

To clarify the standard of evidence used here, I must say that were there nothing to justify the pairing of 32 and 81 save these parallel elements in the two sonnets, the result would be doubtful. Such affinities can be accidental, as anyone knows. But again, a good hedge against accident is a set of multiple factors. Here we have (1) the actual appearance in Q of 81 with 76–86, although—in Q's sonnet order—the connection seems irrelevant; (2) the pointed links between 32 and 76–86, aside from any ties between 32 and 81; (3) the close ties appearing between 32 and 81 after 32 is brought, for independent reasons, to the 76–86 series;

and (4) the remarkable function of 32 81, yet to be considered, as a 'bridge' between 71–74 and 76–86—two sequences adjacent in Q but without apparent affinity *until* the 32 81 bridge connects them.

As 76–86 stands in Q, nothing in it save 81 is clearly relevant to 71–74. And 81 by itself, if placed between the two adjoining sequences, fails to close the gap. But sonnet 32, quite apart from linking independently with 81 and 76–86, joins with 71–74. As noted, 32, 71–74, and 81 are unique in depicting a dead poet with his friend as survivor and inheritor of his verse. Thus if 32 is placed after 71–74, the series continues with an established theme; and if 81 is added (the pairing), unity of statement is simply amplified. But this is not all, for 32 now echoes 71–74 with memorable effect. The singular phrase "deceasèd I" (72.7) sounds again in "deceasèd lover" (32.4), and the context of self-deprecation is the same. "Deceasèd," the adjective, is found nowhere else in the Sonnets. Another linking phrase appears at corresponding points of 74 and 32. After 73 has warned of the poet's impending death—the twilight of his "day"—sonnet 74 offers comfort in an opening line, "But be contented . . . ," which finds its echo in the opening line of 32: "If thou survive my well-contented day [of death]. . . ." And there are less emphatic affinities such as the "surly sullen bell" (71.2) and "that churl Death" (32.2).

So with unique congruity of theme and clear echo, 32 continues 71–74 while leading into and pairing with 81. Simultaneously, it begins the theme of 76–86, the rival poet series. And here it combines introduction of theme with full anticipation (described earlier) of language and metaphor. With this the "wise world" of 71–72, ready enough to mock the poet and his verse, is carried forward into close association with the new "time" of rival poets, "new-found methods . . . compounds strange"—the invidious world of 76–86.

 III C

76 78–80

[76]

   Why is my verse so barren of new pride,
   So far from variation or quick change?
   Why with the time do I not glance aside
   To new-found methods and to compounds strange?
5 Why write I still all one, ever the same,
   And keep invention in a noted weed,
   That every word doth almost tell my name,
   Showing their birth and where they did proceed?
   O know, sweet love, I always write of you,
10 And you and love are still my argument;
   So all my best is dressing old words new,
   Spending again what is already spent;
     For as the sun is daily new and old,
     So is my love still telling what is told.

[78]

   So oft have I invoked thee for my Muse
   And found such fair assistance in my verse
   As every alien pen hath got my use
   And under thee their poesy disperse.
5 Thine eyes that taught the dumb on high to sing
   And heavy ignorance aloft to fly,
   Have added feathers to the learnèd's wing
   And given grace a double majesty.
   Yet be most proud of that which I compile,
10 Whose influence is thine and born of thee;
   In others' works thou dost but mend the style,
   And arts with thy sweet graces gracèd be;
     But thou art all my art and dost advance
     As high as learning my rude ignorance.

[79]

    Whilst I alone did call upon thy aid,
    My verse alone had all thy gentle grace;
    But now my gracious numbers are decayed,
    And my sick Muse doth give another place.
5 I grant, sweet love, thy lovely argument
    Deserves the travail of a worthier pen,
    Yet what of thee thy poet doth invent
    He robs thee of and pays it thee again.
    He lends thee virtue and he stole that word
10 From thy behavior; beauty doth he give
    And found it in thy cheek: he can afford
    No praise to thee but what in thee doth live.
      Then thank him not for that which he doth say,
      Since what he owes thee thou thyself dost pay.

[80]

    O how I faint when I of you do write,
    Knowing a better spirit doth use your name,
    And in the praise thereof spends all his might
    To make me tongue-tied speaking of your fame.
5 But since your worth, wide as the ocean is,
    The humble as the proudest sail doth bear,
    My saucy bark, inferior far to his,
    On your broad main doth wilfully appear.
    Your shallowest help will hold me up afloat,
10 Whilst he upon your soundless deep doth ride;
    Or being wracked, I am a worthless boat,
    He of tall building and of goodly pride.
      Then if he thrive and I be cast away,
      The worst was this: my love was my decay.

III D
82–86

[82]

    I grant thou wert not married to my Muse,
    And therefore mayst without attaint o'erlook
    The dedicated words which writers use
    Of their fair subject, blessing every book.
5   Thou art as fair in knowledge as in hue,
    Finding thy worth a limit past my praise,
    And therefore art enforced to seek anew
    Some fresher stamp of the time-bettering days.
    And do so, love; yet when they have devised
10 What strainèd touches rhetoric can lend,
    Thou truly fair wert truly sympathized
    In true plain words by thy true-telling friend;
      And their gross painting might be better used
      Where cheeks need blood; in thee it is abused.

[83]

    I never saw that you did painting need,
    And therefore to your fair no painting set;
    I found, or thought I found, you did exceed
    The barren tender of a poet's debt;
5   And therefore have I slept in your report,
    That you yourself, being extant, well might show
    How far a modern quill doth come too short,
    Speaking of worth, what worth in you doth grow.
    This silence for my sin you did impute,
10 Which shall be most my glory, being dumb;
    For I impair not beauty, being mute,
    When others would give life and bring a tomb.
      There lives more life in one of your fair eyes
      Than both your poets can in praise devise.

[84]

    Who is it that says most, which can say more
    Than this rich praise, that you alone are you?
    In whose confine immurèd is the store
    Which should example where your equal grew?
5 Lean penury within that pen doth dwell
    That to his subject lends not some small glory,
    But he that writes of you, if he can tell
    That you are you, so dignifies his story.
    Let him but copy what in you is writ,
10 Not making worse what nature made so clear,
    And such a counterpart shall fame his wit,
    Making his style admirèd everywhere.
        You to your beauteous blessings add a curse,
        Being fond on praise, which makes your praises worse.

[85]

    My tongue-tied Muse in manners holds her still
    While comments of your praise, richly compiled,
    Reserve their character with golden quill
    And precious phrase by all the Muses filed.
5 I think good thoughts whilst other write good words,
    And like unlettered clerk still cry 'Amen'
    To every hymn that able spirit affords
    In polished form of well refinèd pen.
    Hearing you praised, I say ' 'Tis so, 'tis true,'
10 And to the most of praise add something more;
    But that is in my thought whose love to you,
    Though words come hindmost, holds his rank before.
        Then others for the breath of words respect,
        Me for my dumb thoughts, speaking in effect.

[86]

Was it the proud full sail of his great verse,
Bound for the prize of all too precious you,
That did my ripe thoughts in my brain inhearse,
Making their tomb the womb wherein they grew?
5 Was it his spirit, by spirits taught to write
Above a mortal pitch, that struck me dead?
No, neither he, nor his compeers by night
Giving him aid, my verse astonishèd.
He, nor that affable familiar ghost
10 Which nightly gulls him with intelligence,
As victors of my silence cannot boast;
I was not sick of any fear from thence.
  But when your countenance filled up his line,
  Then lacked I matter; that enfeebled mine.

III C
76 78–80

III D
82–86

RESTORATION of these two immediately related poems, dividing at 80 82, is a simple matter of detaching 75, 77, and 81 from
the Q sequence. As Q prints it, the famed 'rival poet' series has
two segments, 78–80 and 82–86—each closely unified internally,
each obviously linked with the other. And both recall the isolated
76. The nature of these sequences makes it virtually certain that
they were meant to function together without interruption, that
the standard of coherence set by parts should govern the whole.

Sonnet 75 is equivocal here on several counts. Opening with a "So" clause, it offers itself in any normal reading as a continuation from 71–74. That the sonnet might be a self-contained statement having no backward reference occurs to a reader only after he tries to make clear sense of the apparent development from 74, which turns out to lack the close relevance promised by a 'so' clause. A teasing, possible connection between 74.13 (taken out of context) and 75.1 only compounds the difficulty.

If sonnet 75 does not end a series, perhaps it begins one. As an introduction to 76–86, on the rival poet, its 'alienation' sentiments and its reference to a "filching age" (line 6) have some point, but the sonnet makes no reference to the poet's declining verse and an unpleasant coterie of versifiers competing for the young man's favor, a compound subject that fills every sonnet of the rival poet series. Yet 75 does, perhaps, speak of poetic 'inspiration,' which leads us to Brooke's solution of the difficulty.

Brooke (in his rearrangement) transposed 75 and 76, allowing the former to serve as a long simile amplifying the latter. This might be said to work, but it brings new difficulties; it stands in the way of close linkage between 76 and 78–80 (see below), and it yields an odd poetic logic. In the last of 76 the poet, "still telling what is [already] told," describes his best efforts as "Spending again what is already spent." So if 75 is placed after 76 we move immediately from an image of freely spending love (76.11–14) to one of a miser's hoarding (75.1–4). A paradox? Just possibly: note "telling . . . told" in 76, which could imply 'tallying.' Yet the transitional "So" (75.1) will bring opposites together so pointedly that they will fail to mesh. Paradox or ambiguity, if intended, thus will suffer badly.

Plainly 75 lacks any close relation to 71–74 and any convincing relation to the rival poet series. There is no rule, of course, holding that a sonnet having little or no connection with two sequences may not appear between them, or that a sonnet ampli- fying another (Brooke's order, 76 75) will never cause difficulty. Hence, if there were no problem beyond the one described, I should leave 75 in the 71–86 series. But there is unusual evidence

that 75 belongs as the key sonnet in a poem made up of three
other singles isolated in Q (see II E, pages 86–90). Because of
this, and because the sonnet's role in Q is equivocal to say the
least, I reassign it. At the same time, should more conservative
counsel demand that 75 be left unmolested, I allow for an alternative restoration of poem II E (page 90) that permits the
sonnet to function in the rival poet series as Brooke suggested. I
think, however, that the case for 75 as an element of II E ought to
decide the matter.

The second anomaly here is 77. A single written to accompany
the gift of a table book, it could have been sent to Shakespeare's
friend with the rest of 76–86. But if so, no possible reading can
make it part of the transmitted poem (see page 119). Another
possibility, of course, is that 77 is a stray sonnet with no relationship, even occasional, with 76–86.

Last among the anomalies found in 76–86 is 81. In theme the
rival poet series is invidious, stressing the poet's waning muse and
his fear lest other poets usurp his place. As Q presents it, sonnet
81 interrupts this concentrated anxiety with a serene promise to
the friend of immortality in the poet's verse. Point of view
blandly and suddenly changes, whereupon in 82 the sequence
resumes its course with the old pertinacity.

Essentially, one may justify separation of 75, 77, and 81 from
the rival poet series on two counts: (1) the impressive coherence
shown in 78–80 and in 82–86, units preserved in Q that establish a
norm, and (2) a simple extension of this coherence that appears
when the intrusive sonnets are removed. Sonnet 76 clearly begins
a series by introducing the "new pride" or fashion among versifiers of the "time," by declaring the poet's loyalty to older and
simpler values, and, in the third quatrain, by supplying a reason
for his old-fashioned ways, thus setting a theme later continued:
"O know, sweet love, I always write of you, And you and love
are still my argument" (76.9–10). After its first quatrain, the
sonnet reviews a long relationship between poet and friend during
which the young man has evoked the poet's verse and the verse
has never changed because its animating source has remained the

same. Directly from this statement—when the intrusive 77 is removed—sonnet 78 proceeds: "So oft have I invoked thee for my Muse And found such fair assistance in my verse . . ." And after carrying the friend's involvement with "alien pen[s]" a step beyond the suggestion of 76.1–4, sonnet 78 closes on the opening sonnet's primary note: "But thou art all my art and dost advance As high as learning my rude ignorance." Sonnet 79 now returns to a happy time before the day of rival poets, but the transition echoes 78 unmistakably. At 78.11–14, in a context of rival poets, we have "And arts with thy sweet *graces gracèd* be; But thou art all my art . . . ," and at 79.2 we hear that before the time of rival poets "My verse alone had all thy gentle *grace;* But now my *gracious* numbers are decayed . . ." Further, "my sick Muse" (79.4) echoes "my Muse" (78.1). Next comes an unquestionable double echo of theme-setting lines in the opening sonnet, 76. There we read, *"sweet love,* I always write of you, And *you* and *love* are still my *argument";* at 79.5–6 we find "I grant, *sweet love,* thy *lovely argument* Deserves the travail of a worthier pen."

Sonnet 79 moves from rival poets to the one rival of consequence, and 80 continues in that vein. Except to note that "my decay" of 80.14 echoes 79.3, I shall not comment further on 80 until we come to 86, its companion and co-equal in providing the most interesting statement of the series.

Apparently 82 begins an immediately succeeding poem (discussed below), but the theme remains exactly the same. And as the theme develops there is constant backward reference: sonnet 82 renews the friend-Muse relationship; it echoes in line 5 the friend's role as exemplar of "knowledge" or learning previously stated at 78.5–7, 13–14; and in line 8, with "Some fresher stamp of the time-bettering days," it recalls 76.3–4—"the time," the age of "new-found" modes in verse. Sonnet 83 continues 82 with a direct run-on—"painting" (note 82.13–14), amplified by echoes of "fair" (82.4, 5, 11; 83.2, 13) and "worth" (82.6; 83.8)—all in a precise context that continues from one sonnet to the other. At line 9, sonnet 83 begins the note of muteness carried through 84–86. The friend, his excellence speaking for itself, makes the praise of poets—which unfortunately he is "fond on"—inept, redundant, even a "curse" (84.7–14). Sonnet 85 presents a mute poet who can only "cry 'Amen' " to praise offered by others, who in his love can but "think good thoughts whilst other write good words." It ends, "Then others for the breath of words respect, Me for my dumb thoughts, speaking in effect," lines immediately echoed at the beginning of 86: "Was it the proud full sail of his great verse . . . That did my ripe thoughts in my brain inhearse . . . ?"

Sonnet 86 contains the fine, cryptic phrases that invite endless speculation over Shakespeare's rival. Whose "great verse" under "proud full sail" displaced the poet's own lines in a bid for patronage? Whose was the "spirit, by spirits taught to write"? Who enjoyed the "aid" of "compeers by night"? Who or what was "that affable familiar ghost Which nightly gull[ed] him with intelligence"? Whatever the meaning of all this, the subject of its reference, much of it echoes sonnet 80 with precision, for there the rival's bark likewise bears "the proudest sail" (lines 5–8) and there also a "spirit" writes (line 2), spending his might to confound and silence the poet who once enjoyed favor. But the interaction of sonnets here is not limited to 80 and 86, for "spirit" also appears at 85.7 and "tongue-tied" (80.4) occurs again at 85.1.

Such immediate parallels are tempting. I was convinced for a time that Q 81–84 wrongfully intervenes between 80 and 85–86, an idea consistent with the obvious misplacement of 81 and with a far congruity offered by 82–84 when read as a separate poem. But the Q order (after removal of 81) more than justifies itself. Sonnet 80 speaks in the present tense of a crisis with an impending future: I "faint," knowing a better spirit "doth" use your name, knowing that he "spends" his might to undo me. My bark "doth" willfully appear on your broad main. Your shallowest help "will" hold me afloat while he "doth ride" upon your soundless deep. Or, "being wracked, I am" (I become) a worthless boat—he is a tall ship of great pride. "If he thrive and I be cast away," I can have but one sustaining comfort: "The worst was this: my love was my decay."

Sonnet 86 recalls these contingencies, but there they have become history; the past tense appears throughout. "Was" it his (the rival's) verse that "did . . . inhearse" my thoughts? "Was" it his spirit that "struck" me dead, "astonishèd" (confounded) my verse? See 80.3–4 for the rival's earlier efforts (present tense) to do just this. No, neither he nor his familiars can boast of my silence; I "was" not sick with any fear of them. But when your countenance "filled up" his lines, then I "lacked" a subject. That lack "enfeebled" my own lines.

Clearly two sonnets speaking of identical events with such a disparity of tense are part of the same 'story,' but they need transitional matter between them. Q provides it. If we return to the beginning, we find in 76 and 78 a threat from competing poets and their "new-found methods," but our own poet, although subdued by it all, is still in the picture, still writing. Sonnet 79 in a run-on from 78 makes the avant garde threat more imminent and at the same time centers on a single rival, the one most to be feared. Sonnet 80 continues with the mighty efforts of this "better spirit" to silence the poet, to make him "tongue-tied," and ends by imagining the outcome *if* he is successful, "if he thrive."

So we have what may be called the 'first situation.' Sonnet 82 opens the 'sequel' by granting the friend's right, even his obligation, to look about for "fresher" praise. Yet, when he has it there is something for him to remember. In a former time "Thou . . . wert truly sympathized In true plain words," not in "strainèd touches [of] rhetoric" and "gross painting." Then in 83, linked plainly with 82, we have the transition, the shift from dire possibility (76 78–80) to a fait accompli. The poet is now silent; apparently the better spirit's attempt to tie his tongue (in 80) has succeeded. But—anticipating 86—the poet lets his friend know in 83 that his silence, unfortunately misunderstood, was a matter of voluntary choice. "Being mute" he impairs no beauty by trying to improve on nature. Sonnet 84 wryly implies that the other poet, and the friend too, could profit from that example. In 85 the poet dramatizes his muteness by self-reduction to a role of thinking good thoughts while pathetically saying " 'Tis so, 'tis true" as "others" render glorious praise. As irony, this note in 85 is hard to miss, and it fortifies an ironical reading of 86—a subject of long controversy.

Thus 76 78–79 lead into 80 with its depiction of a rival currently spending "all his might" to silence the poet. And thus 82–85 (83 being central) lead directly to 86, in which the poet *has* been silenced. But not by a rival's might, the proviso suggested from 83 onward and stated with finality in 86. In making this point, 86 redescribes the other poet's talent and power in the very terms of 80, thus linking the end of the story with its earlier development. Backward reference is dramatic, ironical, unmistakable. Sonnets 76 78–80 and 82–86 may be read as one poem with two 'phases' or, preferably I think, as two companion poems, the second a sequel to the first. In either case the series establishes a close unity, the unity both of structure and diction typical of a Shakespearian sonnet group when Q has substantially preserved it.

One tenet of orthodoxy, a very sound one in some ways, is that the Sonnets do not tell a sustained story. In all likelihood they do not, of course, if by 'Sonnets' we mean the whole or most of the 1609 collection and by 'story' something close to autobiography, with the groups as chapters recounting a 'first absence' followed by a 'second absence,' or a cycle of early serenity followed by alienation, sturm und drang, and reconciliation. But if story means fiction and if the stories are not read as chapters in a larger narrative, some of the individual groups—when Q's clutter is removed—tell a story superbly. The rival poet series is one of these. In it Shakespeare uses a lyrical form for narrative purposes, or a narrative form for lyrical purposes—it scarcely matters how we view it so long as we understand that both forms are present, and have a text that properly records the combination.

 GROUP IV
A 62 22–23 102–104 B 97–99 C 100–101
63–68 19 21 105 D 53–55 E 18 F 106 59–60
107–108 115–116

"PRAISE to the End!" would be a good title for this group. The poet speaks in various ways of his muteness, his embarrassed reticence as he feels he ought to render praise but senses that his friend is beyond praise, needs none. In poem C he escapes the impasse by recognizing praise as a duty not to his friend but to the future: the young man becomes "beauty's pattern," an ideal the poet must transmit to "succeeding men." That the friend needs no praise here and now thus becomes pointless as an excuse for silence. And since he embodies only the beauty of truth— never the "ornament" of falsity—he evokes as praise only a faithful description of his virtues. Hence the reticent poet's simple invention and simple style can rise to the occasion.

From this commitment, and continued praise that follows, the poet moves in the last series, F, to a rededication of his affection and talent against all threats of Time, age, or change in poetic fashion. The last sonnet of C (105) anticipates this course.

Thus Group IV shows an orderly structure: apprehension of age and decay, muteness or reticence, rejection of muteness, commitment to praise of the friend as beauty's pattern—praise that will overcome age and decay—and rededication of the friendship in the face of Time and mutability. These are the themes; they come in proper order, recur appropriately, and interact.

 IVA
62 22–23 102–104

[62]

Sin of self-love possesseth all mine eye
And all my soul and all my every part,
And for this sin there is no remedy,
It is so grounded inward in my heart.
5   Methinks no face so gracious is as mine,
No shape so true, no truth of such account,
And for myself mine own worth do define,
As I all other in all worths surmount.
But when my glass shows me myself indeed,
10 Beated and chopped with tanned antiquity,
Mine own self-love quite contrary I read;
Self so self-loving were iniquity.
   'Tis thee (myself) that for myself I praise,
   Painting my age with beauty of thy days.

[22]

My glass shall not persuade me I am old
So long as youth and thou are of one date,
But when in thee time's furrows I behold,
Then look I death my days should expiate.
5   For all that beauty that doth cover thee
Is but the seemly raiment of my heart,
Which in thy breast doth live, as thine in me;
How can I then be elder than thou art?
O therefore, love, be of thyself so wary
10 As I, not for myself but for thee will,
Bearing thy heart which I will keep so chary
As tender nurse her babe from faring ill.
   Presume not on thy heart when mine is slain;
   Thou gav'st me thine not to give back again.

[23]

    As an unperfect actor on the stage
    Who with his fear is put besides his part,
    Or some fierce thing replete with too much rage
    Whose strength's abundance weakens his own heart,
5 So I for fear of trust forget to say
    The perfect ceremony of love's rite,
    And in mine own love's strength seem to decay,
    O'ercharged with burthen of mine own love's might.
    O let my books be then the eloquence
10 And dumb presagers of my speaking breast,
    Who plead for love and look for recompense,
    More than that tongue that more hath more expressed.
      O learn to read what silent love hath writ:
      To hear with eyes belongs to love's fine wit.

[102]

    My love is strengthened though more weak in seeming;
    I love not less though less the show appear;
    That love is merchandized whose rich esteeming
    The owner's tongue doth publish everywhere.
5 Our love was new and then but in the spring,
    When I was wont to greet it with my lays,
    As Philomel in summer's front doth sing
    And stops her pipe in growth of riper days.
    Not that the summer is less pleasant now
10 Than when her mournful hymns did hush the night,
    But that wild music burthens every bough,
    And sweets grown common lose their dear delight.
      Therefore, like her I sometime hold my tongue,
      Because I would not dull you with my song.

[103]

Alack, what poverty my Muse brings forth,
That having such a scope to show her pride,
The argument all bare is of more worth
Than when it hath my added praise beside.
5 O blame me not if I no more can write;
Look in your glass, and there appears a face
That overgoes my blunt invention quite,
Dulling my lines and doing me disgrace.
Were it not sinful then, striving to mend,
10 To mar the subject that before was well?
For to no other pass my verses tend
Than of your graces and your gifts to tell;
     And more, much more than in my verse can sit,
     Your own glass shows you when you look in it.

[104]

To me, fair friend, you never can be old,
For as you were when first your eye I eyed,
Such seems your beauty still. Three winters cold
Have from the forests shook three summers' pride,
5 Three beauteous springs to yellow autumn turned
In process of the seasons have I seen,
Three April perfumes in three hot Junes burned,
Since first I saw you fresh which yet are green.
Ah yet doth beauty like a dial hand,
10 Steal from his figure, and no pace perceived;
So your sweet hue, which methinks still doth stand,
Hath motion, and mine eye may be deceived.
     For fear of which, hear this, thou age unbred:
     Ere you were born was beauty's summer dead.

IVA
62 22–23 102–104

TO restore this poem one must break a Q relationship, 62–63, that admittedly makes sense, for 62 speaks of an aging poet and 63 anticipates a time when the young man shall be as the poet is "now," lined and wrinkled with age. But this relation between two sonnets in Q is far from precise: 62 ends with a private motive for the decrepit poet's praise—to paint or adorn himself with his friend's youthful beauty—while 63 begins a series having a far different if not contrary purpose, to preserve the friend's beauty for all time. Hence the link between 62 and 63 is at best one of associated theme, a connection I preserve by keeping the two sonnets in related poems of the same group. And here, as elsewhere, a new arrangement replaces Q's loose order only because exceptional evidence appears in its favor. This evidence will point to 62 as a sonnet leading into 22 and to 63–68 as a series directly introduced by 100–101.

The paradox ending 62 (praise of "myself" by praise of another) is apt enough but not easy to catch when presented suddenly in a concluding couplet. The concluding paradox is not prepared for as it is, for example, in 42. Nor is there run-on in opening lines of the next sonnet (63) amplifying, explaining, the sudden couplet—a device Shakespeare often uses as a combining element in sonnet pairs (note 34–35, 36–37, or 95–96). Sonnet 63 appears at first to amplify 62; yet, as already described, it ends wide of the mark with no enhancement of 62's gnomic conclusion. Ordinarily such an observation would decide little, but here the circumstances are unusual. In Q, sonnet 22 proceeds vacantly from 21. It happens to amplify trenchantly the statement of 62; and its linkage with 62 is multiple, thus making fortuitous connection unlikely.

Finding himself aged and hence unworthy of praise, the poet says at the end of 62 that he will praise instead his 'other self,' the young man, "Painting my age with beauty of thy days." And in 22, on making his own youth or age contingent upon his friend's youth or age, he explains the matter by pointing to his friend's beauty as "but the seemly raiment" of his own heart: "How can I then be elder than thou art?" Elaboration of the couplet ending 62 could hardly be more pointed; the only change rung is a nice shift in metaphor from the friend's beauty as "painting," in the sense of adornment, to the friend's beauty as "raiment." In addition, 22 expands the sudden note of mutual identity ending 62—"'Tis thee (myself) . . ."—by recourse to the familiar interchange of hearts. But there is more than close thematic unity here; as in typical Shakespearian sonnet pairs a dominant image recurs: "But when my glass shows me [as aging]" (62.9–10)—"My glass shall not persuade me I am old" (22.1). Characteristically, the repeated figure is part of a run-on. The opening statement of 22 proceeds directly from the last six lines of 62, and the repeated "glass" image controls the transition.

After 62 22, I suggest as an experiment that we follow the Q order with 23 and then add 102–104. Although this separates 23 from 24, and 102–104 from 100–101 and 105, no tangible connections are broken.[4] Moreover, in the rearranged sequence (poem A) sonnets 22–23, joined in Q yet apparently unrelated, now function together. In the new context the two, still joined, become a transitional bridge unifying a six-sonnet series.

At 23.9 I retain Q's reading "books" and avoid the frequent emendation to "looks." Either reading can agree with a linking of 23 with 102; but since the case for poem A requires explication of both sonnets, I prefer to base it on the actual Q text.

Like a stricken "actor on the stage" (23.1–2), the poet, unable to speak his lines in the "ceremony of love's rite," invokes his "books" as "dumb presagers of [his] speaking breast." The sonnet having begun with an actor, "dumb presagers" naturally suggests theater usage, a 'dumb show.' But the connection between dumb show and "books" is confusing at first and encourages a revision to "looks"—until we note something repeatedly missed by the many emenders. "Book," in a key sonnet of the rival poet series, means a collection of "dedicated words," lines addressed by "writers" to Shakespeare's friend (82.4; see also 59.7). The dedicated words are those devoted to "their fair subject," not words of an appended 'dedication,' in the modern sense. And that the fair subject is the young man becomes plain from the rest of 82, especially lines 11–14. Hence the poet of 23, wordless in actual speech and calling on his "books," calls on his poems of praise (not on his 'looks' or countenance, as the emenders have it) to stand as silent "presagers" of what he, like the poor actor, wants to say—is expected to say, but cannot. To hold that a 'dumb show' in Shakespeare's theater is visual, not lingual, and hence must not be "books" is all very well, but the truism ignores a simple language of paradox in which written speech, ordinarily the opposite of 'dumb show,' becomes—pleasantly enough—its equivalent in "presaging" silently what the poet-actor will convey in person when he is able to speak his proper lines. In any event, this in effect is what Q says, and it makes apt sense.

So in 23 the poet, bereft of speech, invokes his "books," his poems, to prefigure an "eloquence" he hopes to attain. Yet in the very act of speaking through his written lines he adds (23.11–12) that they too, by comparison, lack expressive power. His poems, silent declarations, "plead for love" and seek "recompense" more than does a certain other "tongue that more hath more expressed." Thus sonnet 23, having begun with the poet's mute speech, ends on a note of his comparatively mute verse, or "books." And this is the note 102 immediately continues and develops.

Sonnet 102's relation to 23, so pointed and elaborate, so typical of an authentic run-on, must be taken seriously. In Q, 23 plays an orphan's role in the miscellany running from 18 through 28. But if we carry it along with 22—in restoring the pair, 62 22—and then follow it with 102–104, we find signs of original linkage running forward and backward through the series. And these ties are additional to those joining 62 and 22. I list them numerically to show their variety and cumulative force. (1) The theme, a poet's muteness, is uniform through 23, 102, and 103; all three sonnets in different ways say that muteness can be, or is, more eloquent than eloquence. (2) In both 23 and 102 strength of love is the ironical cause of muteness; and rhythmic, purposeful repetition of "love" through 23.5–14, echoed immediately with identical repetition in 102.1–5, gives the thematic carry-over unusual point. The effect is special, not routine or casual, as a reading of the lines will show. (3) We now find more specific echoes. Compare "My *love* is *strengthened* though more *weak* in *seeming*" (102.1) with "in mine own *love's strength seem* to decay" (23.7) and "*strength's* abundance *weakens*" (23.4). (4) In addition to this pointed echo of 23 at 102.1, the first four lines of 102 show a run-on that vividly recalls the phrasing of 23.11–14 while continuing its statement. Note the rhetorical balancing of "Who [my books] plead for love . . . More than that tongue that *more* hath *more* expressed" (23.11–12) with "I love not *less* though *less* the show appear" (102.2). And compare the overly expressive "tongue" that expects "recompense" (23.11–12) with the endlessly "publish-[ing]" "tongue" that "merchandize[s]" love (102.3–4). Then, read 23.9–14 followed by 102.1–4 to sense the continuing statement in which these links of image and phrase play a part. (5) Not only is the voluble rival called "that tongue" (23.12) and "owner" of the "tongue" (102.4); the poet's ending of the rivalry by deliberate choice of reticence (102.13–14) also comes in terms of "tongue"—this time his own. (6) Sonnet 103 extends the muteness theme of 23 102 by placing the friend's graces beyond articulate praise, and it caps this at line 14 by recalling the "glass" image so dominant as a connective between 62 and 22. Then 104 opens with a line, ". . . you never can be old," that balances with the opening line of 22, ". . . shall not persuade me I am old," and in so doing relates 103's glass image to the theme it served in both 62 and 22—that of age and Time's ruin. Except for instances in sonnets 3 and 77, obviously apart from the present context, these are the only appearances of "glass" (mirror) with reference to age and change. In a multiply joined series, sonnets 62 22 and sonnets 103–104 thus become parallel opening and closing passages, each expressing the poet's impulsive dependence on his friend's youth, as he perceives almost simultaneously that age and change will take their toll. In each passage the young friend, symbol of youth, changes suddenly into a prefigurement of age and mutability, and in each the "glass" image (22.1 and 103.14) is prominent. (7) In the series restored here, 62 22 and 23 102–104 can be read as immediately related poems or as two phases of a single poem. In either case a continuous series is verified by the preservation in Q of the 'bridge': 22–23.

IV B

97–99

[97]

How like a winter hath my absence been
From thee, the pleasure of the fleeting year;
What freezings have I felt, what dark days seen,
What old December's bareness everywhere.
5 And yet this time removed was summer's time,
The teeming autumn, big with rich increase,
Bearing the wanton burthen of the prime,
Like widowed wombs after their lords' decease.
Yet this abundant issue seemed to me
10 But hope of orphans and unfathered fruit;
For summer and his pleasures wait on thee,
And thou away, the very birds are mute;
   Or if they sing 'tis with so dull a cheer
   That leaves look pale, dreading the winter's near.

[98]

From you have I been absent in the spring,
When proud-pied April dressed in all his trim
Hath put a spirit of youth in everything,
That heavy Saturn laughed and leaped with him.
5 Yet nor the lays of birds nor the sweet smell
Of different flowers in odor and in hue
Could make me any summer's story tell,
Or from their proud lap pluck them where they grew;
Nor did I wonder at the lily's white,
10 Nor praise the deep vermilion in the rose;
They were but sweet, but figures of delight,
Drawn after you, you pattern of all those.
   Yet seemed it winter still; and you away,
   As with your shadow I with these did play.

[99]

The forward violet thus did I chide:
Sweet thief, whence didst thou steal thy sweet that smells,
If not from my love's breath? The purple pride
Which on thy soft cheek for complexion dwells
5   In my love's veins thou hast too grossly dyed.
The lily I condemnèd for thy hand,
And buds of marjoram had stol'n thy hair;
The roses fearfully on thorns did stand,
One blushing shame, another white despair;
A third, nor red nor white, had stol'n of both,
10 And to his robb'ry had annexed thy breath;
But, for his theft, in pride of all his growth
A vengeful canker eat him up to death.
    More flowers I noted, yet I none could see
    But sweet or color it had stol'n from thee.

IV B
97–99

THIS poem of three sonnets has its difficulties of structure and
logic: the seasons unfold in a puzzling chronology; the 'yet'
clause beginning with 97.9 seems to be meant as a 'so' or 'thus'
clause; and 98 seems to start the poem all over again after 97 has
launched it. One can experiment with a revised sequence running
98–99 97, but there is still trouble. Yet the three sonnets join
closely in the expression of a single theme; and while 98 is a
somewhat repetitive complement of 97, it is clear that 99 continues 98.

Sonnets 97–99 are discrete, and nothing is disturbed by placing
them immediately after 102–104. In this position they continue
the muteness theme of 102–103 with its subtheme of birds muted

in song; compare 102.5–14 with 97.12–14 and with 98.5–7 in which the "lays of birds" contrast with a poet's silence. More, the play throughout on the four seasons echoes a strong note found in both 102 and 104.

Placed as they are, 97–99 retain their Q relationship with 100–101 which will introduce the next poem, one that continues the celebration found here of Shakespeare's friend as the "pattern" of all natural grace (98.11–14 and the whole of 99).

IV C

100–101 63–68 19 21 105

[100]

Where art thou, Muse, that thou forget'st so long
To speak of that which gives thee all thy might?
Spend'st thou thy fury on some worthless song,
Dark'ning thy power to lend base subjects light?
5 Return, forgetful Muse, and straight redeem
In gentle numbers time so idly spent;
Sing to the ear that doth thy lays esteem
And gives thy pen both skill and argument.
Rise, resty Muse, my love's sweet face survey,
10 If Time have any wrinkle graven there;
If any, be a satire to decay,
And make Time's spoils despisèd everywhere.
　　Give my love fame faster than Time wastes life;
　　So thou prevent'st his scythe and crooked knife.

[101]

O truant Muse, what shall be thy amends
For thy neglect of truth in beauty dyed?
Both truth and beauty on my love depends;
So dost thou too and therein dignified.
5 Make answer, Muse: wilt thou not haply say,
'Truth needs no color, with his color fixed,
Beauty no pencil beauty's truth to lay,
But best is best if never intermixed'?
Because he needs no praise wilt thou be dumb?
10 Excuse not silence so, for 't lies in thee
To make him much outlive a gilded tomb
And to be praised of ages yet to be.
　　Then do thy office, Muse—I teach thee how—
　　To make him seem long hence as he shows now.

[63]

Against my love shall be as I am now,
With Time's injurious hand crushed and o'erworn:
When hours have drained his blood and filled his brow
With lines and wrinkles, when his youthful morn
5   Hath travailed on to age's steepy night,
And all those beauties whereof now he's king
Are vanishing or vanished out of sight,
Stealing away the treasure of his spring;
For such a time do I now fortify
10 Against confounding age's cruel knife,
That he shall never cut from memory
My sweet love's beauty, though my lover's life.
   His beauty shall in these black lines be seen,
   And they shall live, and he in them still green.

[64]

When I have seen by Time's fell hand defaced
The rich proud cost of outworn buried age;
When sometime lofty towers I see down-rased,
And brass eternal slave to mortal rage;
5   When I have seen the hungry ocean gain
Advantage on the kingdom of the shore,
And the firm soil win of the wat'ry main,
Increasing store with loss and loss with store:
When I have seen such interchange of state,
10 Or state itself confounded to decay,
Ruin hath taught me thus to ruminate
That Time will come and take my love away.
   This thought is as a death, which cannot choose
   But weep to have that which it fears to lose.

[65]

Since brass nor stone nor earth nor boundless sea
But sad mortality o'ersways their power,
How with this rage shall beauty hold a plea,
Whose action is no stronger than a flower?
5 O how shall summer's honey breath hold out
Against the wrackful siege of batt'ring days,
When rocks impregnable are not so stout,
Nor gates of steel so strong, but Time decays?
O fearful meditation; where, alack,
10 Shall Time's best jewel from Time's chest lie hid?
Or what strong hand can hold his swift foot back,
Or who his spoil of beauty can forbid?
    O none, unless this miracle have might:
    That in black ink my love may still shine bright.

[66]

Tired with all these, for restful death I cry:
As to behold desert a beggar born,
And needy nothing trimmed in jollity,
And purest faith unhappily forsworn,
5 And gilded honor shamefully misplaced,
And maiden virtue rudely strumpeted,
And right perfection wrongfully disgraced,
And strength by limping sway disablèd,
And art made tongue-tied by authority,
10 And folly, doctor-like, controlling skill,
And simple truth miscalled simplicity,
And captive good attending captain ill;
    Tired with all these, from these would I be gone,
    Save that to die I leave my love alone.

[67]

Ah wherefore with infection should he live
And with his presence grace impiety,
That sin by him advantage should achieve
And lace itself with his society?
5   Why should false painting imitate his cheek,
And steal dead seeing of his living hue?
Why should poor beauty indirectly seek
Roses of shadow, since his rose is true?
Why should he live, now Nature bankrout is,
10   Beggared of blood to blush through lively veins?
For she hath no exchequer now but his,
And proud of many, lives upon his gains.
        O him she stores to show what wealth she had
        In days long since before these last so bad.

[68]

Thus is his cheek the map of days outworn
When beauty lived and died as flowers do now,
Before these bastard signs of fair were born
Or durst inhabit on a living brow,
5   Before the golden tresses of the dead,
The right of sepulchres, were shorn away
To live a second life on second head,
Ere beauty's dead fleece made another gay.
In him those holy antique hours are seen
10   Without all ornament, itself and true,
Making no summer of another's green,
Robbing no old to dress his beauty new;
        And him as for a map doth Nature store
        To show false Art what beauty was of yore.

[19]

Devouring Time, blunt thou the lion's paws,
And make the earth devour her own sweet brood;
Pluck the keen teeth from the fierce tiger's jaws,
And burn the long-lived phœnix in her blood;
5 Make glad and sorry seasons as thou fleet'st,
And do whate'er thou wilt, swift-footed Time,
To the wide world and all her fading sweets;
But I forbid thee one most heinous crime:
O carve not with thy hours my love's fair brow,
10 Nor draw no lines there with thine antique pen;
Him in thy course untainted do allow
For beauty's pattern to succeeding men.
    Yet do thy worst, old Time; despite thy wrong,
    My love shall in my verse ever live young.

[21]

So is it not with me as with that Muse
Stirred by a painted beauty to his verse,
Who heaven itself for ornament doth use
And every fair with his fair doth rehearse,
5 Making a couplement of proud compare
With sun and moon, with earth and sea's rich gems,
With April's first-born flowers, and all things rare
That heaven's air in this huge rondure hems.
O let me true in love but truly write,
10 And then believe me, my love is as fair
As any mother's child, though not so bright
As those gold candles fixed in heaven's air.
    Let them say more that like of hearsay well;
    I will not praise that purpose not to sell.

[105]

Let not my love be called idolatry,
Nor my belovèd as an idol show,
Since all alike my songs and praises be
To one, of one, still such and ever so.
5 Kind is my love today, tomorrow kind,
Still constant in a wondrous excellence;
Therefore my verse to constancy confined,
One thing expressing, leaves out difference.
'Fair, kind, and true' is all my argument,
10 'Fair, kind, and true' varying to other words;
And in this change is my invention spent—
Three themes in one which wondrous scope affords.
'Fair, kind, and true' have often lived alone,
Which three till now never kept seat in one.

IV C

100–101 63–68 19 21 105

OF the first 126 sonnets, those presumably addressed to Shakespeare's friend, the great majority (118) clearly mention him. Of
these, 104 employ direct second-person address or (infrequently)
combine such address with third-person reference. Only fourteen
refer to the young man exclusively in the third person; and three
of these (5, 25, and 33) pair with, introduce, immediately following sonnets of second-person address. The remaining eleven sonnets limited to third-person reference are those brought together
here in poem C.

Such a consistent mode of address places these sonnets in a rare
class although, in itself, not necessarily a significant one. But the
eleven sonnets joined here agree in another respect: they desig-
nate Shakespeare's friend with a uniform epithet, "my love" or its
variants such as "my beloved." See for example 100.9, 13; 63.1, 12;

105.2, 5. In 67 the epithet appears through pronoun reference—he, his, him—in a direct run-on from 66.14, and it continues by the same means through 68 which proceeds syntactically (line 1) from 67. Only once (65.10) is any other epithet added.

Now according to Brooke (pages 17–18 of his commentary), "my love" or its variant "love" is the "commonest epithet" in the first 126 sonnets. Yet it occurs in but ten aside from the sonnets of our restored poem; and of these ten, five are worth noting. Sonnets 22 and 107 show the epithet, but they belong, on the strength of other evidence, to Group IV and are thus cognate with the restored poem here in question. Sonnets 76, 79, and 82 contain the epithet, but in them Shakespeare uses it just as he does in 63–68—to unify an authentic series preserved in Q.

At any rate, appearance of the epithet elsewhere is hardly significant, in view of an unusual set of facts: all eleven sonnets of poem C address Shakespeare's friend wholly in the third person; all speak of him as "my love"; and throughout the 1609 Quarto they are the only sonnets that combine these two modes of address. (A few sonnets of third-person address use a different epithet and some sonnets use the epithet in the second person.) So, beyond doubt the eleven sonnets are unique, but can we say that they appeared originally as stanzas of a unified poem? In part, the answer is plain, for six of the sonnets make up two triads, 63–65 and 66–68, in which clear run-on and phrasal echo support a continuity of theme. Preservation of the sequence in 63–68 of Q makes it clear that Shakespeare wrote a series closely unified in the usual manner, and then unified it even more closely by third-person address combined with the uniform epithet. Since he used this double device in joining six sonnets, the only question left is whether its appearance in five other sonnets connects them with the 63–68 cluster. The alternative, plausible enough at first, is that they merely reproduce, without its connective function, the device found in 63–68. And in three of the five, part of the usage is readily explained, for in 100–101 and 19 second-person address to the Muse or Time requires third-person reference to the friend in order to avoid confusion. Yet it does not, of course, require a use of the "my love" epithet. Still, under these circumstances the parallels become doubtful as connectives, and strong added evidence will be needed to join the five scattered sonnets with the 63–68 'nucleus.'

In the restored poem internal evidence points to a sonnet order of 100–101, 63–68, 19, 21, 105. I shall limit discussion at first to the internal unity of 100–101 and of 63–68, the two elements surviving in Q as intact sequences. As a result we shall have (1) an example of sonnet linkage clearly in the Shakespearian mode because it is drawn from passages in Q that no one can seriously question, and (2) a responsibility to meet: a requirement that Shakespeare's own standard of linkage derived from 100–101 and 63–68 be matched in restoring any links Q may have broken. In short, if two authentic sequences and three isolated sonnets are to be joined in a single poem, the whole poem ought to show the coherence found in continuous parts of it that Q preserves.

First, 100–101. Compare the standard of linkage set by this pair with the standard that might be drawn from 18–19. In each case two consecutive sonnets speak of immortality given the friend by the poet's verse. But in 18–19 this conventional theme, reduced to generality, is the only connective, while from 100 to 101 the theme is carried over in terms both multiple and specific. Both sonnets are addressed formally to a Muse who neglects her duty; both begin with an accusing question from which ensuing lines develop; both speak of the Muse as wholly dependent for inspiration on the friend; both refer to the friend as "my love." And beyond all this there is unmistakable run-on. The second sonnet does not merely parallel a statement made in the first; it continues and completes it.

Now, the second series preserved in Q. A first reading of 63–65 reveals a continuing theme, Time's ruin, and the more specific links of third-person–"my-love" address to the friend. Certainly this interconnection justifies the Q order, but it does not account for the whole design. Sonnet 65 opens with an epitome of 64: "Since brass nor stone nor earth nor boundless sea . . ." Recall in 64.1–8, the "brass," the "lofty towers" (stone), the "firm soil," the "wat'ry main"—all now brought with identical context into the first two lines of 65. Besides, in 65.3–4 "this rage," the rage of "sad mortality" (line 2) carries over from the "mortal rage" of 64.4; in 65.6 the "wrackful siege of batt'ring days" calls up the "lofty towers . . . down rased" of 64.3; and the "fearful medita-tion" of 65.9 renews the "thought" equivalent to "death" in 64.13. Finally, after its development of 64, sonnet 65 returns with its couplet to the couplet of 63: "That in black ink my love may still shine bright" (65.14) echoes "His ["my sweet love's"] beauty" that "shall in these black lines be seen"; and "still shine" (65.14) recalls "still green" (63.14).

Although 66–68, the next three sonnets in Q, continue the third-person–"my-love" mode of address (at 66.14, and with pronoun reference thereafter), they appear at first to be distinct from 63–65. But even in Q as it stands the two triads are related, for their respective themes, Time's ruin (63–65) and the Former Age, a pristine earlier world now in ruin and decay (66–68), were conventionally associated in Shakespeare's day.

Whatever the connection between these three-sonnet units may turn out to be, 66–68 has its own sequential logic. The singular and widely quoted 66 recites a litany of abuses from which the poet would "be gone" were it not that his death would "leave my love alone." Sonnet 67 moves directly from this turn of couplet by asking why the friend himself should continue living merely to grace with his presence "impiety" and "infection" (the abuses recited in 66). The subject then shifts easily from the world of infection to a world of artifice, and the question is asked again: "Why should he live" now that Nature is "bankrout" and artifice prospers? Then the answer: the young man must live because Nature "stores" him "to show what wealth she had In days long since before these last so bad." This couplet summation of 67 now links with the opening line of 68 in a run-on: "Thus is his cheek the map of days outworn." The opening statement of 68 then echoes in the couplet of 68 (the "map"), which turns full circle back to the couplet of 67—"him . . . doth Nature store" (68.13) and "him she stores" (67.13).

Such is the standard of linkage found in the two sequences of poem C that Q preserves. Now the ultimate question: if we place 100–101 before 63–68, and allow 19, 21, and 105 to complete the series, will it show, not only throughout but at each point of restored connection, the kind of intensive linkage found in the surviving Q sequences?

Although a number of Shakespeare's sonnets mention his Muse, only 100–101 are written in the style of formal invocation. The two sonnets are surely designed to introduce a series by declaring its subject and purpose; yet in their deliberate, formal manner they introduce nothing but confusion when they precede 102–105,[5] as they do in the 1609 edition. But if we take our cue from their third-person–"my-love" reference to Shakespeare's friend, and allow 100–101 to introduce 63–68, we find the two sonnets invoking the Muse to do precisely what is done. In theme and style these introductory sonnets fit nowhere as they do here. Time's ruin, immortality conferred by verse, preservation of the friend as beauty's pattern, double uniformity in the mode of address—everything agrees. But remembering that fortuitous connection is always possible, and that a loose thematic relation appears in Q between 62 and 63 (page 147), we had better look further. "Confounding age's cruel knife" (63.10) echoes Time's "crooked knife" (100.14). Elsewhere in the Sonnets, oddly enough, this image is approximated only at 74.11. Time's "spoil" (65.12), echoing "Time's spoils" (100.12), is another figure we might expect to reappear often, but we find it in no other sonnet. The remaining link between 100–101 and 63–68 appears at the immediate point of contact when the separated units are brought together. It is a last-line–first-line transition, Shakespearian in its combination of rhetorical balance with phrasal echo. Sonnet 101 describes the friend's beauty as beyond written praise but insists on present praise as a record for the future; sonnet 63 introduces the ruin Time will make of this beauty and repeats the poet's intent to preserve it. And when the two sonnets are placed together the transitional echo appears: the couplet of 101 directs the Muse "To make him ["my love" of line 3] seem long hence *as he shows now*"; introducing Time's ruin, 63 begins, "Against *my love* shall be *as I am now* . . .*" The transition is like the one between 67 and 68 in which last-line–first-line run-on is supported by the same kind of verbal echo: "In *days* long since"—"of *days* outworn."

Now we come to sonnet 19, the first of three scattered singles in Q which share the unusual third-person–"my-love" mode of address. (The problem of separating 19 from 18 and 20 is discussed, with similar questions raised by poem C, in note 5, page 299). Beyond continuing the Time's ruin theme of 63–65, sonnet 19 (lines 9–10) repeats the "hours"-"brow"-"lines" cluster of 63.3–4 with identical images in the same compact order and in the same precise context. And at 19.6 we have "swift-footed Time" which echoes Time's "swift foot" (65.11) in a repetition we might expect frequently but which, again, occurs nowhere else in the Sonnets. Besides recalling the theme and imagery of 63–65, sonnet 19 refers directly to the second triad, 66–68. Sonnet 68 ends with the friend as a "map" (pattern) stored by Nature "To show false Art what beauty was of yore"; at 19.11–12 Time is called upon to spare the young man that he may continue "untainted" in that very role, "beauty's pattern."

Although, as noted before, the themes of 63–65 and 66–68 were conventionally related in Shakespeare's time, the two triads, as they appear in Q, seem to stand apart from one another. But when sonnet 19 is placed after 68, the apparently separate elements take on a very close and complementary relationship. The theme of 63–65 is the poet's Time-conquering verse that will preserve the friend's beauty for a future age, while the theme of 66–68 is the friend preserved by Nature as beauty's pattern to show a present age of sin and false artifice "what beauty was of yore." Sonnet 19 fuses the two themes, first by calling on Time to spare the friend as "beauty's pattern to succeeding men"—an apt extension into the future of his role in the present age, announced by 66–68. Then sonnet 19 'hedges' on this in the couplet: "Yet do thy worst, old Time . . . , My love shall in my verse ever live young"—an apt renewal of the theme declared in 63–65. Here the poet's verse becomes a preserver not merely of the young man's beauty (63–65) but of beauty's veritable pattern (66–68). Sonnet 19 thus brings together themes stated in the first two triads, and in doing this it begins a third and final triad: 19 21 105.

In Q, 21 is separated from 19 only by 20, a bit of scandalous pleasantry unrelated to any adjacent sonnet. If we allow 21 to follow 19 directly, the two sonnets not only become linked rhetorically but combine in referring back to 101 and 67–68. Sonnet 19 ends with the poet's resolve, "My love shall in *my verse* ever live young"; sonnet 21 opens: "So is it not with me as with that Muse Stirred by a painted beauty to *his verse*." The comparison becomes exact: we know from 101.3–4 that the poet's Muse "depends" on his friend, as does all "truth and beauty." Thus, ironically, the poet can immortalize his friend (the main theme here) only because his friend sustains his Muse. And the young friend does so because (67–68) he lives on—in a world that desecrates the true rose by "false painting"—as beauty's "map" or pattern. Hence, again, the last four lines of 19: "*my* verse" shall immortalize "beauty's pattern"; then the first lines of 21: "*So*" is my verse not inspired "as with that Muse Stirred by a *painted* beauty to *his* verse. . . ." Nor, sonnet 21 continues, do I traffic—as does "that Muse" (line 1)—in extravagant "*ornament*" (line 3); let me but "*truly* write" (line 9). With this compare the friend of 68.9–10 who subsists as primal beauty "Without all *ornament*, itself and *true*." I emphasize, of course, not the conventional single words but the repetition of pairing and context.

In 21 the poet scorns the use of "heaven itself" as ornament. "True in love," he will "but truly write" and then his "love [will be] as fair As any mother's child, though not so bright As those gold candles fixed in heaven's air." As a summation of this, the opening lines of 105 could not be more apt: "Let not my love be called idolatry, Nor my belovèd as an idol show." Here the immediate reference to idolatry, following the 'other' poet's equation in 21 of "his fair" with the glories of "heaven itself," is cogent enough. But as usual, a close thematic connection is accompanied by other links: the heavenly stars as "gold candles" (21.12) fits nicely into Elizabethan associations of idolatry with certain 'outward forms' of religious worship; the play in 105.1–2 on "love" in two senses, the emotion and the beloved object, echoes the usage in 21.9–10; and the poet's "verse" appears again at 105.7, so that in 19, 21, 105 the series begins with "my verse," considers "his verse" (another poet's), and then in peroration returns to "my verse."

Two concluding sonnets, 21 and 105, thus continue the previous note of falsity and painted beauty (67–68), extending it to a rejection of idolatry in favor of true love and true writing; and thus they enhance the rededication in 19 of the poet's verse to his friend's perpetuation. But 105 becomes even more pertinent as it caps the theme of truth and beauty embodied in the friend (101; 67.5–8; 68.9–12; 21.9–10) by adding a third and inclusive quality, kindness, to the dual attribute. Here, in "Fair, kind and true"—thrice repeated in 105, called "Three themes in one," and then made attributes of one man—a secular trinitarianism opposes itself to the sonneteer's idolatry scorned in 21, and stands forth as a simple article of faith that "wondrous scope affords." Is it accidental that this trinitarian credo, recited three times as a structural device in 105, appears to be an organizing principle in the poem as a whole? After 100–101, the two sonnets of invocation, we have in 63–65, 66–68 and 19 21 105 three distinct but interrelated units, each composed of three closely joined sonnets.

In any event, such is the result when eleven sonnets, unique in Q by virtue of their mode of address, are brought together with minimum preconception and manipulation. As an invocation, 100 and 101 fit naturally at the beginning; they are succeeded by the Q nucleus, 63–68, left intact; the nucleus is logically followed by 19 21, and they lead directly to 105 with its unmistakable note of summation. At least seven wholly independent factors support restoration of poem C. They are listed in Chapter I (pages 35–37) as an example of multiple, cumulative evidence.

 **IV D**

53–55

[53]

> What is your substance, whereof are you made,
> That millions of strange shadows on you tend?
> Since every one hath, every one, one shade,
> And you, but one, can every shadow lend.
> 5 Describe Adonis, and the counterfeit
> Is poorly imitated after you;
> On Helen's cheek all art of beauty set,
> And you in Grecian tires are painted new;
> Speak of the spring and foison of the year,
> 10 The one doth shadow of your beauty show,
> The other as your bounty doth appear,
> And you in every blessèd shape we know.
> > In all external grace you have some part,
> > But you like none, none you, for constant heart.

[54]

> O how much more doth beauty beauteous seem
> By that sweet ornament which truth doth give;
> The rose looks fair, but fairer we it deem
> For that sweet odor which doth in it live.
> 5 The canker-blooms have full as deep a dye
> As the perfumed tincture of the roses,
> Hang on such thorns and play as wantonly
> When summer's breath their maskèd buds discloses.
> But for their virtue only is their show,
> 10 They live unwooed and unrespected fade,
> Die to themselves. Sweet roses do not so;
> Of their sweet deaths are sweetest odors made.
> > And so of you, beauteous and lovely youth,
> > When that shall vade, by verse distills your truth.

[55]

Not marble nor the gilded monuments
Of princes shall outlive this powerful rhyme,
But you shall shine more bright in these contents
Than unswept stone besmeared with sluttish time.
5   When wasteful war shall statues overturn,
And broils root out the work of masonry,
Nor Mars his sword nor war's quick fire shall burn
The living record of your memory.
'Gainst death and all-oblivious enmity
10 Shall you pace forth; your praise shall still find room
Even in the eyes of all posterity
That wear this world out to the ending doom.
    So till the judgement that yourself arise,
    You live in this and dwell in lovers' eyes.

IV D
53–55

HERE, after poem C, three clearly linked sonnets continue the poet's verse as an enhancement of his friend "in the eyes of all posterity." Neither "sluttish time" nor death shall prevail to diminish his memory. Sonnet 53 finds the young man pervading every "blessèd shape," present in "all external grace" or outward beauty, but turns nicely in the last line to honor his inner quality, constancy. The first two lines of 54 then define constancy (truth) in terms of beauty itself; it becomes beauty's "sweet ornament." In the ensuing metaphor of roses and "canker-blooms," the substance-shadow opposition of 53 becomes at 54.9 a balancing of "virtue" (inner worth) against "show." And at the end of 54 virtue turns into essence, the young man's inner truth which the poet's verse "distills" and so preserves. From this turn of couplet the fine concluding statement of 55 proceeds.

Sonnets 53–55 (IV D) are separated in Q from 59–60 (of IV F), 62 (of IV A), and 63–68 (of IV C) only by 56–58 and 61, which are firmly placed by internal evidence in Group II. In theme 53–55 link closely with 60 and 63–68. There is a clear note of the friend as "beauty's pattern"; compare 53 with 67–68. There is the note of beauty enhanced by truth; compare 54 with the same two sonnets, noting especially the relation of truth to "ornament," the key word in both 54.2 and 68.10. And there is the essential note of 53–55, preservation for posterity of the friend's truth and beauty in the poet's verse; compare 54–55 with 60 and 63–65. Singly, these themes are sonneteers' clichés, of course, but where they appear combined in each of two sequences almost contiguous in Q, an editor must preserve the grouping he finds already present in the text. This is done here by placement of 53–55 as poem D, succeeding poem C which contains 63–68, and preceding (with E) poem F which contains 60.

It is interesting that although sonnets conferring immortality in verse are thought to abound indiscriminately, they are found, with two exceptions, in three 'clusters' of Q: 18–23, 53–68, and 100–107. One exception is 81, strongly tied to Group III (see pages 129–131); the other exception is 15–17, belonging clearly in the special context of Group I. The three clusters just mentioned represent the 'segments' of Q (pages 238–250) in which elements of Group IV, regardless of the immortality-in-verse theme, are found.

IV E

[18]

    Shall I compare thee to a summer's day?
    Thou art more lovely and more temperate.
    Rough winds do shake the darling buds of May,
    And summer's lease hath all too short a date;
5 Sometime too hot the eye of heaven shines,
    And often is his gold complexion dimmed;
    And every fair from fair sometime declines,
    By chance or nature's changing course untrimmed;
    But thy eternal summer shall not fade,
10 Nor lose possession of that fair thou ow'st;
    Nor shall Death brag thou wander'st in his shade,
    When in eternal lines to time thou grow'st.
      So long as men can breathe or eyes can see,
      So long lives this and this gives life to thee.

IV E
18

A COMMON theme of immortality conferred by enduring verse suggests a relationship between 18 and the sonnets of poems C and D, above. But between 18 and these sonnets one finds none of the multiple connectives supporting the restoration of poem C.

    Sonnet 18 scarcely belongs with Group I (1–17), for its ingenuous promise of immortality in verse is a negation of 15–17 which question such innocent magic. The negation is no paradox or antithesis; occurring as it does in Q, it is fatuous (see note 5, pages 299–300). The sonnet is, however, contiguous with 19 which presents the same theme, and this requires that it remain at least in proximity with 19, even though the two sonnets lack the cogent and multiple affinity that places 19 (and 21) within poem C. Again, as with 53–55, 60, and 63–68, when sonnets on the same theme, but without multiple affinity, are adjacent or almost adjacent in Q, they must be kept at least within the same group in any restored sequence. This condition is satisfied here by placement of 18 (E) but five sonnets removed from 19 (in C). Perhaps 18 should precede 53–55 (D). But its couplet happens to be an echo of the couplet in 55: note "So till," "You live in this," "dwell in lovers' eyes" in 55.13–14 and "So long as," "lives this," "eyes can see" in the corresponding lines of 18. The triple couplet echo and the identity of theme could well justify placing 53–55 and 18 in the same poem, a disposition requiring no change of the revised sonnet order as it now appears.

The parallel use of "this" in couplets, just noted, also serves to relate both 55 and 18 to other sonnets of Group IV. Compare the couplet of 107 (poem F): "And thou in this [these lines] shalt find thy monument"; note also the couplet of 63: "shall in these black lines be seen, And they shall live. . . ." Hence, the "this" construction appears in the couplets of four sonnets brought into Group IV on the basis of other evidence. Its only other appearance is in the couplet of 74, which clearly belongs with the sonnets of Group III.

IV F

106 59–60 107–108 115–116

[106]

When in the chronicle of wasted time
I see descriptions of the fairest wights,
And beauty making beautiful old rhyme
In praise of ladies dead and lovely knights,
5   Then in the blazon of sweet beauty's best,
Of hand, of foot, of lip, of eye, of brow,
I see their antique pen would have expressed
Even such a beauty as you master now.
So all their praises are but prophecies
10 Of this our time, all you prefiguring;
And for they looked but with divining eyes,
They had not skill enough your worth to sing;
    For we which now behold these present days
    Have eyes to wonder, but lack tongues to praise.

[59]

If there be nothing new, but that which is
Hath been before, how are our brains beguiled,
Which laboring for invention bear amiss
The second burthen of a former child.
5   O that record could with a backward look
Even of five hundred courses of the sun
Show me your image in some antique book,
Since mind at first in character was done,
That I might see what the old world could say
10 To this composèd wonder of your frame;
Whether we are mended or whe'r better they,
Or whether revolution be the same.
    O sure I am the wits of former days
    To subjects worse have given admiring praise.

[60]

Like as the waves make towards the pebbled shore,
So do our minutes hasten to their end:
Each changing place with that which goes before,
In sequent toil all forwards do contend.
5   Nativity once in the main of light
Crawls to maturity, wherewith being crowned,
Crookèd eclipses 'gainst his glory fight,
And Time that gave doth now his gift confound.
Time doth transfix the flourish set on youth
10   And delves the parallels in beauty's brow,
Feeds on the rarities of nature's truth,
And nothing stands but for his scythe to mow;
   And yet to times in hope my verse shall stand,
   Praising thy worth despite his cruel hand.

[107]

Not mine own fears nor the prophetic soul
Of the wide world dreaming on things to come
Can yet the lease of my true love control,
Supposed as forfeit to a confined doom.
5   The mortal moon hath her eclipse endured,
And the sad augurs mock their own presage;
Incertainties now crown themselves assured,
And peace proclaims olives of endless age.
Now with the drops of this most balmy time
10   My love looks fresh, and Death to me subscribes,
Since spite of him I'll live in this poor rhyme,
While he insults o'er dull and speechless tribes;
   And thou in this shalt find thy monument
   When tyrants' crests and tombs of brass are spent.

[108]

    What's in the brain that ink may character
    Which hath not figured to thee my true spirit?
    What's new to speak, what now to register,
    That may express my love or thy dear merit?
5 Nothing, sweet boy, but yet like prayers divine,
    I must each day say o'er the very same,
    Counting no old thing old, thou mine I thine,
    Even as when first I hallowed thy fair name.
    So that eternal love in love's fresh case
10 Weighs not the dust and injury of age,
    Nor gives to necessary wrinkles place,
    But makes antiquity for aye his page,
        Finding the first conceit of love there bred,
        Where time and outward form would show it dead.

[115]

    Those lines that I before have writ do lie,
    Even those that said I could not love you dearer;
    Yet then my judgement knew no reason why
    My most full flame should afterwards burn clearer.
5 But reckoning Time whose millioned accidents
    Creep in 'twixt vows and change decrees of kings,
    Tan sacred beauty, blunt the sharp'st intents,
    Divert strong minds to th' course of alt'ring things—
    Alas, why fearing of Time's tyranny
10 Might I not then say 'Now I love you best,'
    When I was certain o'er incertainty,
    Crowning the present, doubting of the rest?
        Love is a babe; then might I not say so,
        To give full growth to that which still doth grow.

[116]

    Let me not to the marriage of true minds
    Admit impediments; love is not love
    Which alters when it alteration finds,
    Or bends with the remover to remove:
5 O no, it is an ever-fixèd mark
    That looks on tempests and is never shaken;
    It is the star to every wand'ring bark,
    Whose worth 's unknown although his height be taken.
    Love's not Time's fool, though rosy lips and cheeks
10 Within his bending sickle's compass come;
    Love alters not with his brief hours and weeks,
    But bears it out even to the edge of doom.
      If this be error and upon me proved,
      I never writ nor no man ever loved.

IV F
106 59–60 107–108 115–116

IN theme, 106–108 are at most collateral with 105, and such a
relationship continues so long as the sonnets remain in the same
restored group. Separation of 59 from 58 and of 60 from 61
breaks no continuity. Sonnet 106 has a loose connection with the
pair 107–108 (see below). Far from interfering with this relationship, a placement of 59–60 between 106 and 107 enhances it.

When joined, the closely parallel 106 and 59 not only balance
one another but become a single continuing statement. Sonnet
106: when I read "descriptions of the fairest wights" in "old
rhyme," I sense that poets of times past tried to express the ideal
of beauty you now embody; hence "their praises are but prophecies . . , all you prefiguring"; but since they lacked you, the
model, they could only "divine" such beauty, could only intuit

what it would be. As for ourselves (poets of the present), we have you as a model before our eyes, but our tongues cannot express what we see. Now, sonnet 59: if nothing is really new, that is, if the old poets managed to "prefigure" you (106.10), our labors "for invention" only "bear amiss" (compare 106.14) a "former child." If I might but read what the old poets "could say To this composèd wonder of your frame" (what they could have written with your actual form before them), then I might know whether "they" or "we" are the better, or whether poets of all ages are the same. I can never know, of course, but of one thing "sure I am": whether or not the old poets were better, the "subjects" they praised were "worse."

In short, if the two sonnets are brought together we have 106 declaring that the old poets, aware of an ideal, could only "divine" the actuality, while present-day poets faced with the glorious actuality cannot do it justice. What a marvel it would be (59.5 ff.) if the contest could be made equal—if one "might see" what the old poets "could say" with the true model before them? But one cannot, so 'no contest,' except that the old poets lose (how could they help losing?) when it comes to a choice of subjects. The restored pair 106 59 has all of the pertinence and easy wit typical of Shakespearian pairs preserved in Q.

Sonnets 106 and 59 are linked by much more than a shared idea, for the conventional theme, ancient poets and new ones, appears in a specific context that remains the same in both sonnets. In its first quatrain 59 starts, moreover, with a tentative conclusion drawn from the last six lines of 106 and, proceeding to 'test' it, ends in a couplet that balances nicely with the one ending 106. Both couplets are of the kind that purports to sum up a sonnet but instead neatly changes the subject. And the couplet of 106 points to the handicap of modern poets—inferior "tongues," while the couplet of 59 notes the handicap of ancient poets—inferior "subjects."

Beyond these unifying elements the two sonnets show verbal connectives repeatedly found in authentic pairs. With the echoing couplets of 69–70 in mind as an example, compare the two couplets here, noting the balance of phrase, "present days" (106)—"former days" (59), and the identical couplet rhymes, "days"-"praise." The repetition of "wonder" (106.14 and 59.10) also serves to balance the two sonnets, for in each of them it denotes a quality of the young man that challenges poets, tests their "tongues" in one instance and what they "could say" in the other. Another significant echo is "antique pen"-"antique book" (106.7 and 59.7), parallel phrases within parallel second quatrains. Finally, the pitting of old poets against new ones has a personal immediacy in both sonnets, its ultimate statement in terms of "we" and "they."

Next, the continuation of 106 59 with 60 107–108. Sonnet 108 reasserts, in a different context, the note of 'old and new' praise found in 106. This works against any extensive separation of the two and calls, moreover, for retaining 107 in the scheme since it clearly belongs with 108 (beyond ordinary congruity, note "My love looks fresh . . ." at 107.10 and ". . . in love's fresh case" at 108.9). At the same time, nothing in the loose link between 106 and 107–108 prevents the insertion of 59 by pairing it, as we have done, with 106. But if 59 is to come after 106, what of 60, its companion in Q? Although unrelated to 61, sonnet 60 continues 59 to an extent of projecting the poet's verse into the future (lines 13–14) after 59 has compared it (and that of his contemporaries) with verse of the past. Besides, the couplet of 60 echoes the "worth"-"praise" association found in the last three lines of 106. So, if we restore the pair 106 59, we must add 60 and then continue with 107–108. This should be a good check on the linking of 106 and 59, for although an interposed 59 in no way breaks a connection between 106 and 107–108, the addition of 60 could do so and thus put the whole matter in doubt. Fortunately, the retention of 60 after 59 has an entirely opposite result: far from disturbing continuity, it serves aptly to introduce and state the theme of 107–108 (see below). Thus Q's 59–60 turns out to be an authentic fragment—displaced but intact—consisting of two sonnets, the first pairing with 106 and the second belonging with

107–108. Like 22–23 of poem A, 59–60 is found to be a missing bridge between elements of a series.

Generalized, the link between 60 and 107–108 is a conventional theme, Time-the-destroyer—verse-the-preserver, introduced formally by 60 and continued by 107. But the actual connection is far more pointed. Ordinarily, after Shakespeare presents Time's ruinous course he invokes his verse almost desperately to preserve youth and beauty against the grimmest of odds: in 63–65, for example, the very thought of ravaging Time is "as a death" (64.13), a "fearful meditation" of destruction that only a "miracle" of "black ink" can withstand (65.9–14). In 60 we find a different note; after twelve excellent lines on relentless Time, a dramatic shift introduces "times in hope"—a future still within Time and the scope of "his cruel hand," yet prior to Finality. Time the unhappy absolute will prevail at last but meanwhile there are "times" that may well prove benign, at least to the poet's lines standing as his friend's monument. In place of the old troubled defiance of Time appears a quiet confidence in the future. This new note found in the couplet of 60 is just what 107 develops, for as 60 ends with its reference to "times in hope," 107 opens by exorcising hope's opposite, "fears" and prophetic anxiety over "things to come." Neither fear nor prophecy can limit the "lease [duration] of my true love." So enough of the doomsday cult! The "mortal moon" has endured her eclipse without promised disaster and the "sad augurs" are left to mock themselves. "Incertainties" have turned into assurance; peace proclaims itself as "endless." And in this "most balmy time" (double-entendrists may explicate any pun on 'barmy'), "My love looks fresh, and Death to me subscribes." I will live "in this poor rhyme" and it will be your eternal monument. The vision at the end of 60 of times in hope within cruel Time thus receives in 107 the enlargement it needs.

Nor is the usual echo of metaphor lacking here, for in the second quatrain of each sonnet "eclipse," in an astrological sense, is the principal figure standing for an onset of Time or Mutability; and the successfully "endured" eclipse of 107.5–8 may represent deliverance from the dire eclipses of 60.5–8. "Eclipse" occurs elsewhere in the Sonnets but once (35.3), and in a different context. Still, the truly unique parallel between 60 and 107 is an immediate association in both sonnets of "eclipse" with "crown": in 60 nativity "crowned" with maturity suffers eclipse and in 107 the mortal moon endures her eclipse, whereupon "Incertainties now crown themselves assured."

The link this double metaphor establishes between 60 and 107 becomes involved with a widely accepted equation of the "mortal moon" in eclipse (107.5–8) with Queen Elizabeth, for in such a context the crown image of 107 is especially apt, and that of 60 may possibly anticipate it. But anticipation does not mean equivalent meaning, and nothing requires that the eclipse-crown allusion in 60 be read as a reference to the queen; it may be nothing more than a free association of images that precedes an eclipse-crown association in 107. But if so, the implication of linkage is still there. Although repetition of image combinations can be fortuitous, it remains as one of the distinguishing elements in Q's existing, authentic sequences. And when accompanied by other signs of linkage it can be prime evidence for restored sequence.

Restoration of poem F ends with the placement of 115–116 after 107–108. Persuasive evidence, if I may call it that, points to an intrusion of two discrete pairs, 113–114 and 115–116, between fragments of a unified series. This disrupted series, when restored, becomes Poem 5 (page 183) comprising sonnets 109–112 117–121. Internal evidence places 113–114 with Group II (page 69); so we relocate the first intrusive pair. Then, if we move 109–112 to a position immediately before 117–121 we have Poem 5, as described. But we also have an interesting 'by-product'—115–116 left in a position immediately following 107–108. The result is encouraging, for independent evidence now supports the new position of 115–116, just as it supported the relocation of 113–114 and 109–112.

The declared subject of 107–108 is old love reawakened, newly dedicated (107.1–3, 10–11; and all of 108), a theme elaborately continued throughout 115–116. In 107–108 love becomes "fresh" with the passing of time (the same phrasing at 107.10 and 108.9); despite the "dust and injury of age," love "makes antiquity for aye his page." Likewise in 115–116 love is "a babe" that continues to grow in the face of "Time's tyranny," is never "Time's fool," and never alters with Time's "brief hours and weeks." As in 23 102 of poem A, a purposeful if not contrived repetition—the word "love" made to echo and reecho—sharpens in both 107–108 and 115–116 what would otherwise be a commonplace resemblance. But beyond this, phrasal echo is doubled, compounded. In the deliverance from his "fears," celebrated in 107, the poet finds that *"Incertainties* now *crown* themselves assured" (line 7). In 115 he looks back to a former time, presumably before this deliverance, "When [he] was certain o'er *incertainty, Crowning* the present, doubting of the rest" (lines 11–12). In other words, at that time he was so doubtful of the future ("the rest") that he lived in the present, finding there a certainty he could affirm "o'er" the incertainty that plagued him. The word "incertainty" appears only in sonnets 107 and 115, and in both instances the "crown" metaphor accompanies it, a matter of more than incidental interest when we recall that the crown metaphor twice joins with "eclipse" to form a compound link between 60 and 107. Thus in the same restored poem the eclipse-crown combination continues from 60 into 107–108, and the incertainty-crown association carries over from 107–108 into 115–116.

In the series restored here the first two lines of 115 may appear to contradict the essential statement of 60 and 107, for if we read 115.1 as giving the lie to all lines the poet has written, what becomes of their immediately prior role (107.13) as a lasting "monument" to his friend? But the 'retraction' in 115 has no such scope; the lines that lie are "Even those that said I could not love you dearer" (115.2). "Even" here does not mean 'even including' but 'namely' or 'to wit'; see the usage, now virtually obsolete, in 81.14 and 111.14. Developing statement throughout 115 is consistent only with such a reading. So, with the retraction applying only to lines that once "said I could not love you dearer," the statement of 115 supports the theme of love increasing with time and newly rededicated. It introduces no contradiction.

The restored sequence now includes three elements: 106 59; 60 107–108; and 115–116—elements we may read as three divisions of a single poem or as three poems, separate but closely related. It makes little difference so long as we recognize an order and continuity of the whole. The surviving 'frame' in Q (106, 107–108, . . . 115–116), and the displaced but intact 'bridge' (59–60) between 106 and 107–108, plainly suggest an originally integrated series.

 POEM 5

109–112 117–121

[109]

O never say that I was false of heart,
Though absence seemed my flame to qualify;
As easy might I from myself depart
As from my soul which in thy breast doth lie.
5 That is my home of love; if I have ranged,
Like him that travels I return again,
Just to the time, not with the time exchanged,
So that myself bring water for my stain.
Never believe, though in my nature reigned
10 All frailties that besiege all kinds of blood,
That it could so preposterously be stained
To leave for nothing all thy sum of good;
    For nothing this wide universe I call,
    Save thou, my rose; in it thou art my all.

[110]

Alas, 'tis true I have gone here and there
And made myself a motley to the view,
Gored mine own thoughts, sold cheap what is most dear,
Made old offences of affections new.
5 Most true it is that I have looked on truth
Askance and strangely; but by all above,
These blenches gave my heart another youth,
And worse essays proved thee my best of love.
Now all is done, have what shall have no end;
10 Mine appetite I never more will grind
On newer proof to try an older friend,
A god in love to whom I am confined.
    Then give me welcome, next my heaven the best,
    Even to thy pure and most most loving breast.

[111]

O for my sake do you with Fortune chide,
The guilty goddess of my harmful deeds,
That did not better for my life provide
Than public means which public manners breeds.
5 Thence comes it that my name receives a brand,
And almost thence my nature is subdued
To what it works in, like the dyer's hand.
Pity me then and wish I were renewed,
Whilst like a willing patient I will drink
10 Potions of eisel 'gainst my strong infection;
No bitterness that I will bitter think,
Nor double penance, to correct correction.
    Pity me then, dear friend, and I assure ye
    Even that your pity is enough to cure me.

[112]

Your love and pity doth th' impression fill
Which vulgar scandal stamped upon my brow;
For what care I who calls me well or ill,
So you o'ergreen my bad, my good allow?
5 You are my all the world, and I must strive
To know my shames and praises from your tongue;
None else to me, nor I to none alive,
That my steeled sense or changes right or wrong.
In so profound abysm I throw all care
10 Of others' voices that my adder's sense
To critic and to flatterer stoppèd are.
Mark how with my neglect I do dispense:
    You are so strongly in my purpose bred
    That all the world besides methinks are dead.

[117]

  Accuse me thus: that I have scanted all
  Wherein I should your great deserts repay,
  Forgot upon your dearest love to call,
  Whereto all bonds do tie me day by day;
5 That I have frequent been with unknown minds,
  And given to time your own dear-purchased right;
  That I have hoisted sail to all the winds
  Which should transport me farthest from your sight.
  Book both my wilfulness and errors down,
10 And on just proof surmise accumulate;
  Bring me within the level of your frown,
  But shoot not at me in your wakened hate;
    Since my appeal says I did strive to prove
    The constancy and virtue of your love.

[118]

  Like as to make our appetites more keen,
  With eager compounds we our palate urge;
  As to prevent our maladies unseen,
  We sicken to shun sickness when we purge;
5 Even so, being full of your ne'er-cloying sweetness,
  To bitter sauces did I frame my feeding,
  And sick of welfare found a kind of meetness
  To be diseased ere that there was true needing.
  Thus policy in love, t'anticipate
10 The ills that were not, grew to faults assured,
  And brought to medicine a healthful state,
  Which rank of goodness would by ill be cured.
    But thence I learn, and find the lesson true,
    Drugs poison him that so fell sick of you.

[119]

    What potions have I drunk of Siren tears,
    Distilled from limbecks foul as hell within,
    Applying fears to hopes and hopes to fears,
    Still losing when I saw myself to win.
5 What wretched errors hath my heart committed,
    Whilst it hath thought itself so blessèd never;
    How have mine eyes out of their spheres been fitted
    In the distraction of this madding fever.
    O benefit of ill; now I find true
10 That better is by evil still made better,
    And ruined love when it is built anew
    Grows fairer than at first, more strong, far greater.
      So I return rebuked to my content,
      And gain by ills thrice more than I have spent.

[120]

    That you were once unkind befriends me now,
    And for that sorrow which I then did feel
    Needs must I under my transgression bow,
    Unless my nerves were brass or hammered steel.
5 For if you were by my unkindness shaken,
    As I by yours, you've passed a hell of time,
    And I, a tyrant, have no leisure taken
    To weigh how once I suffered in your crime.
    O that our night of woe might have rememb'red
10 My deepest sense, how hard true sorrow hits,
    And soon to you, as you to me, then tend'red
    The humble salve which wounded bosoms fits.
      But that your trespass now becomes a fee;
      Mine ransoms yours, and yours must ransom me.

[121]

'Tis better to be vile than vile esteemed
When not to be receives reproach of being,
And the just pleasure lost, which is so deemed
Not by our feeling but by others' seeing.
5 For why should others' false adulterate eyes
Give salutation to my sportive blood?
Or on my frailties why are frailer spies,
Which in their wills count bad what I think good?
No, I am that I am, and they that level
10 At my abuses reckon up their own;
I may be straight though they themselves be bevel;
By their rank thoughts my deeds must not be shown,
    Unless this general evil they maintain,
    All men are bad and in their badness reign.

POEM 5
109–112 117–121

IN Q there is a lapse of continuity between 108 and 109, and
between 121 and 122. Hence restoration of this poem requires
merely that a separable pair, 113–114, and an element of IV F,
115–116, be removed from the Q sequence 109–121. Sonnets
109–112 and 117–121 thus come together.

But if the suggested changes are minor and simple, their effect
is to transform two fragments into a single poem of remarkable
unity. The first fragment, 109–112, concerns renewal of an in-
tense friendship (real or assumed) after alienation and public
scandal. Caste barriers intensify the speaker's predicament, but he
refers only incidentally (some say not at all) to another theme

often thought of as primary—his sense of degradation as a play-wright. This theme seems clear in 111 but remains subordinate to the note of renewed friendship after disloyalty and disgrace (see the Variorum commentary on sonnet 110). In 109–110 the speaker "returns" bringing water (tears?) to cleanse his stain; he has made a public fool of himself, has "gone here and there" bestowing "affections new" only to find himself guilty of "old offences"; he has "sold cheap what is most dear." But these "blenches" (wandering glances) have given his heart "another youth" (a pun?); never again, "On newer proof," will he "try [test] an older friend." He asks to be received and welcomed. Sonnet 111 continues the theme of cleansing and renewal by urging the friend to chide the poet's ill fortune—"public means which public manners breeds"—to redeem him with pity, "Whilst like a willing patient [he] will drink Potions of eisel 'gainst [his] strong infection." After continuing the note of pity expressed in 111, sonnet 112 declares the poet deaf to "others' voices" and subject only to his friend's judgment: "You are my all the world, and I must strive To know my shames and praises from your tongue."

If we remove Q's disruptive 113–116, we find in 117 a direct run-on from 112. As just noted, the speaker avows in 112 that he will seek praise or censure only from his friend—and sonnet 117 begins its address to the friend with "Accuse me thus. . . ." Then comes the censure the poet invites, prescribes; and it parallels exactly his self-accusation in the first fragment. Say "That I have frequent been with unknown minds, . . . have hoisted sail to all the winds." My "appeal" (plea, excuse) is that I sought "to prove" (test or assess) your constancy and love. Compare these statements in 117 with parallel statements in 110. Two linked sonnets, 118–119, now explain what this means: "full of your ne'er-cloying sweetness, To bitter sauces [unworthy friendships] did I frame my feeding"; "sick of welfare," I took bitter medicine to "anticipate" an illness not yet present. But I have learned my "lesson true." "Drugs poison him that so fell sick of you." Sonnet 119 completes the metaphor of drugs ("potions"), and its couplet,

"So I return . . ," fulfills the earlier statement of 109—"Like him that travels I return again." Sonnet 120, "That you were once unkind befriends me now," recalls a past transgression by the friend whose repentance on that occasion, "humble salve," now invokes the poet's own charity. Sonnet 121 needs separate discussion that will follow shortly.

Supplementing thematic links between these sonnets is an interaction of phrase and image. Compare 109.3-4, "As easy might I from myself depart As from my *soul* which in thy *breast* doth lie," with 110.13-14, "Then give me welcome, next my *heaven* the best, Even to thy pure and most most loving *breast*." Compare also the play of "ill" in 118.10, 12 and 119.9, 14; and note the poet's "errors" in 117.9 and 119.5. More important than these connectives, of course, are those which bridge the two fragments separated in Q. See "proof," "prove," in the same special sense (110.11 and 117.13), and—previously cited—"I return again," "So I return" (109.6 and 119.13). Compare "potions of eisel . . . ; No bitterness that I will bitter think" (111.10-11) and "bitter sauces" (118.6), foul "potions" of Siren tears (119.1-2). Note also the poet's "steeled sense" (112.8) and "nerves" of "hammered steel" (120.4). Finally, compare the images of disease and medicine in 111.9-10 with those of 118.2-14.

Sonnet 121 ends the series in the manner of an 'envoy' by generalizing, grimly, on the note of 112: the "rank thoughts" of other men are unfit to judge my deeds—unless they grant that "All men are bad" and that evil is everywhere. This last sonnet echoes phrasing of both fragments disjoined in Q. Compare "frailties," "frailer" (121.7) with "frailties" (109.10); "level At my abuses" (121.9-10) with "level of your frown" (117.11). Note "blood" linked with moral "frailty" (121.5-7 and 109.9-10). In 112 the poet declares himself deaf to the censure of "others' voices"; in 121 he denounces "others' false adulterate eyes" and deems it better actually "to be vile" than in their prurient view to be "vile esteemed." (I would rather be everything they think me than submit myself—and you(?)—to their leering judgment.) With this *defi* the prodigal caps his "return" by casting out devils who are creatures at once of sin and false judgment of sin. Reconciliation is an affair wholly between the poet and his friend.

As for disruption by 113–116 of the closely joined 109–112 and 117–121, I trust that a reading of the Q sequence will make the matter fairly obvious. Sonnets 113–114 shift from a speaker who has "returned" (109–111) to one who is still absent, and wander into new and involved conceits; 115–116, excellent sonnets, introduce peripheral generalities. The effect is such that no poet could expect the close interplay between 109–112 and 117–121 to survive the interruption. It is possible, as usual, for loose thematic interpretation to attempt a justification of 113–116 in their 1609 position: "monsters and things indigest" (114.5) can serve to recall the infected world of Poem 5 (a forced connection, however, in view of the context and tone of 113–114); and the finality of devotion expressed in 115–116 can agree with a return, a reconciliation. Yet, even if we allow for such vague linkage, Q's mangling of 109–112 117–121 will remain: the cohesion of this series, including the carry-over from 112 to 117, either has purpose or it has not. If it has, sonnets 113–116 ruin it, and those skeptical of change in the Q order must affirm either that Shakespeare intended the disaster or that he wrote half of a multiply unified poem while oblivious of the other half. Such affirmations are hardly suited to the skeptic's position. He may reason, of course, that sonnets 117–121 continue 109–112 but were written later—that the extraneous 113–114 and 115–116 were composed in the interim. Yet if this were somehow provable, should a modern text reproduce the sonnets chronologically or should it print the completion of a poem so that it follows the beginning? Or, if the two segments can be thought of as companion pieces, should they remain separated by extraneous sonnets or should they appear together? The answer to either question is that if clear authorial intention can be inferred from internal evidence, it should govern. There is no external evidence, for Q has no authorial sanction.

Poem 5 remains here in its Q position where its theme of a prodigal's return precedes an assertion of final, irrevocable allegiance in 122–126. Yet it may belong with Group II as the terminal poem (K) of that series. The theme of Group II is separation of poet and friend, intensified in the group's latter poems (F through J) by alienation, and progressively related to some misdeed or misdeeds contaminating both men and forming a barrier between them. In these Group II poems, moreover, allusion to repentance, forgiveness, reunion, and 'oneness' consistently accompanies reference to injury, disloyalty, divisive guilt, and the necessity of staying apart. Hence, Poem 5 with its declared "return" from absence and alienation, its note of remorseful confession, its account (in 120) of mutual injury and mutual atonement, could aptly end the Group II series. It has little or no relation to the other 'alienation' series (Group III, on the rival poet) or to other statements of absence (such as 97–99) unconcerned with alienation or injury.

Further, Poem 5 and Group II (89, 90, 96, 33–35, 40—of poems G, H, J) share a vocabulary unique in the Sonnets. There is "stain" (both noun and verb), referring to guilt or sin, found only in 109.8, 109.11, 33.14 (twice), and 35.3. There is "error" in its special sense of sin or misdeed, found in 117.9, 119.5, and 96.7 (the one example not occurring in Poem 5 or Group II appears at 141.2). And denoting a relationship between poet and friend, the word "hate" appears only in 117.12, 35.12, 40.12, 89.14 and 90.1. Finally, there is a repeated 'cluster': "salve"–"ransom"–"trespass," the first word meaning to compensate for a wrong, the second to 'buy back' a wrong and thus atone for it. In the Sonnets the three words appear in conjunction and only in the following places:

"salve"	"ransom"	"trespass"
120.12	120.14	120.13
34.7	34.14	
35.7		35.6

The three consecutive lines, 12–14, of sonnet 120 present a continuing statement in Poem 5, and the two consecutive sonnets, 34–35, present another in poem J of Group II. Moreover, if Poem

5 belongs with Group II, its 'finality' requires that it be the end poem (K), which would place it directly after J. Hence the "salve"–"ransom"–"trespass" cluster in 34–35 and the same cluster in 120 would appear in successive poems.

Another hint that Poem 5 is a part of Group II appears in Q's arrangement, or rather disarrangement, in which a fragment of Group II (113–114) is lodged between the two fragments of Poem 5 (109–112 and 117–121). As we shall see later, fragments of related poems in the restored order are commonly found together in Q.

Thus parallel themes, parallels of style, and a bit of collateral evidence all point in the same direction. In addition, there may be a parallel of incident, of situation: in 120 the "trespass" once committed by the friend and atoned for with "humble salve," the wrong that now "ransoms" the poet's trespass, could readily be the wrong described, likewise in terms of trespass, salve, and ransom, in sonnets 34 and 35.

A single factor, however, opposes the linking of Poem 5 with Group II, and while it may be an accident of Q's disarrangement, it will have to be decisive. I have allowed the Q order to stand wherever it shows a cogent relation between sonnets. And even where the connection is loosely thematic, I have tried to preserve a group relation found in Q although, in trying to restore cogency, I may have altered the sonnet order. Poem 5's relation to Group II is multiple, probable. But in its Q position between 107–108 and 122–126, Poem 5, if not cogent, is plainly coherent. These sonnets, with 115–116, all celebrate a 'late,' a terminal reconcilation and a rededication of the threatened friendship. So does Poem 5. Its note of reunion with 'finality' could properly end Group II but happens also to be appropriate in the context Q furnishes. And in Q's context Poem 5 may still refer back in time to the events and situation Group II has depicted. One might say that sonnets 107–108, 115–116, and 122–126 are serene, while Poem 5 recounts some very unserene experiences. Just the same, Poem 5 resolves previous stress by facing it, by describing it. And to hold that final statement in the Sonnets should be entirely serene would carry us into pseudo-biography—'out of the depths, on the heights.'

Editorial consistency requires that Poem 5 be restored (by removal of 113–116), but that it remain in the context Q gives it. Editorial obligation, however, requires a statement of the strong case for assigning this poem to Group II, and a reminder that consistency, necessary though it is, can be mistaken. Put it this way: had Q happened to place the sonnets of Poem 5 directly after those of II J, then removal of the poem—because of its 'finality'—to a later position (Q's actual placement) would break an 'inviolable' link and substitute one merely appropriate or 'reasonable.'

# POEM 6

122–126

[122]

Thy gift, thy tables, are within my brain
Full charactered with lasting memory,
Which shall above that idle rank remain
Beyond all date, even to eternity;
5 Or at the least, so long as brain and heart
Have faculty by nature to subsist,
Till each to rased oblivion yield his part
Of thee, thy record never can be missed.
That poor retention could not so much hold,
10 Nor need I tallies thy dear love to score;
Therefore to give them from me was I bold,
To trust those tables that receive thee more.
    To keep an adjunct to remember thee
    Were to import forgetfulness in me.

[123]

No, Time, thou shalt not boast that I do change;
Thy pyramids built up with newer might
To me are nothing novel, nothing strange;
They are but dressings of a former sight.
5 Our dates are brief, and therefore we admire
What thou dost foist upon us that is old,
And rather make them born to our desire
Than think that we before have heard them told.
Thy registers and thee I both defy,
10 Not wond'ring at the present nor the past,
For thy records and what we see doth lie,
Made more or less by thy continual haste.
    This I do vow, and this shall ever be:
    I will be true despite thy scythe and thee.

194

[124]

    If my dear love were but the child of state,
    It might for Fortune's bastard be unfathered,
    As subject to Time's love or to Time's hate,
    Weeds among weeds, or flowers with flowers gathered.
5 No, it was builded far from accident;
    It suffers not in smiling pomp, nor falls
    Under the blow of thrallèd discontent,
    Whereto the inviting time our fashion calls.
    It fears not policy, that heretic
10 Which works on leases of short-numbered hours,
    But all alone stands hugely politic,
    That it nor grows with heat nor drowns with showers.
      To this I witness call the fools of Time,
      Which die for goodness, who have lived for crime.

[125]

    Were 't aught to me I bore the canopy,
    With my extern the outward honoring,
    Or laid great bases for eternity,
    Which proves more short than waste or ruining?
5 Have I not seen dwellers on form and favor
    Lose all and more by paying too much rent,
    For compound sweet forgoing simple savor—
    Pitiful thrivers in their gazing spent?
    No, let me be obsequious in thy heart,
10 And take thou my oblation poor but free,
    Which is not mixed with seconds, knows no art
    But mutual render, only me for thee.
      Hence, thou suborned informer; a true soul
      When most impeached stands least in thy control.

[126]

    O thou, my lovely boy, who in thy power
    Dost hold Time's fickle glass, his sickle, hour;
    Who hast by waning grown, and therein show'st
    Thy lovers withering as thy sweet self grow'st;
5 If Nature, sovereign mistress over wrack,
    As thou goest onwards still will pluck thee back,
    She keeps thee to this purpose, that her skill
    May time disgrace and wretched minutes kill.
    Yet fear her, O thou minion of her pleasure;
10 She may detain but not still keep her treasure:
      Her audit, though delayed, answered must be,
      And her quietus is to render thee.

POEM 6

122–126

THE usual reading of 123–125 disregards 122 which, like 77, is interpreted as a sonnet standing by itself, the acknowledgement of a gift, a notebook ("thy tables"). Beyond doubt, sonnet 122 has this simple function, but its implications are far from simple. In it the written word, so far as it commemorates "dear love," is dismissed as "idle," as a mere "adjunct" (lines 3, 13), in favor of the intangible but far more genuine record preserved in "brain and heart" (line 5). Like other sonneteers, Shakespeare is not above being artful in comparing his art unfavorably with 'true feeling.' And in sonnets 16–17 he holds verse in lower esteem than procreation as a means of preserving his friend's memory. Nevertheless, the tone of 122 seems different, more genuine. Do we have here the beginning of a 'retraction' that continues through 123–126 as a final statement denying art—sonneteers' art—as an expression of enduring 'truth?'

Sonnet 122 has its ambiguities. The "tallies," entered or to be entered in the table book (line 10) have to do with "thy dear love," and presumably, although judged inadequate for the purpose, were supposed to commemorate that love. Thus it appears that the tables were to contain poems. But from the sonnet itself we cannot tell whether the notebook as given away (line 11) contained writing by the young man, whether it contained writing by Shakespeare, or whether it remained blank because the poet chose to record his feelings only in his heart. I agree with Ingram and Redpath (*Shakespeare's Sonnets*, page 280) that the first possibility is unlikely, for if the tables contained written tribute from his friend, the poet's statement in 122 and his disposal of the book would have been tactless if not insulting. But I cannot agree that the second possibility is less probable than the third. Shakespeare often "tallies" his friend's "dear love." And Meres tells us that the Sonnets were in circulation, which implies a possible giving away of "tables" containing them (lines 11–12). It really makes little difference, for beyond the second and third possibilities lies a fourth—that the whole occasion, gift and all, was fictional.

Yet the sentiment of 122, rejection of the written word in its commemorative role, remains quite 'real.' And if I interpret 123–126 correctly, 122 becomes the lead sonnet in a series of five that repudiates everything spurious in the sonnet tradition—its banal idolatry, its petulant anxiety, its derivative ingenuity, and its depressing claim to a victory over Time and dissolution.

Sonnets 123–125 have been read as commentary on architectural fads, court life, politics, the Jesuits, and the Gunpowder Plot. Allusion to the more general of these matters would be hard to deny, but it is well to remember that topical allusion can serve as metaphor. Thus, whatever Time's "pyramids built up with newer might" (123.2) may call up from the contemporary scene, they graphically represent innovation that, straining for a newer might, merely reproduces the old. Shakespeare constantly presents the 'new writing' in this light. See, for example, sonnets 59 and 106, both done in the manner of 123; see also 68, 76, 82, and

108. In fact, whenever a sonnet compares new things unfavorably with old, the reference is to falsity or deficiency in poetry or art. Characteristic phrasing in 123 falls within the scheme: Time's newer pyramids, "nothing novel, nothing strange," are "but *dressings* of a *former* sight." Compare this with 76.11: "So all my best is *dressing* old words new"; and with 68.12: "Robbing no old to *dress* his beauty new"—the only other instances of "dress" in the Sonnets save one in a wholly different context at 98.2. Consider also 59.4, 13—"*former* child," "wits of *former* days," referring respectively to poetry and poets. In 123.5–8, the old things we will not admit to having "*heard*" before would seem to be something verbalized, recounted. In 123.9–11 the lie is given to Time's "registers" and "records," a sentiment that can have general meaning, but see 108.3 for the only other occurrence in the Sonnets of "register"; it means to record tribute in a sonnet. As for "record," in its three appearances elsewhere (55.8, 59.5, 122.8) the context, if not the direct reference, is invariably one of written tribute to the young man.

Hence, if usage in the Sonnets themselves is a reliable guide, the characteristic metaphors and vocabulary of 123 strongly suggest a poet dissociating himself from poets and poetry of a spuriously new order. In addition to saying that his devotion will not change, he appears to say that the "new" style of expressing devotion is neither new nor worth his attention. Sonnet 124, which follows, declares the poet's love immune from Time's "accident" and the "thrallèd discontent, Whereto *the inviting time our fashion* calls." The phrasing here bears one of the hallmarks of Shakespearian satire addressed to 'new poetry': see 32.5, 76.3, and 82.8 on "*the time*," the current fashion in versifying, and the "strainèd touches" (82.10) it evokes in poets. And "thrallèd discontent," the accompanying phrase in 124, is scarcely a misdescription of the stance assumed by sonneteers. The couplet of 124 is one of those gnomic statements that invite deciphering from one generation to the next. In the present context it remains gnomic but readily adaptable to the pervasive subject matter. The "fools of Time" who are called to "witness" the poet's constancy in a swirl of change and innovation (compare the "Time's fool" passage, 116.9) can readily be understood as sonneteers who, like Shakespeare, have renounced a perverse and endless anxiety over fads of "the time" and Time's threat to their patrons, their status, and their verse. They are now in a state of grace and can "die for goodness" after a life of "crime." The light touch is not lacking.

Through 122, 123, and 124 allusion seems to point constantly in the same direction, and the reference becomes still more pointed in 125. A "suborned informer" apparently has charged the poet with "outward honoring" of his patron, with having "laid great bases for eternity" which, the poet concedes, "proves more short than waste or ruining." As Dowden observed, this recalls and negates Shakespeare's promise to his friend—recurrent in earlier sonnets on Time's ruin—of immortality, eternity in verse. In 125.5–8 the progressive reference to sonnets and those who write them now ends in another typical image: "Have I not seen dwellers on form and favor Lose all and more by paying too much rent, For *compound sweet* forgoing simple savor—Pitiful *thrivers* in their gazing spent?" For application of this to sonneteers, see 76.4—"new-found methods . . . *compounds strange*" contrasted with poetic simplicity—and 79 in which the rival poet, who wants to "thrive" in 80.13, becomes like the "Pitiful thrivers" of 125—spent in his gazing, unable to transmit more than the beauty he actually sees. Sonnet 125 forswears all such pathetically contrived "art" (compare lines 9–12, especially, with sonnets 78–79), and casts the suborned informer "hence." Then, with finality, 126 reverses a dominant note, recurrent from sonnet 1 onward, by actually surrendering the "lovely boy" to Time. Nature's audit must be answered; "her quietus is to render thee."

 GROUP V

A 127 130   B 144 143 135–136 131–134
C 138(?) 139–140   D 137 141–142 147–152
E 129 146   F 153–154   G 128(?) 145(?)

LIKE Group I, Group V is distinctive in theme and shows no sign of intermingling with other groups or independent poems. But unlike Group I, Group V obviously has suffered internal disarrangement, although its sonnets remain together. The lack of intermingling suggests that the two groups have a manuscript history and a provenience separate from those of sonnets 18–126, an implication supported by Q's isolation of Group I as the first seventeen sonnets and Group V as the last twenty-eight.

Group V is concerned with the poet's relations—whether real, fictional, or both—with a woman or perhaps a number of women. A man, who may be the one celebrated in other groups, appears here in a few sonnets as the poet's friend, sensually involved with the woman and, like the poet, trapped by her. Save for the close relationship of poems D and E, internal evidence and the evidence of Q's arrangement suggest little more than cognate ties between the restored poems of Group V, and point to no necessary order for their appearance. Nevertheless they belong together in loose association. On the other hand, linkage *within* the individual poems restored here is far from loose; internally they show a concentration of theme and detail rarely exceeded by other restored poems or by Q's 'intensive units.'

V A

127–130

[127]

In the old age black was not counted fair,
Or if it were it bore not beauty's name;
But now is black beauty's successive heir,
And beauty slandered with a bastard shame:
5 For since each hand hath put on nature's power,
Fairing the foul with art's false borrowed face,
Sweet beauty hath no name, no holy bower,
But is profaned, if not lives in disgrace.
Therefore my mistress' eyes are raven black,
10 Her eyes so suited, and they mourners seem
At such who not born fair no beauty lack,
Sland'ring creation with a false esteem;
    Yet so they mourn, becoming of their woe,
    That every tongue says beauty should look so.

[130]

My mistress' eyes are nothing like the sun;
Coral is far more red than her lips' red;
If snow be white, why then her breasts are dun;
If hairs be wires, black wires grow on her head.
5 I have seen roses damasked red and white,
But no such roses see I in her cheeks;
And in some perfumes is there more delight
Than in the breath that from my mistress reeks.
I love to hear her speak, yet well I know
10 That music hath a far more pleasing sound;
I grant I never saw a goddess go;
My mistress when she walks treads on the ground;
    And yet, by heaven I think my love as rare
    As any she belied with false compare.

V A
127 130

EVEN a casual reading of these two sonnets will link them in theme: inversion of the sonneteer's ideal of fair beauty by extolling its opposite—black eyes, black hair—in comic lines having just a trace of the serious. The two sonnets also come together in a run-on beginning with "my mistress' eyes" at the start of the last quatrain in 127 and continuing with the identical phrase at the first line of 130.

The thematic parallels are, of course, commonplace and would scarcely link two widely separated sonnets. But here the sonnets are almost adjacent in Q; they are separated, moreover, by 128 and 129 which obviously have as little to do with 127 and 130 as with one another. Those who find the meandering Q order 'loosely unified but appropriate' never, apparently, find themselves unhinged by laughter when reading 129, that grim and amazing sonnet on lust, in close context with 128 and 130. We await an explication of this impasse as 'the interplay of contraries.'

If 128 and 129 are deemed out of place and removed, Q does the rest by bringing 127 and 130 together.

V B

144 143 135–136 131–134

[144]

Two loves I have of comfort and despair,
Which like two spirits do suggest me still;
The better angel is a man right fair,
The worser spirit a woman colored ill.
5 To win me soon to hell, my female evil
Tempteth my better angel from my side,
And would corrupt my saint to be a devil,
Wooing his purity with her foul pride.
And whether that my angel be turned fiend
10 Suspect I may, yet not directly tell;
But being both from me, both to each friend,
I guess one angel in another's hell;
    Yet this shall I ne'er know, but live in doubt,
    Till my bad angel fire my good one out.

[143]

Lo, as a careful housewife runs to catch
One of her feathered creatures broke away,
Sets down her babe and makes all swift dispatch
In pursuit of the thing she would have stay,
5 Whilst her neglected child holds her in chase,
Cries to catch her whose busy care is bent
To follow that which flies before her face,
Not prizing her poor infant's discontent;
So runn'st thou after that which flies from thee,
10 Whilst I thy babe chase thee afar behind.
But if thou catch thy hope, turn back to me
And play the mother's part, kiss me, be kind;
    So will I pray that thou mayst have thy *Will,*
    If thou turn back and my loud crying still.

[135]

Whoever hath her wish, thou hast thy *Will*,
And *Will* to boot and *Will* in overplus;
More than enough am I that vex thee still,
To thy sweet will making addition thus.
5   Wilt thou whose will is large and spacious
Not once vouchsafe to hide my will in thine?
Shall will in others seem right gracious,
And in my will no fair acceptance shine?
The sea, all water, yet receives rain still,
10 And in abundance addeth to his store;
So thou being rich in *Will*, add to thy *Will*
One will of mine, to make thy large *Will* more.
    Let no unkind, no fair beseechers kill;
    Think all but one, and me in that one *Will*.

[136]

If thy soul check thee that I come so near,
Swear to thy blind soul that I was thy *Will*,
And will, thy soul knows, is admitted there;
Thus far for love my love-suit, sweet, fulfil.
5   *Will* will fufil the treasure of thy love,
Ay fill it full with wills, and my will one.
In things of great receipt with ease we prove
Among a number one is reckoned none;
Then in the number let me pass untold,
10 Though in thy store's account I one must be;
For nothing hold me so it please thee hold
That nothing me a something, sweet, to thee.
    Make but my name thy love, and love that still,
    And then thou lov'st me, for my name is *Will*.

[131]

Thou art as tyrannous, so as thou art,
As those whose beauties proudly make them cruel;
For well thou know'st to my dear doting heart
Thou art the fairest and most precious jewel.
5 Yet in good faith some say that thee behold,
Thy face hath not the power to make love groan;
To say they err I dare not be so bold,
Although I swear it to myself alone.
And to be sure that is not false I swear,
10 A thousand groans, but thinking on thy face,
One on another's neck do witness bear
Thy black is fairest in my judgement's place.
    In nothing art thou black save in thy deeds,
    And thence this slander, as I think, proceeds.

[132]

Thine eyes I love, and they as pitying me,
Knowing thy heart torments me with disdain,
Have put on black and loving mourners be,
Looking with pretty ruth upon my pain.
5 And truly not the morning sun of heaven
Better becomes the grey cheeks of the east,
Nor that full star that ushers in the even
Doth half that glory to the sober west,
As those two mourning eyes become thy face.
10 O let it then as well beseem thy heart
To mourn for me, since mourning doth thee grace,
And suit thy pity like in every part.
    Then will I swear beauty herself is black,
    And all they foul that thy complexion lack.

[133]

Beshrew that heart that makes my heart to groan
For that deep wound it gives my friend and me.
Is 't not enough to torture me alone,
But slave to slavery my sweet'st friend must be?
5 Me from myself thy cruel eye hath taken,
And my next self thou harder hast engrossed:
Of him, myself, and thee I am forsaken,
A torment thrice threefold thus to be crossed.
Prison my heart in thy steel bosom's ward,
10 But then my friend's heart let my poor heart bail;
Whoe'er keeps me, let my heart be his guard;
Thou canst not then use rigor in my jail.
    And yet thou wilt, for I being pent in thee,
    Perforce am thine, and all that is in me.

[134]

So now I have confessed that he is thine
And I myself am mortgaged to thy will,
Myself I'll forfeit, so that other mine
Thou wilt restore to be my comfort still.
5 But thou wilt not nor he will not be free,
For thou art covetous and he is kind;
He learned but surety-like to write for me
Under that bond that him as fast doth bind.
The statute of thy beauty thou wilt take,
10 Thou usurer that put'st forth all to use,
And sue a friend came debtor for my sake;
So him I lose through my unkind abuse.
    Him have I lost, thou hast both him and me:
    He pays the whole, and yet am I not free.

V B
144 143 135–136 131–134

SONNET 143 is clearly related to the "Will" pair, 135–136, a
witty, bewildering tour de force that plays on the poet's first
name, the friend's first name (presumably), and "will" in its
Elizabethan sexual connotation. The opening line of 135–136,
"Whoever hath her wish, thou hast thy *Will*," amounts to an
immediate echo of 143.13, "So will I pray that thou mayst have
thy *Will*" (italics are in the 1609 text). Hence the three sonnets
are sometimes lumped together without concern for others. But
note that 143 and 144, its companion in Q, are closely related;
both sonnets depict a 'triangle' in which the speaker pursues the
pursuer of another. Q, however, seems to have reversed the order,
for 144 obviously introduces a situation—the triangle—and 143
proceeds from it. If we allow 144 to appear first, we have a
familiar device: an introductory sonnet followed by a long simile
that amplifies it. See, for example, Shakespeare's authentic pair,
117–118. Thus, previous evidence linking 143 with 135–136 is
matched by evidence linking 143 with 144. Fortunately, the two
pieces of evidence are consistent, one specifying that 143 precede
135–136, and the other specifying that 144 precede 143. The
reversed order, 144 143, makes the 143 135–136 sequence possible.

But we cannot stop with this recombination. Although 144
introduces the sequence 143 135–136, it has a special relation to
the paired sonnets 133–134 with *their* triangle of speaker, friend,
and mistress. Reference in 133.2 to "my friend and me" seems to
assume a relationship already introduced. If so, the reference must
be to 144, for 131–132, the sonnets preceding 133–134 in Q,
neither mention nor allude to the friend. Since the order previously formed has been 144, 143 135–136, the allusion in 133 to
144 calls for placement of 133–134 after 136. The tentative sequence becomes 144 143 135–136 133–134.

Again, internal evidence turns out to be consistent, for if sonnet 133 assumes previous exposition by 144, sonnet 134, its twin, assumes prior statement by 143 135–136, the restored "Will" triad. Without reference to these sonnets the second line of 134, "And I myself am mortgaged to thy will," cannot carry the "will" connotations. But with such reference the line is cogent. Thus additional data in the text bears out the location of 133–134 after 135–136 in the tentative sequence.

Now, after noting that independent bits of evidence support a restored series running 144 143 135–136 133–134, we find that further evidence enlarges it. The last two sonnets, 133–134, cannot be separated from 131–132, for the heart beshrewed for deeply wounding in 133.1–2 is the heart just called upon to show pity in 132.10–14. And the speaker's groaning heart of 133.1 echoes his "groans" introduced in 131. So the full restored series will have to be 144 143 135–136 131–132 133–134—four interlocking pairs. Yet, as before, the varied internal evidence remains consistent, for 144 now becomes an antecedent of 131–132, our final addition to the series. The "worser spirit a woman colored ill" (144.3–4), anticipates the "tyrannous" dark woman of 131–132, whose "black is fairest in my judgement's place." This off-hand reference in 131.12–14 to "black" as a blemish misjudged as beauty (compare lines 5 ff.), a blemish of "deeds" as well as countenance, is the kind of reference effective only if the subject has been introduced before. In Q's sonnet order the malignancy of "black" suddenly appearing in 131 is not prepared for by 130. In the restored series it is nicely prepared for in 144 by the "female evil" colored "ill."

I have promised to give warning when a restored sequence breaks a plausible link in the Q order. Here, a joining of the "Will" sonnets, 143 135–136, breaks a seeming run-on in Q from 134.13–14 through 135.1–2. I justify this on several grounds. First, the three "Will" sonnets are intensively related not only in manner but tone, a relationship lacking between 133–134 and 135–136. Second, when the "Will" sonnets are linked, a remarkable end-couplet–first-line run-on carries from 143 into 135, and it is based on "Will," the intricate, dominant connective (see above). Finally, although I separate 133–134 and 135–136, they remain as elements of a single poem.

At the same time, if a reader wants to retain Q's linkage at 134–135, he may do so by casting V B as 144 143 131–136 in place of the sequence as I restore it. Either order at least remedies the fragmentation in Q by bringing together sonnets of a distinctive series. I believe, of course, that multiple evidence favors the restored order.

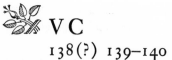 V C

138(?)   139–140

[138]

    When my love swears that she is made of truth,
    I do believe her though I know she lies,
    That she might think me some untutored youth,
    Unlearnèd in the world's false subtleties.
5   Thus vainly thinking that she thinks me young,
    Although she knows my days are past the best,
    Simply I credit her false-speaking tongue:
    On both sides thus is simple truth suppressed.
    But wherefore says she not she is unjust?
10   And wherefore say not I that I am old?
    O love's best habit is in seeming trust,
    And age in love loves not to have years told.
       Therefore I lie with her and she with me,
       And in our faults by lies we flattered be.

[139]

    O call not me to justify the wrong
    That thy unkindness lays upon my heart;
    Wound me not with thine eye but with thy tongue;
    Use power with power, and slay me not by art.
5   Tell me thou lov'st elsewhere, but in my sight,
    Dear heart, forbear to glance thine eye aside;
    What need'st thou wound with cunning, when thy might
    Is more than my o'erpressed defence can bide?
    Let me excuse thee: ah, my love well knows
10   Her pretty looks have been mine enemies,
    And therefore from my face she turns my foes,
    That they elsewhere might dart their injuries.
       Yet do not so; but since I am near slain,
       Kill me outright with looks, and rid my pain.

[140]

Be wise as thou art cruel; do not press
My tongue-tied patience with too much disdain,
Lest sorrow lend me words and words express
The manner of my pity-wanting pain.
5 If I might teach thee wit, better it were
Though not to love, yet, love, to tell me so:
As testy sick men when their deaths be near
No news but health from their physicians know;
For if I should despair I should grow mad,
10 And in my madness might speak ill of thee.
Now this ill-wresting world is grown so bad,
Mad sland'rers by mad ears believèd be;
    That I may not be so, nor thou belied,
    Bear thine eyes straight though thy proud heart go wide.

VC
138(?) 139–140

IF these three sonnets are taken in their Q order, we find the speaker in 138 justifying "my love's" false oath of "truth"—"though I know she lies"—on the ground that "seeming trust," tact, is better, after all, than the unpleasantness of plain speech. In the opening lines of 139 he then rejects this expedient by preferring the hurt of plain speaking to that inflicted by wandering eyes. Then, at 139.9, "Let me excuse thee . . . ," he doubles back to a justification of "my love's" tactful disloyalty much like the one he contrived in 138. In turn, he impulsively rejects this notion at 139.13–14. Finally, in 140, he overrules the appeal to blunt honesty found in 139, and returns despairingly to the idea of tactful falsehood justified in 138.

In paraphrase, the three sonnets thus work together on a coherent theme 'dramatically' rendered as the speaker changes and rechanges his mind. But this interesting structure becomes doubtful when paraphrase yields to direct reading. When 139 calls for an honest tongue, it does retract a statement made in 138. Yet the full retraction is "Wound me not with thine eye but with thy tongue" (139.3)—and although "not with thine eye" seems to have direct reference to a previous statement (as though to modify it), it relates to no statement made in 138. More, the speaker's rejection of plain speaking in 140 is hard to read as reversing his sentiments in 139 and returning to his prescription in 138. In 140.5 ff. ("If I might teach thee wit . . ."), he seems to be recommending pragmatic falsehood as though he had not mentioned it before and feels that it needs full introduction and explanation. Yet the two previous sonnets have almost exhausted the subject.

Besides, if the warning against "too much disdain" in 140.1–2 is a warning against disdain from wandering eyes (as it seems to be from its relation to 139.5–14), it then turns out, at 140.5–8, to be a warning against the disdain of plain speaking (unless "tell me so" at 140.6 means 'tell me so with your eyes'—which strains the text).

I suspect, without much conviction, that the Q sequence 139–140 has reversed the proper order. If we start this pair with 140 we have the case made for tactful falsehood. Such falsehood prescribed for the woman's tongue (lines 5–8) is then prescribed for her eyes (lines 13–14). Then, if 139 follows 140, the speaker will deny his previous justification offered in 140.5 ff. of a lying tongue, but still must ask (139.5 ff.) for untruthful eyes, eyes that do not stray even though the woman's tongue admits her falsity. And in the end he will ask to be killed outright by that straight gaze. This, although heavily precious, is at least climactic. But again I fear that paraphrase is more coherent than the text. One gives up; the two sonnets are scarcely worth the strain.

Still there is no doubt that 139 and 140 are paired, no matter in what order they are meant to be read. There is enough confusion in the Q order to suggest a transposed reading, but since there are difficulties in either order, naturally it is best to let Q stand.

The problem of 138 is similar. Although, with Pooler, I am not convinced that this sonnet links cogently with 139–140, I can find no evidence of other linkage and for want of a better order must accept Q here also.

VD

137   141–142   147–152

[137]

Thou blind fool Love, what dost thou to mine eyes
That they behold and see not what they see?
They know what beauty is, see where it lies,
Yet what the best is take the worst to be.
5   If eyes, corrupt by over-partial looks,
Be anchored in the bay where all men ride,
Why of eyes' falsehood hast thou forgèd hooks,
Whereto the judgment of my heart is tied?
Why should my heart think that a several plot
10   Which my heart knows the wide world's common place?
Or mine eyes seeing this, say this is not,
To put fair truth upon so foul a face?
　　In things right true my heart and eyes have erred,
　　And to this false plague are they now transferred.

[141]

In faith I do not love thee with mine eyes,
For they in thee a thousand errors note;
But 'tis my heart that loves what they despise,
Who in despite of view is pleased to dote.
5   Nor are mine ears with thy tongue's tune delighted,
Nor tender feeling to base touches prone,
Nor taste nor smell desire to be invited
To any sensual feast with thee alone;
But my five wits nor my five senses can
10   Dissuade one foolish heart from serving thee,
Who leaves unswayed the likeness of a man,
Thy proud heart's slave and vassal wretch to be.
　　Only my plague thus far I count my gain,
　　That she that makes me sin awards me pain.

[142]

    Love is my sin, and thy dear virtue hate,
    Hate of my sin grounded on sinful loving.
    O but with mine compare thou thine own state,
    And thou shalt find it merits not reproving;
5   Or if it do, not from those lips of thine
    That have profaned their scarlet ornaments
    And sealed false bonds of love as oft as mine,
    Robbed others' beds' revénues of their rents.
    Be it lawful I love thee as thou lov'st those
10 Whom thine eyes woo as mine impórtune thee.
    Root pity in thy heart, that when it grows,
    Thy pity may deserve to pitied be.
      If thou dost seek to have what thou dost hide,
      By self-example mayst thou be denied.

[147]

    My love is as a fever, longing still
    For that which longer nurseth the disease,
    Feeding on that which doth preserve the ill,
    Th' uncertain sickly appetite to please.
5   My reason, the physician to my love,
    Angry that his prescriptions are not kept,
    Hath left me, and I desperate now approve
    Desire is death, which physic did except.
    Past cure I am, now reason is past care,
10 And frantic-mad with evermore unrest;
    My thoughts and my discourse as madmen's are,
    At random from the truth vainly expressed;
      For I have sworn thee fair and thought thee bright,
      Who art as black as hell, as dark as night.

[148]

O me, what eyes hath Love put in my head,
Which have no correspondence with true sight;
Or if they have, where is my judgment fled,
That censures falsely what they see aright?
5   If that be fair whereon my false eyes dote,
What means the world to say it is not so?
If it be not, then love doth well denote
Love's eye is not so true as all men's no.
How can it? O how can Love's eye be true,
10   That is so vexed with watching and with tears?
No marvel then though I mistake my view;
The sun itself sees not till heaven clears.
    O cunning Love, with tears thou keep'st me blind,
    Lest eyes well-seeing thy foul faults should find.

[149]

Canst thou, O cruel, say I love thee not
When I against myself with thee partake?
Do I not think on thee when I forgot
Am of myself, all tyrant for thy sake?
5   Who hateth thee that I do call my friend?
On whom frown'st thou that I do fawn upon?
Nay, if thou lour'st on me do I not spend
Revenge upon myself with present moan?
What merit do I in myself respect
10   That is so proud thy service to despise,
When all my best doth worship thy defect,
Commanded by the motion of thine eyes?
    But, love, hate on, for now I know thy mind;
    Those that can see thou lov'st, and I am blind.

[150]

    O from what power hast thou this powerful might
    With insufficiency my heart to sway,
    To make me give the lie to my true sight,
    And swear that brightness doth not grace the day?
5 Whence hast thou this becoming of things ill,
    That in the very refuse of thy deeds
    There is such strength and warrantise of skill
    That in my mind thy worst all best exceeds?
    Who taught thee how to make me love thee more,
10 The more I hear and see just cause of hate?
    O though I love what others do abhor,
    With others thou shouldst not abhor my state.
      If thy unworthiness raised love in me,
      More worthy I to be beloved of thee.

[151]

    Love is too young to know what conscience is,
    Yet who knows not conscience is born of love?
    Then, gentle cheater, urge not my amiss,
    Lest guilty of my faults thy sweet self prove;
5 For thou betraying me, I do betray
    My nobler part to my gross body's treason.
    My soul doth tell my body that he may
    Triumph in love; flesh stays no farther reason,
    But rising at thy name doth point out thee
10 As his triumphant prize. Proud of this pride,
    He is contented thy poor drudge to be,
    To stand in thy affairs, fall by thy side.
      No want of conscience hold it that I call
      Her 'love' for whose dear love I rise and fall.

[152]

   In loving thee thou know'st I am forsworn,
   But thou art twice forsworn, to me love swearing;
   In act thy bed vow broke, and new faith torn
   In vowing new hate after new love bearing.
5 But why of two oaths' breach do I accuse thee
   When I break twenty? I am perjured most,
   For all my vows are oaths but to misuse thee,
   And all my honest faith in thee is lost;
   For I have sworn deep oaths of thy deep kindness,
10 Oaths of thy love, thy truth, thy constancy,
   And to enlighten thee gave eyes to blindness,
   Or made them swear against the thing they see.
     For I have sworn thee fair; more perjured eye,
     To swear against the truth so foul a lie.

VD

137 141–142 147–152

SONNETS 138–140 appear to be a discrete series of three without tangible attachment to 137 or 141. Sonnets 143–144 have been recombined with others addressed distinctively to the poet-woman-friend triangle. The most casual reading of 145 separates it from either 144 or 146. And however close the relation between 146 and 147, the 1609 order of the two sonnets is wholly questionable, for 146 resolves, transcends, the crisis described in 147; Q's placement of the resolving sonnet before the one it seems to resolve offers nothing but confusion. In short, the internal evidence suggests that 138–140 and 145 are discrete, separable, and that 143–144 and 146 are out of place.

What happens when we simply remove these sonnets from their places in the Q order? Left standing in uninterrupted se-

quence are 137, 141–142, 147–152—nine sonnets so clearly and
variously linked that a purposeful series must be assumed. One is
not always sure of the right order, but little doubt remains that
the sonnets once formed a coherent poem.

Removal of 138–140 from the Q series brings together 137 and
141. Sonnet 137 introduces the poem's theme in two opening lines
followed by an arraignment of the eyes and then of the heart.
The first four lines of 141 echo the beginning of 137 ("mine
eyes") and directly qualify the joint indictment of heart and eyes
found in 137 by clearing the eyes of guilt and placing blame on
the heart alone. Finally, the echo of couplets ("plague") in the
two sonnets is unmistakable. Sonnets 137 and 141 show the close,
multiple linkage typical of Shakespearian pairs like 57–58.

The two opening lines of 142 follow directly from the couplet
of 141: they amplify the cryptic statement, "she that makes me
sin awards me pain" (141.14), by pointing to love as the speaker's
sin and to ill-becoming hatred of his sin as the pain or penance
inflicted on him by his seductive accomplice. Sonnet 142 ends
with a plea for her pity, a more appropriate feeling for her fellow
sinner.

If, as previously suggested, 143–146 are misplaced in Q, the
series left after their removal resumes with 147, a sonnet continuing the theme of compulsive sensuality on a note of "fever,"
"disease," "ill," and "sickly appetite"—rounded out with "reason"
as an angry "physician" whose "prescriptions are not kept." With
Q's intervening miscellany removed, this elaborate statement expands the already repeated "plague" metaphor found in the couplets of 137 and 141. Plague is the sickness of sin and at the same
time a punishment for sin. Sonnet 147 also caps the first 'half' of
the poem with a striking couplet on the speaker's judgment of
hell's blackness as "fair," a couplet echoing 137.11–12—the beginning sonnet—and, as we shall see, anticipating the couplet of
152—the end sonnet.

Any suspicion that the ties between 137, 141, and 147 are
accidental disappears with a reading of 148, a sonnet so clearly

parallel to 137 that demonstration would be pointless. What needs to be said, perhaps, is that the two parallel sonnets have parallel functions in introducing respective halves or divisions of the poem, and that the two divisions, like their introductory sonnets, are parallel in structure as well as subject matter. Sonnet 148 resumes with the question posed originally by 137: what has Love done to blind the eyes, to demoralize the "judgment"? (compare the heart-judgment equation in 137.8). But while doubling back to the opening question asked in 137, sonnet 148 moves forward to an answer: Love has blinded the eyes with tears. Sonnet 149 now resumes the note of perversity in terms identical with those of 137: worship of ugliness ("defect"), confusion of "best" and "worst" (compare 149.9–11 and 137.3–4, 11–12). The couplet of 149 recalls, moreover, the opening lines of 142: "But, love, hate on," the summation of 149, harks back to the "hate" rendered vividly by 142.1–2 as "thy dear virtue" ("dear" means 'most characteristic,' 'intrinsic,' and—with a likely overtone—'costly').

Now comes 150 directly recalling 149 with "insufficiency" (compare "defect," 149.11), and echoing 148 with "true sight" (see 148.2). Yet with this immediate reference there is also reference back to 137 and 141–142. The 'best-worst' note, recurring at 150.8 and immediately recalling 149.11, points again to 137.4. And 150 serves in the second half of the series just as 141 does in the first half; it is the point where equivocal distribution of blame stops and the miserable lover lays his delusion to his heart which gives the lie to his true-seeing eyes.

After thus recalling 141, sonnet 150 (lines 11–14) resumes the note of mutual guilt—the injustice of one sinner judging another—which revives the theme of 142 in the first part of the series. Here, note two passages: "shouldst not abhor my state" (150.12) and "with mine compare thou thine own state" (142.3)—the same phrasing, in the same basic context (the right to judge), in the same special context ("love" not just opposed to "hate" but linked with it), and with the same rhymes ("hate"—"state"). This theme of 150 is then expanded by 151–152. In the last half of 151 a grimly comic equation of "flesh"

with phallus restates the main theme of the series, sensual enslave-
ment, which 152 concludes in the now familiar context of willful
blindness and mutual perjury, the latter note strongly reminiscent
again of 142 in its context of love-hate and shared guilt. See also
"bed vow" (152.3) and "beds' revénues" (142.8). Significantly,
the couplet of 152, ending the second half of the series, echoes the
couplet of 147, ending the first half: both couplets begin, "For I
have sworn thee fair . . ." In 152.13 I retain the Q reading
"perjured eye" in place of the usual emendation "perjured I" (the
emenders apparently ignore lines 11–12). Q's phrase is plainly apt
after the continuous heightening of perjury as a sworn denial of
what the eyes clearly see, or should see.

In a sense, reinstatement of this series is a by-product of the
disposition of 138–140, 143–144, 145, and 146, and is thus a further
instance of one body of evidence confirming another. For comparison, note II B, E, and G: strong internal evidence linking
46–47 with 24; 48 with 75, 56, 52; and 49 with 87–90 leads to the
relocation of 46–49, which leaves a residual series 43–45 50–51,
which in turn is supported by equally strong, and independent,
internal evidence.

I have left poem D in the Q order remaining after intrusive
sonnets are removed, a procedure that at least brings a fragmented
sequence together. For immediate interconnection the optimum
order might be 137, 148, 141–142, 149–152, 147.[6] But the un-
touched Q order scarcely lacks pointed development with its two
halves introduced respectively by parallel sonnets, 137 and 148,
and concluded respectively by sonnets having parallel couplets,
147 and 152. The parallel halves recall, moreover, a structural
division found elsewhere in Q: note the relationship between 76
78–80 and 82–86 (pages 138–142).

As noted before, my editorial commitment is to leave un-
touched any cogent relationship in the Q sonnet order, and to
allow noncogent but plausible Q relationships to stand, except at
points where evidence quite outweighs authority of the 1609 text.
In these exceptions, very few in number, I undertake to give
warning that a plausible link in Q has been broken.

The only link so broken in restoring poem D is the possible one between 142 and 143. One might read 143 as a long simile expanding lines 9–10 of 142—". . . I love thee as thou lov'st those Whom thine eyes woo as mine importune thee"—and as calling again for the pity asked for at 142.11–12.

I reject Q's possible link for several reasons. (1) If the delightful 143 is not out of tune with 142 standing alone, it clashes with poem D as a whole—and 142 clearly belongs with poem D (see again its echo of 141.13–14, and its anticipation of 150 and 152). To include 143 with the sonnets of D, addressed as they are to nausea at the blindness and perjury of loving what the speaker "abhors"—to 'illustrate' these sonnets with 143's winsome simile of a crying child pursuing its mother who pursues an errant fowl, one of her "feathered creatures"—would accept the kind of fatuity Q ascribes to Shakespeare in its sequence 128, 129, 130 (see the discussion of poem A, above). (2) Besides, 143 (its couplet leading into 135.1–2) obviously belongs with the "Will" sonnets (poem B); so if 143 goes into poem D, the "Will" sonnets go with it, and that would be the end of poem D, and likewise of the "Will" sequence. (3) Sonnet 143 is a perfect expansion by simile of 144. The parallel of situation is wholly apposite, the tone unerring (see poem B).

V E
129 146

[129]

    Th' expense of spirit in a waste of shame
    Is lust in action; and till action lust
    Is perjured, murd'rous, bloody, full of blame,
    Savage, extreme, rude, cruel, not to trust;
5 Enjoyed no sooner but despisèd straight,
    Past reason hunted, and no sooner had,
    Past reason hated, as a swallowed bait
    On purpose laid to make the taker mad:
    Mad in pursuit and in possession so;
10 Had, having, and in quest to have, extreme;
    A bliss in proof, and proved, a very woe;
    Before, a joy proposed; behind, a dream.
      All this the world well knows, yet none knows well
      To shun the heaven that leads men to this hell.

[146]

    Poor soul, the center of my sinful earth,
    . . . . these rebel powers that thee array,
    Why dost thou pine within and suffer dearth,
    Painting thy outward walls so costly gay?
5 Why so large cost, having so short a lease,
    Dost thou upon thy fading mansion spend?
    Shall worms, inheritors of this excess,
    Eat up thy charge? Is this thy body's end?
    Then, soul, live thou upon thy servant's loss,
10 And let that pine to aggravate thy store;
    Buy terms divine in selling hours of dross;
    Within be fed, without be rich no more.
      So shalt thou feed on Death that feeds on men,
      And Death once dead, there's no more dying then.

V E
1 29 146

PLACEMENT in Q of these two sonnets is more than suspect. For the bitter 129, the dainty, affected air of 128 and 130 furnishes a context at once distressing and absurd. Sonnet 146 is related to 147–152 but, as noted before, the Q order 146–147 cannot be right. And Q's joining of 145 with 146 yields patent nonsense.

The relation between 129 and the nine sonnets of poem D involves more than general theme. In 129, as in poem D, lust is obsessive in its mad progress from craving to revulsion. But in both contexts lust has another, an unusual attribute; in 129.3 it is "perjured," and perjury also distinguishes sexual obsession in sonnets 142, 147 (see the couplet), 150, and 152.

Sonnet 146 also links with sonnets of poem D. In 151.5–10 the speaker's "nobler part," his "soul," is betrayed to his "gross body's *treason*," while in 146 his "Poor soul" is treasonably beset by "*rebel* powers" representing his body—see line 8. (This much of the meaning is certain, in spite of Q's corrupt line 2.) Further, in 147, note the association in continued metaphor of "feeding" (line 3), "desire," and "death"; then, in 146, note the prescribed victory over desire and death in terms of feeding—this time a feeding not of the body but the soul. "Within be fed. . . . So shalt thou feed on Death that feeds on men, And Death once dead, there's no more dying then." Apt backward reference to 147 is hard to deny.

Sonnets 129 and 146 thus link pointedly with 137 141–142 147–152; and neither fits cogently elsewhere. As I have placed them, the two sonnets appropriately follow poem D as a summation, but no one can be sure that they originally functioned together in exactly that way. Plainly, 146 is a 'resolving' sonnet and thus should come at the end of a poem or series, but 129 could have begun the series as a statement of theme, or it could have appeared at some intermediate position. For what it is worth, however, note that 128 and 145 may be related (see poem G). If 128 and 145 were once together, their attachment in Q respectively to 129 and 146 can imply that 129 and 146 were also once joined, that they intruded between 128 and 145, and that the resulting miscellany of four separated, on further dispersal, into two fragments which became Q 128–129 and 145–146.

The blank space in line 2 of 146 represents deletion of Q's "My sinful earth," a repetition of the last three words of line 1. In Q, line 2 lacks coherence and takes on two extra syllables. Mistranscription or misprinting is more than likely, but none of the dozen or more emendations is better than a guess.

V F

153–154

[153]

Cupid laid by his brand and fell asleep:
A maid of Dian's this advantage found,
And his love-kindling fire did quickly steep
In a cold valley-fountain of that ground;
5   Which borrowed from this holy fire of Love
A dateless lively heat, still to endure,
And grew a seething bath which yet men prove
Against strange maladies a sovereign cure.
But at my mistress' eye Love's brand new-fired,
10   The boy for trial needs would touch my breast;
I, sick withal, the help of bath desired,
And thither hied, a sad distempered guest,
    But found no cure: the bath for my help lies
    Where Cupid got new fire, my mistress' eyes.

[154]

The little Love-god lying once asleep
Laid by his side his heart-inflaming brand,
Whilst many nymphs that vowed chaste life to keep
Came tripping by; but in her maiden hand
5   The fairest votary took up that fire
Which many legions of true hearts had warmed;
And so the general of hot desire
Was sleeping by a virgin hand disarmed.
This brand she quenchèd in a cool well by,
10   Which from Love's fire took heat perpetual,
Growing a bath and healthful remedy
For men diseased; but I, my mistress' thrall,
    Came there for cure, and this by that I prove:
    Love's fire heats water, water cools not love.

V F
153–154

THESE two sonnets, obviously paired, are apart from the poem ending at 152 and show no close connection with other sonnets of Q's final series beginning with 127. But there is no reason for doubting their rightful place in Group V; the motif, "my mistress' eyes" (153.9, 14) associates them with others of the series, especially 127 and 130.

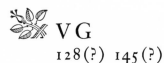 V G
128 (?) 145 (?)

[128]

How oft when thou, my music, music play'st
Upon that blessèd wood whose motion sounds
With thy sweet fingers, when thou gently sway'st
The wiry concord that mine ear confounds,
5   Do I envy those jacks that nimble leap
To kiss the tender inward of thy hand,
Whilst my poor lips, which should that harvest reap,
At the wood's boldness by thee blushing stand.
To be so tickled they would change their state
10   And situation with those dancing chips
O'er whom thy fingers walk with gentle gait,
Making dead wood more blest than living lips.
        Since saucy jacks so happy are in this,
        Give them thy fingers, me thy lips to kiss.

[145]

Those lips that Love's own hand did make
Breathed forth the sound that said 'I hate'
To me that languished for her sake;
But when she saw my woeful state,
5   Straight in her heart did mercy come,
Chiding that tongue that ever sweet
Was used in giving gentle doom;
And taught it thus anew to greet:
'I hate' she altered with an end
10   That followed it as gentle day
Doth follow night, who like a fiend
From heaven to hell is flown away;
        'I hate' from hate away she threw,
        And saved my life, saying 'not you.'

V G
128(?) 145(?)

IT is interesting that, when reordered, all sonnets of the Q series 127–154 fit into closely unified poems, save 128, 145, and perhaps 138. Still, 128 and 145 are not alien to the group, since each is addressed to a woman. Just possibly, as a residue after disposition of the other sonnets, the two form a pair. The mannered content and tone are similar, and in the order of printing here the "lips" motif of 128 (lines 7, 12, and 14) continues, approximating a characteristic run-on, with the opening line of 145. As they appear in this edition, 128 and 145 can be read either as a possible pair or as two miscellaneous singles; persuasive signs of linkage are lacking. Shakespeare's authorship, in fact, has been questioned, but that matter is also conjecture.

❧ III. ❧ VERIFICATION

UNLESS someone discovers a reliable manuscript, verification of a restored sonnet order will never be objective in a literal sense. Yet this does not mean that 'subjective' evidence leading to an amended order must stand unconfirmed by other factors. Internal evidence for such a restored text is, on the whole, circumstantial evidence, which responds to well-understood tests. Are the elements composing it actually various, that is, do they differ in kind; are they independent, nonredundant? Do they agree in what they imply? Good circumstantial evidence can be so many-sided and yet so consistent that the chance of error, fundamental error at least, steadily lessens. In some cases the result may approach certainty; in others it will scarcely be so impressive. But the principle behind verification will remain the same: a consistency of all details in pointing to a single conclusion will be the essential matter.

Verification, in a quite usual sense of the word, has actually been with us from the start. The last part of Chapter I defines a standard of evidence and invites readers to sample it in the restoring of Group III and several poems from groups II and IV. From these illustrations it appears that one finding can corroborate another, that a given fragment, for example, may link independently with two others already adjacent in Q. Or its relocation may have double results: a new coherence not only in the Q series to which we assign it but also in the one from which we remove it. Hence the appearance, at this stage, of a chapter called 'Verification' may seem to begin an old story. But although parts of it will be familiar, the story is not complete. Certain details need to be transferred from isolation into full context, and some larger matters, so far only suggested, need full explanation. This final chapter deals with three aspects of verification: first, the full extent to which Q 'automatically' yields one restoration as the simple consequence of another ('interacting restoration'); next the disarrangement of restored groups in Q by parcels or segments implying a once-intact sonnet order; and last, the consistency of manuscript forms implied by Q's fragmentation of the restored poems.

ONE RESTORATION AS CONSEQUENCE OF ANOTHER

Unless hopelessly fragmented, a disarranged sequence—a new pack of cards cut several times, a newspaper column in Linotype accidentally disturbed—often 'restores itself.' Reordering the garbled news column, whether it concerns market quotations or civil insurrection, gives pleasure because when we move a set of lines to a position that allows it to make sense, our judgment is confirmed by other lines restored to sense as they come together. Our discernment in making the first move is borne out by a windfall that supplies the second. And more than two reciprocal moves may be involved.

Forgive a reminder that the disordered news column could never respond so neatly to adjustment in the absence of an original line order corresponding to the restored one. The suggested analogy is only figurative, however, for sonnets in sequence and consecutive lines of type are hardly alike when it comes to deciding whether they read coherently or whether they do not. But if discrimination is used in reordering sonnets—if, for example, we limit new connection to 'intensive,' highly specific linkage—the analogy begins to have point. As one such restoration continues to yield another simply as 'by-product,' it should become more and more likely that Q *is* the disarrangement of an original sonnet order, a disarrangement that responds 'logically' when restoration happens to be on the right track. We have met this response before in isolated cases; now we can view all examples together.

Since one class of examples extends widely through Q, a listing is in order. When sonnets in the left-hand column of the following table are relocated as shown there (or set off as independent poems—another form of relocation), the sonnets immediately

Sonnets Relocated	Closely Related Sonnets Thus 'Brought Together' (left in Q order without intervening sonnets)
20 (set off as Poem 1) [a]	19 21 (a key element of IV C)
36–39 (II I, linked with 96 and others of II H)	33–35 40–42 (II J)
46–47 (linked with 24, forming II B) 48 (linked with 75 56 52, forming II E) 49 (linked with 87–90, forming II G)	44–45 50–51 (II D)
53–55 (placed as IV D)	52, 56 (adjacent sonnets of II E, but in reversed order, 56 52)
77 (set off as Poem 4) 81 (linked with 32, forming III B)	76 78–80 82–86 (III C D)
113–114 (II A, linked with II B) 115–116 (linked with 107–108 and others of IV F)	109–112 117–121 (Poem 5)
128 (set off as independent, or linked with 145, forming V G) · 129 (linked with 146, forming V E)	127 130 (V A)
138–140 (set off as V C) 144 143 (linked with 135–136 131–134, forming V B) 145 (set off as independent, or linked with 128, forming V G) 146 (see 129, above)	137 141–142 147–152 (V D)

[a] In addition, Poem 2 (25–26) and Poem 3 (29–31) may be related (page 63). If so, they come together in proper order with the relocation of 27–28 as an element of II C (61 27–28 43).

opposite in the right-hand column 'come together' by virtue of their Q order. They are left without formerly intervening sonnets, those relocated in the first column.

Evidence independent of that linking sonnets in the first column then shows affinity between those coming together in the second column. One restored sequence verifies another. Nat-

urally, such verification depends on good primary evidence justifying each of the sequences; one may test this in any instance by
reference to the "Text and Commentary."

Thus in the first example shown in the table, sonnet 20 is the
intervening element between 19 and 21. Its relocation (as an
independent poem) brings 19 together with 21, and the unit so
formed turns out to be one of the key links in restored poem
IV C.

All elements in the table are disarranged fragments of the
restored sonnet order as it is shown on pages 40–41. That is—
whether the element is a single isolated sonnet (20 or 48), an
intact series representing a whole poem (36–39), or an intact
series representing part of a poem (46–47 or 33–35)—it is separated in Q's sonnet order, presumably a disarrangement, from
other elements that accompany it in the restored sonnet order.
Thus poem V D in the second column of the table appears in Q as
three fragments: a single sonnet, a pair, and a run of six.

The number of 'relocated' fragments in the table (first column)
comes to sixteen; the number of fragments 'brought together'
(second column) comes to eighteen. If 27–28 and Poems 2 and 3
are included, as suggested, the two totals become seventeen and
twenty, a combined total of thirty-seven fragments involved in a
process of 'mutual' or reciprocal verification.

The examples above (a first class or category of verification)
involve two elements or fragments in Q that become adjacent,
and closely related, when a third fragment, relocated, is removed
from its place between them. An opposite but analogous kind of
verification (a second class) occurs when the third element, instead of being removed, is inserted between two fragments already adjacent in Q. It then is found related not just to one of
them but independently to both. Thus, in the formation of II H,
the fragment 69–70 is placed after 91–93, forming a close relationship; the inserted fragment then also ties in closely and
independently with two succeeding ones: 95–96 and 94. In forming Group III, when the restored pair 32 81 (two fragments) is

placed before 76 78–80 82–86, the resulting close relationship is matched by an independent relationship of 32 81 extending 'back' to 71–74 (75 is relocated in II E). In the restoration of IV F, sonnet 59 (of the fragment 59–60) links with 106, forming a clear pair (106, 59); 60 is then found to anticipate 107–108, and the whole series becomes interrelated. And in forming IV C, when the fragments 63–68, 19, and 21 are relocated in close relationship after 100–101, they are also found closely related to 105, which sums up the entire series. (On the removal of 102–104, see the third class of verification, below.) Good evidence supports the initial 'move' in each of these cases, and in each the independent additional links 'automatically' set up are also strong and multiple.

Several fragments involved in this second class of verification also appear in the first (that is in the table, page 233). Not counting these (19, 21, 81, 76, 78–80, 82–86), the number of fragments involved in the second class comes to twelve. When they are added to the thirty-seven of the first class, the total is forty-nine.

In verifications of the second class elements already adjacent in Q show independent ties with an element inserted between them. Now we come to a third class. Here, none of the elements involved are adjacent in Q, but one of them (we may call it Y) links independently and closely with each of the others (X and Z). And the sonnets of Y—consecutive in the 1609 text, although they apparently lack close affinity—happen to continue X and introduce Z. This relationship suggests, tentatively, a restored sequence in the order X, Y, Z. When the tentative sequence is assembled, additional, independent signs of linkage show it to be unified throughout.

There are two clear-cut examples of this. In Q we find 22 and 23 consecutive but seemingly unrelated; 22 links closely with 62, plainly in the order 62, 22; and 23 links independently with 102–104, plainly in the order 23, 102–104. Put together tentatively with 22–23 as a connective, the series provides a third set of links that unifies it as poem A of Group IV: 62 22–23 102–104.

Relation between the consecutive 43 and 44–45 is loose. But 43 links intensively, clearly as the end sonnet, with 61 27–28. And 44–45 links intensively, clearly as two beginning sonnets, with 50–51. The result, based on additional evidence, is a pair of closely related poems with 43–44 as the 'bridge'—surviving in Q—between them: 61 27–28 43(II C) and 44–45 50–51 (II D). And again, each stage of restoration is based on independent evidence.

Not counting fragments involved here but already counted in one of the first two classes (27–28, 44–45, 50–51), we find four additional fragments in this last class. Thus, the number involved in all three classes of verification becomes fifty-three.

Although many relationships listed here receive isolated comment in other places, they have been brought together in the last few pages to show a full range of verification available from the 1609 text. With some added explanation the result can speak for itself. Each of the three classes of verification just considered involves a set relation of some kind in the Q sonnet order, an objective fact independent of wish or bias. In every instance, internal evidence leads to one restored sequence; then the Q order, simply by being what it is, points to another—either a separate sequence or a marked extension of the first. Then further internal evidence, independent of that used at the outset, confirms the overall result, the 'accidental' bonus. This is just what ought to happen when we undertake to repair an actual disarrangement representing an original, once intact sonnet order. It is just what should not occur consistently if we try to repair the imaginary disarrangement of an imaginary original sequence.

In the disarrangement of a genuine sequence, pieces or fragments will show frequently the logic of relationship appearing in our three classes of verification. And here we have found, in Q, that fifty-three fragments of the restored order are directly involved in at least one of the three classes. Since the restored order is represented in Q by sixty-two discrete pieces or units (single sonnets or intact sequences),[1] it would seem then that nine of its fragments are unaccounted for. But the number is deceptive: two of the nine (1–17 and 122–126) represent Group I and Poem 6. These two units need no verification since they appear in the restored order exactly as they appear in Q—intact, and at the beginning and end of the major series (1–126). They are not, in fact, fragments.

Two more of the nine residual units are intact poems preserved by Q substantially in their contexts: as an intact pair, 57–58 (II F) follows 56 and 52 (concluding sonnets of II E); and 153–154 (V F) remains as a unique pair directly following 147–152 which end V D.

Since each of the four units just listed remains intact in Q, and since each appears there either exactly or substantially in its presumed original context, it is hardly surprising that none plays a significant part in disarrangement patterns of the kind we have found. Units of a text undergoing little or no disarrangement are unlikely to appear in a verification scheme based on the logic of disarrangement. And the same can be said of certain intact fragments belonging to disrupted poems. Two (131–134 and 135–136) representing the bulk of V B remain substantially in position, and intact save for Q's transposition of their order.

Thus, of the nine units apparently 'left over' after verification, only three, sonnets 18, 24, and 75, remain. The placement of 18 in Group IV, of 24 in II B, and of 75 in II E can rest on internal evidence and other kinds of verification to follow.

VERIFICATION OF GROUPS: DISARRANGEMENT
   BY 'SEGMENTS'

Notwithstanding differences, all forms of verification are tests of the same negative possibility—that a poem or series of poems one thinks he has restored never existed, that he has been fooled by accidental affinities of the kind thought to abound in the Sonnets. In testing this possibility, an editor must assume Q as the disarrangement of his original sonnet order, and if that order never existed he finds himself consulting Q for signs of a disarrangement that never took place. In such a case it is unlikely, so long as he plays the game by rules, that he will find in Q a sequence of fragments having ultimate order in its apparent confusion. But if he has been lucky, if he has restored a series somewhat as Shakespeare wrote it, he may expect to find Q reflecting its original make-up in a rational although perhaps singular manner.

Having put the revised sonnet order to one such test, we may now put restored groups II, III, and IV to another, with Group IV as paradigm. Since this test, like the previous one, must check the results of primary, or 'qualitative' evidence against other evidence, it presupposes a fairly close reading of Group IV and the commentary (pages 143 ff.). Consulting the poems themselves and attending strictly to their internal signs of coherence, we find the usual links, various and pointed, that combine to support the revised order. Whether or not these are convincing will naturally be a matter of opinion.

So here, as in the first part of this chapter, we move to objective matters—not to objective 'proof' but to indications of probability drawn entirely from the physical arrangement of the 1609 edition. As restored, Group IV, with its constituent poems, is made up of sonnets numbered thus in Q:

Poem A	62	
	22–23	
	102–104	
Poem B	97–99	
Poem C	100–101	
	63–68	
	19	
	21	
	105	
Poem D	53–55	
Poem E	18	
Poem F	106	
	59–60	
	107–108	
	115–116	

Viewed in one way, this group of poems has been dispersed through Q over nearly the maximum range possible within the first 126 sonnets. Yet in spite of the scattering there are signs of order. With its organization obliterated and with its three longer poems unrecognizable, Group IV still has identity. Except for the last two sonnets, all of its elements are found in three compact segments of Q: 18–23, 53–68, and 97–108. Here I define a segment as a concentration, a clustering in Q of sonnets—often in disarranged order—from a single restored group. A segment is not necessarily an unbroken sequence of elements from a given group, but within any segment these elements will appear consistently except for very minor interruptions. Thus, in the first segment only 20, an independent poem, interrupts a continuous run of fragments from Group IV; in the second segment only 56–58 and 61, both from Group II, break the sequence of Group IV fragments; and in the third segment no break occurs. I exclude 115–116 from the third segment because the interruption between 108 and 115 is extensive in proportion to the segment's length.

Such a relation between restored Group IV and Q is provocative. But it is not simple or neat, a fact best illustrated by describing two hypothetical cases from which it differs. Suppose that instead of supporting Group IV as it appears above, the evidence had indicated an original group of three related poems running (19 18 21–23) (59–60 53–55 62–68) and 99 97–98 100–108). Here the three poems would appear in Q with internal disarrangement only, plus the intrusion of 20, 56–58, and 61 (presumably from other restored units), and each poem would appear in a single Q segment. This one-to-one correspondence of poems and segments might be impressive at first glance, but the pattern by itself would not point to the three poems as linked with one another, as elements of an original group. Qualitative, or primary evidence might establish such a group relationship, but it would lack any verification from the Q arrangement.

Now suppose as a second possibility that the primary evidence had led to a restored group of three poems in the sonnet order just assumed, but with the first poem ending with 59 and the second with 99, thus: (19 18 21–23 59) (60 53–55 62–68 99) (97–98 100–108). Here the group's disarrangement pattern in Q would offer much better confirmation of the primary or qualitative evidence, for we should have the group split into three segments of Q with each of its first two poems ending in a sonnet (59, 99) that introduces a new segment. This 'overlapping' would imply that the three segments were once joined, that if the poems are authentic, so is the group.

But the evidence behind Group IV supports nothing packaged so neatly or conveniently (I remember once wishing that it did). Far from being a series that appears almost in order when three concentrations of Q are brought together, Group IV (again, see page 238) is represented in the 1609 edition as follows: the first Q segment (18–23) contains fragments representing poems A, C, and E; the second (53–68), fragments representing A, C, D, and F; the third (97–108), fragments representing A, B, C, and F. Poems A and C are scattered among all three Q segments; only the shorter poems are confined to single segments. The last two sonnets of F are outside the three-segment scheme. Three of the poems thus lose identity in Q and, needless to say, in Q's arrangement the group as a whole has apparently disintegrated. Under the circumstances, does the qualitative or 'subjective' case for Group IV's original existence lack support from the objective data, from Q's distribution of the fragments? Or, more pointedly, does Group IV's fragmentation and *random* distribution among three Q segments make it less probable as an authentic series than either of the neatly distributed hypothetical groups we have considered?

If we allow for a leafed manuscript permitting internal disarrangement, the presence of random fragments instead of largely intact poems in the segments of Group IV actually points to its authenticity. What we have here should be clearly understood. In a state of disorder, but nevertheless compacted into three well-defined 'runs' of Q, are twenty-nine sonnets having such affinity for one another that we can recombine them into a highly unified group of poems. And to a surprising degree the potential connection between one fragment and another— between, for example, 62 and 22 or 100–101 and 63–68—is not loose but intensive. So we recombine the scattered fragments into a tentatively restored series. But although the series has a cogent unity, it could be fortuitous; perhaps it never had actual identity. So we may call it 'ostensible.' Now, if unlike restored Group IV, an ostensible sonnet series should appear almost consecutive in Q save for a split into three segments, its authenticity might be hard to estimate. I suppose no one would question authenticity of the individual segments, but if we join them in a series, what verification would the Q arrangement supply? Possibly not much more than showing that an ostensible group can divide into three parts, a revelation not very helpful in distinguishing a fortuitous series from a genuine one. Any direct affinity between the end fragment of one segment and the beginning fragment of another (overlapping) would strengthen the case for verification, but the primary evidence behind Group IV's sonnet order leads to no relationship of this kind.

Yet what the evidence actually prescribes is quite remarkable: a restored series whose presumed disarrangement in Q is extreme, but whose fragments, still compacted, occupy three distinct segments. Thus, if we assume that Group IV and its poems are based on persuasive but nevertheless spurious affinities, we assume that an extensive miscellany of actually unrelated fragments—the smallest a single sonnet and the largest a sequence of six—could appear in three distinct parcels from which, wholly by chance, an intensively unified series can be derived. We assume, moreover, that in this random assemblage only three extrinsic elements (20, 56–58, and 61) entered the combination.

There is a temptation to speak of random pottery fragments, seemingly disparate bits found in the same vicinity but in three separate concentrations, that just happen to combine into a well-wrought urn that probably, we are told, never existed. But analogies almost always beg the question, so I prefer to let Group

IV justify itself. The accompanying diagram shows the close affinity between elements of the ostensible group and, at the same time, their random separation as they divide among the Q segments.

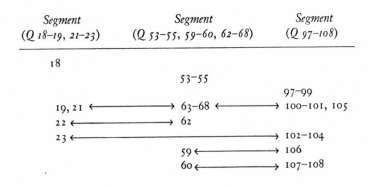

Segment (Q *18–19, 21–23*)	Segment (Q *53–55, 59–60, 62–68*)	Segment (Q *97–108*)
18		
	53–55	
		97–99
19, 21 ⟵⟶	63–68 ⟵⟶	100–101, 105
22 ⟵	⟶ 62	
23 ⟵		⟶ 102–104
	59 ⟵	⟶ 106
	60 ⟵	⟶ 107–108

Sonnets are arranged here according to segments in Q (vertical groupings) and according to cogent relationships (horizontal groupings). Thus, if a reader wishes to check the internal evidence (pages 160 ff.), he will find that 19, 21 of the first segment, 63–68 of the second segment, and 100–101, 105 of the third segment are all intensively linked and interrelated as elements of poem C. The diagram points only to intensive connection between elements in different segments (see the arrows); it takes no account of simple cognate ties (these pervade the group), or even of close ties between elements in the same segment (such as the one between 97–99 and 102–104). Nor does the diagram actually reveal some extraordinary links that materialize when one fragment of Q is placed between two other fragments: when, for example, 22 and 23, seemingly unrelated to one another, are placed between 62 and 102–104, also seemingly unrelated, thus forming A, a poem with fragments from all three segments. And naturally there is no suggestion in the diagram of a pervasive unity, a quality sensed on reading the group as a unit. But the diagram points extensively, if crudely (again, see the arrows), to a close affinity between widely dispersed elements, to a random distribution of these elements among segments (which in Q conceals most of the affinity), and to a concentration of all but one element (115–116) in three clusters of the 1609 text.

So we are ready again for the question. If restored Group IV is fortuitous, if its scattered elements only seem to be connected, what strange accident brought a collection of random fragments into three concentrations that, between them, can supply the varied materials of an intensively unified series? What accident allowed but three extraneous fragments to enter the concentrations? If Group IV as restored is merely imaginary there is no accounting for the accident; one can say only that it was strange.

The alternative is to infer that elements of Group IV were once together in a coherent series; that the series underwent extensive internal disarrangement, a shuffling of manuscript leaves, but held together as a group; and that it later divided into three parts to appear finally, as Q prints it, in three internally disordered clusters. This, I think, was the accident and, if so, there was nothing strange about it. Random dispersal of fragments among the three segments of Group IV points to its continued identity (authenticity), for the longer a series undergoing purely internal disarrangement remains otherwise intact (not dispersed), the more internally disarranged its fragments will be. But although in random order, they will still be packed together in clusters (segments) after the group splits three ways.

Now we have a further question. As previously noted, we must assume internal disarrangement of Group IV to account for its sonnet order prior to a three-way partition, and—consequently—for the sonnet content of the three segments after partition occurs. Will the nature of this disarrangement turn out to be simple, plausible, or must we explain it gratuitously with a statement that almost anything can happen to a sonnet sequence?

In order to divide into its three segments, Group IV must become virtually unrecognizable. But extensive disorder is not necessarily implausible; it may defy any rational explanation or it may be understood in quite simple terms. If the explanation we need here is to be simple it must start with Group IV's restored (original) sonnet order and produce Q's disorder—the random division of Group IV fragments among three segments—by a few key 'moves.' If this can be done, our hypothesis is still in good condition; if it cannot be done, the hypothesis could raise a problem as serious as the one it appears to solve.

The table on the following page shows restored Group IV with its sonnet order intact (see 'Elements Left Intact . . .'), except for the four displacements (first column) required to bring all fragments of each Q segment together, as, for example, 19, 21, 18, 22–23 of segment one (in the first and second columns). Each sonnet in the table appears both in terms of its Q number and its position in the restored group; thus sonnets 59–60 (in Q) are also designated sonnets 2–3 of poem F (first column). The four key displacements, shown at the left, produce a group disarrangement in which all sonnets of each segment are brought together, although not always in their final Q order. Hence we have a series that can divide into three parts, each containing the sonnets of one Q segment. Further minimal disarrangement (third column), required in but two cases, puts all sonnets exactly in their Q order within the segments.

In this tabular arrangement three factors stand out. First, in terms of Q numbers (the ultimate, objective disarrangement), an intact block of eight sonnets from restored poem C (63–68, 19, 21) fits (numerically) between the opening sonnet of A (62) and A's next two sonnets (22–23). For this, see the first two columns. Second, the collection of fourteen sonnets involved in the 'key displacements' (first column) is no random gathering; instead it contains elements from four consecutive poems of the restored group: C 3–10, D intact, E intact, and F 2–3. Third, displacement of these virtually adjacent elements assumes no displacement of remaining elements ('Elements Left Intact'), all of which remain in their presumed original order.

Hence, despite Group IV's scattered condition in Q, its presumed disarrangement becomes strangely rational, simple. To account for it 'mechanically,' simply assume, as shown in the table,

DISARRANGEMENT OF GROUP IV REQUIRED
FOR SEGMENT FORMATION

Group IV with Minimum Disarrangement Required for Segment Formation			Group IV as Finally Disarranged in Segments	
Key Displacements Required for Segment Formation	Elements Left Intact and in Group Order			

(D intact)	53–55→		Forms	53–55	Segment
(F 2–3) [a]	59–60→	(A 1) [a]		59–60	in Q
	62			62–68	Order
(C 3–10) {	63–68→				
	19→		After movement of 18, will form	18	
	21→			19	Segment
(E intact)	18→			21	in Q
	22–23	(A 2–3)		22–23	Order
	102–104	(A 4–6)	After movement of 102–104, will form..	97–99	
	97–99	(B intact)		100–101	Segment
	100–101	(C 1–2)		102–104	in Q
	105	(C 11)		105	Order
	106	(F 1)		106	
	107–108	(F 4–5)		107–108	
	115–116	(F 6–7)		115–116	'Anomaly' [b]

[a] Relates the fragment to the restored poem originally containing it. 'F 2–3' indicates that 59–60 comprise the second and third sonnets of poem F. 'A 1' indicates that 62 is the first sonnet of poem A.

[b] That is, included in no segment.

that C 3–10 and E (first column) intruded between A 1 and A 2–3 (second column), and that D intact, with F 2–3 (first column) lodged at the top of a loose-leaf manuscript—a common form of disarrangement. With these simple displacements the entire group is ready for a three way split into its Q segments. And to account for Q's ultimate order of sonnets within the three segments (third column), but two further dislocations are required: those of 18 and 102–104. These two minimal displacements, not necessary to account for segment content at the time of partition, could have occurred either before or after the split into segments.

Naturally, disarrangement of Group IV could have been more devious, with the same result, but my point is that it need not have been; that, in fact, apparent disarrangement confined to a 'block'—involving C 3–10 and adjacent elements D, E, and F 2–3—favors an assumption of simplicity. Simple, plausible dislocation provides the segmentation of Group IV, and the only remaining problem concerns dispersal in Q of the segments themselves. We shall consider that later.

For tactical reasons I should like to summarize in terms addressed to skeptics—not those of a dogmatic cast but actual doubters willing to experiment with Thorpe's 1609 text and yet wholly aware of the difficulties in it. We are told that if we range through the Sonnets we can find so many recombinations that they lose meaning. If this refers to sequences with 'intensive' linkage, I think we have been misinformed, but suppose we take the statement at face value. Suppose that 'ranging through the Sonnets' we can find affinities impressive enough to 'justify' poems and groups that never existed. Even if this were true, it would scarcely meet the issue as restored Group IV now frames it. For if the skeptic wishes to discredit such a group, he must believe not merely that we can perform at random almost any tour de force of so-called restoration, but that we can perform it and at the same time fulfill a strict condition: that we can produce cogent sequences like Group IV at will, and then expect to find that Q presents them—as it does Group IV—normally and plausibly disarranged, and confined in the text to three concentrations. This is an unlikely prospect unless the 'control' just described is falsely set up, a possibility we need to consider.

With such a control or limitation, the chance of delusion lessens substantially unless, of course, one unconsciously 'plans' his restored series so that its elements fit into segments of the Q sonnet order. Unless Q is an actual disarrangement of the restored order, this kind of planning would be difficult without recourse to loose or spurious linkage, but since even a charitable reader will suspect that I have produced such a tautology, and since an awareness of the fallacy is no sure means of avoiding it, I shall describe the manner in which Group IV was intuited, formed, reformed, and perhaps verified. An autobiographical account of the process has the advantage of directness and, unlike an idealized account, will show some possibly false moves that need watching. But it should not be understood as an attempt to set forth good motives. I offer it, in fact, so that motives may be examined critically as possible hidden factors in the logic.

For ready reference, here again is Group IV in tabular outline:

Poem A 62
        22–23
        102–104
Poem B 97–99
Poem C 100–101
        63–68
        19
        21
        105
Poem D 53–55
Poem E 18
Poem F 106
        59–60
        107–108
        115–116

And the 'three Q segments' containing all but the last two sonnets of Group IV are: (18–19, [20], 21–23) (53–55, [56–58], 59–60, [61], 62–68) (97–108). The bracketed sonnets are extraneous to the group.

I first became involved with poem C, which by coincidence is one of the two Group IV poems with fragments in all three segments. Perhaps this ought to have suggested a disarrangement pattern, but it did not. In any event, the initial or trial basis for poem C was the fact that its eleven sonnets are unique, the only ones in the entire cycle to combine third-person address with the epithet, "my love." This basis of trial selection, which remains as primary evidence for the restored poem, excludes any chance of C being formed with a numbers game in mind, with an eye out for clusters in Q, such as 18–23. Sonnets with a specific, a unique mode of address are found only where they happen to be. And much of the further internal evidence for this poem (pages 162 ff.) is likewise independent of a bias in favor of Q number patterns.

My next concern was with poem F. The key to this restored poem was, and is, a singular unity of theme, detail, and continuing statement found in a pairing of 106 and 59 (pages 176–178). Such an intensive relation between two sonnets has nothing to do with the lucky position of either in Q's numerical order and must control any decision to pair them.

After combining 106 and 59 I turned to 60. Its relationship with 59 is far from cogent, but there is enough connection to warn against a separation. Hence in the pairing of 106 and 59 I tentatively carried 60 into the revised order. So placed after 106 59, sonnet 60 revealed its capacity to introduce 107–108 in combination with 115–116. Thus poem F emerged, and from the internal evidence it appeared to be a natural. Now, at this point and with poem C freshly in mind, no one could fail to note that sonnets from two Q segments, roughly 59–68 and 100–108, seemed to be combining.

Thus from here on a motive may have affected my judgment; so the question now is whether internal evidence for poems other than C and F is strong enough to join them in Group IV no matter what the motive for inclusion may be. Clearly, 62 and 102–104 (of A) must remain in their Q contexts. Although 62 is separable from 63–65, a thematic link between these sonnets (page 147) requires at least the retention of a proximity that Q provides. And 103 of the unified series 102–104 has a connection with

100–101 much like 62's with 63–65. So again, if this thematic connection is apparent, a proximity or group relationship that Q presents must be retained. But what of 22–23, the transitional fragment joining 62 with 102–104 to form poem A? Without these two sonnets, the segment 18–23 would be minimal; but they cannot be linked with Group IV on slight grounds just to favor the segmentation hypothesis. Fortunately, the grounds are far from slight (pages 147 ff.), and virtually demand linkage whether a segment results or not. The case for linking 22 with 62 and 23 with 102–104 is quite similar to that for placing 59–60 between 106 and 107–108 (pages 176 ff.).

The inclusion of poem B (97–99) in Group IV is based on its ties with 102–104 (page 153) and the fact that Q presents the two sequences in proximity. If the sonnets of B and 102–104 of A were not proximate in Q, the affinity between them, though tangible, would not justify bringing them together. The same can be said of the proximate elements, 53–55 (poem D) and 63–68 (of C), and, additionally, of 18 (E) and 19 (of C). But in each instance the two factors, affinity and proximity in Q, are present; and one of the rules of this edition is that no relationship involving both factors may be disturbed in its essentials. So I have had no choice in the matter; poems B, D, and E must be included in Group IV whether or not they reinforce the segmentation pattern. In fact, none of them turns out to be 'advantageous' to the scheme, for the segment pattern would actually be more clear-cut without D and would be perfectly viable without B and E. The longer poems—A, C, and F—sustain the scheme of distribution by segments.

Finally, I must add that in forming Group IV the use of primary evidence has been consistent. Such evidence calls for including 115–116 in poem F, and the fragment is included, perhaps to cast doubt on the whole matter. It is seven sonnets removed from 108 and thus outside the three-segment distribution of Group IV fragments in Q. With 20, 56–58, and 61, which appear within the segments but cannot belong to the group, 115–116 will have to be 'explained.'

What can be said, then, for Group IV as an authentic series? Multiple links, all of them described in the "Text and Commentary," bring sonnets together into 'poems' and relate the poems to one another in a basic sequence. When tested for hidden assumptions, this recombination seems essentially free from any tendency, conscious or unconscious, to link sonnets from predetermined clusters, or segments, in the 1609 edition. Thus when the group is formed, any interesting relation its sonnet order may have to the 1609 sonnet order is not a result of circular inference. When we find that all but two of the sonnets brought together to form Group IV come from three distinct segments of Q, the discovery is not negligible in verifying previous estimates of linkage. For accident scarcely explains how fragments so lacking in order and yet so closely related could appear in three such concentrations. The only 'rational' explanation seems to be that the fragments were once together in an intact manuscript which, after serious internal disarrangement, divided into three parts. And although serious, the internal disarrangement assumed in this explanation is itself rational: far from being complex, it turns out to be minimal and normal.

Separate a deck of cards into four packets, each containing all the cards of one suit arranged in proper order; shuffle each packet separately; then merge the packets into a full deck. Finally, cut the deck several times, not by halves but by smaller fractions culled at random and reassembled at random. The result will be clusters of the same suit, a 'segment' of spades, for example, followed by one of diamonds, followed perhaps by another of spades, and so on. Some of the clusters will be extensive; others will be limited. A single diamond may occasionally interrupt a spade sequence. None of the segments, or 'flushes,' may be in 'straight' order throughout, but there will be short runs of the straight-flush pattern. Allowing for obvious differences between playing cards and loose-leaf manuscripts having, say, two sonnets to a leaf, the process just described may represent what happened to the manuscripts behind Q. Although the analogy is only illustrative, it has point, of course, to the extent that originally intact suits of cards are something like originally unified sonnet groups in a loose-leaf manuscript; individual shuffling of the intact suits is something like internal disarrangement of a group manuscript; and cutting of the reassembled deck is something like a mingling of one intact but disarranged manuscript with another. Our relation to the Sonnets may be like our relation to the shuffled and cut deck of cards should we encounter it with no knowledge of its history. We should know only that it shows a pattern of segments each containing cards substantially of the same suit and often in proper order. But chances are good that from the pattern we may infer that spades or hearts were once together in proper sequence, and that a process of shuffling and cutting occurred.

Having considered Group IV as a paradigm, we can appraise Group II much more readily. In terms of Q numbers this restored series runs:

Poem A 113–114
Poem B 24
46–47
Poem C 61
27–28
43
Poem D 44–45
50–51
Poem E 48
75
56
52
Poem F 57–58
Poem G 49
87–90
Poem H 91–93
69–70
95–96
94
Poem I 36–39
Poem J 33–35
40–42

In disarrangement, fragments of Group II also appear in distinct segments of the 1609 sonnet order. Adapting the analysis of Group IV, the following diagram shows the distribution of Group II fragments according to segments found in Q (vertical arrangement), and a close affinity of the fragments separated by the segmentation (horizontal arrangement with arrows). Distribution according to restored poems is also represented (by capital letters), and all anomalies (fragments outside the segment pattern) are listed. Thus the last arrowed lines in the diagram indicate that sonnets 33–42 (in the first Q segment), 91–96 (in the second segment), and 69–70 (an anomaly, in neither segment) are all intensively linked and, further, that they are from poems H, I, and J. As in the similar diagram for group IV, the affinity indicated here is primarily between fragments found in different Q segments; some extremely close ties within the same segment, such as those between poems C, D, and E, are not represented.

Segment	*Segment*	*Anomalies (in no*
(*Q 24, 27–28, 33–52, 56–58, 61*)	(*Q 87–96*)	*segment*)
24 46–47 (B) ⟵⟶		113–114 (A) ᵃ
61 27–28 43 (C)		
44–45 50–51 (D)		
48 56 52 (E) ⟵⟶		75 (E)
57–58 (F) }⟵⟶	87–90 (G)	
49 (G)		
36–39 (I) }⟵⟶	91–93 95–96 94 (H) ⟷	69–70 (H)
33–35 40–42 (J)		

ᵃ Sonnets 109–112 117–121 may be the terminal poem (K) of this group (pages 191 ff.), instead of an independent poem. If so, the diagram should represent a third segment (109–114, 117–121) formed by conjunction in Q of the terminal poem K and poem A (113–114). In that case, the close linkage (arrowed line) between 24 46–47 and 113–114 would extend between segment 1 and segment 3, instead of between segment 1 and the anomaly column as above. And the anomaly column would contain only 69–70 and 75.

After considering Group IV at length, any reader will be aware of the case for authenticity based on its distribution by segments in the 1609 edition. Hence, for an extension of the principle to Group II no more than a brief statement will be needed. As the diagram shows, Group II appears in two segments (or three, if 'poem K' is added). And there is intensive linkage (the arrows) between a variety of elements found in separate segments. For the nature of this linkage, see the Group II text and commentary. Such various and independent connection between fragments in diverse segments is substantially like that of Group IV. Although Group II is limited to two segments, the distribution between them of all save three of its twenty-two fragments supplies verification at key points of the restored order.

Group III remains. In terms of Q sonnet numbers, it is restored in this order:

> Poem A 71–74
> Poem B 32
> 81
> Poem C 76
> 78–80
> Poem D 82–86

Group III is unlike II and IV. Except for 32 of poem B, all of its elements appear in a single segment of Q: 71–74, 76–86. Although 77 is surely out of place between 76 and 78, it may have accompanied the group (page 119); hence only 75 (from II E) clearly intrudes. And within the one segment of III, there is minimal disarrangement: aside from the doubtful 77, only 81, which pairs with 32, is out of place. Thus it may appear that Group III is substantially intact as Q prints it, and that no question of verification need be raised. Why not forget about 32 and accept the 1609 publisher's implied word for the rest? But without 32, sonnet 81 has no relevance to the group; in fact, its presence in the 'rival poet' series has been questioned repeatedly. And without poem B (32 81), no bridge exists between poem A

(71–74) and poems C, D. With B restored, however, the entire series comes together with precision (page 131). Sonnet 32 is the linchpin of Group III; yet it appears as the single anomaly, the one sonnet Q fails to place in a concentrated series with the rest.

Q's placement of 32 is one of five lapses from the otherwise orderly scheme of groups disarranged by segments. And to sustain verification we must consider all such anomalies, for if any restored group is questionable, or partly so, they ought to show it. If they cannot be brought into the segment design, and readily, doubtless something is wrong.

The single anomaly of Group III is 32, just discussed; that of Group IV is 115–116 (page 239). Group II, on the other hand shows three anomalies: 69–70, 75, and 113–114 (page 252). An anomaly as defined here is a fragment seriously isolated from any segment of its group.

Sonnets 69–70, a fragment of II H, and 75, a fragment of II E, are respectively eight and twelve sonnets removed from the nearest Q segment representing their group. Sonnet 32, a fragment of III B, is thirty-nine sonnets removed from the single gathering in Q of its group. It happens that just as 32 becomes the pivotal sonnet of Group III, so 75 becomes the center of poem E in Group II (pages 87 ff.). And the fragment 69–70 is essential to II H. Sonnets 113–114 (II A) and 115–116 (a fragment of IV F) are not so critical, but they lay strong claims to their positions in the restored order and must be accounted for in Q's presumed disarrangement. If dislocation of these five fragments cannot be explained as 'rational' displacement strictly in terms of the disarrangement hypothesis, then the 1609 text will fail to support the restored text in places where support is much needed.

What we need now is a collective representation of restored Groups II, III, and IV just as Q appears to have disarranged them—a representation showing where their segments appear in relation to one another and where the five anomalies, elements resisting the segment pattern, happen to fall. Table A, on the following page, gives this information. This table makes it clear that segments of the three groups alternate in the Q sonnet order,

TABLE A: GROUPS II, III, AND IV AS FOUND IN Q

Longer uninterrupted sequences are shown by vertical lines. Concentrations, or segments, are designated.

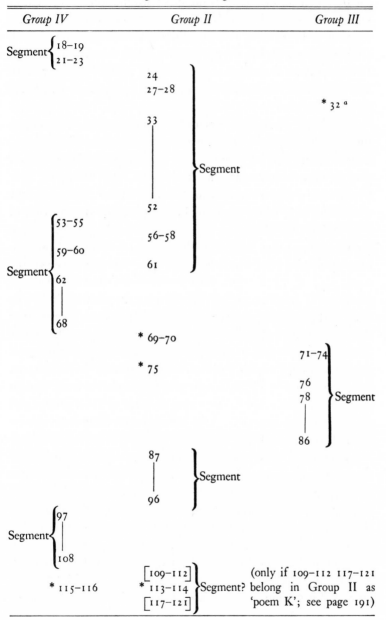

Group IV	Group II	Group III
Segment { 18–19, 21–23		
	24, 27–28	* 32 ᵃ
	33	
	} Segment	
	52	
Segment { 53–55, 59–60, 62 ... 68	56–58, 61	
	* 69–70	
	* 75	71–74, 76, 78 ... 86 } Segment
	87 ... 96 } Segment	
Segment { 97 ... 108		
* 115–116	[109–112], * 113–114, [117–121] } Segment?	(only if 109–112 117–121 belong in Group II as 'poem K'; see page 191)

ᵃ Anomalies, elements falling outside segments, are indicated by asterisks.

and that segments are distinct save for some overlapping where the first segment of Group II mingles with the second segment of Group IV. Beginning with sonnet 18, the Q order presents a segment of IV (18–19, 21–23) followed by a long segment of II, after which—with the overlapping—appears another segment of IV. Then come the single segment of III, another segment of II, and another of IV. A final segment of II (with Poem 5 as II K) remains doubtful.

Now if the restored sonnet order happens to be authentic, or substantially so, the segment order of Table A can be ascribed only to a mingling of manuscripts—those representing the three groups—into a composite manuscript, the one behind Q. Our hypothesis of disarrangement must assume this to account for the alternation in Q of a portion of IV, a portion of II, a portion of IV, the bulk of III, and so on. And once made, the assumption should explain other matters. If the hypothesis is not to lapse into one explanation after another (a new one wherever needed), the combining of manuscripts must account not only for the segments in Q but for radical disarrangement whether inside or outside the segment pattern. The hypothesis must assume first that the groups originally were intact. It can then take minor disarrangement (within confined sequences) for granted at any stage, but it must explain major dislocation of two kinds: first, the wide separation in Q of closely related fragments even though they are found in regular segments of their restored group, and second, the appearance of any anomaly, any fragment clearly isolated from segments of its group.

For example, much of the sonnet order within segments of Group II can be explained by minor, internal disarrangement. And a glance at Table A shows, roughly, how Group II was split into two segments by a mingling of its elements with elements of III and IV. All this, the hypothesis can explain, but how will it explain the drastic separation in Q of 49 and 87–90 (components of II G) or the radical parting of 33–42 (components of II I and J) from 91–96 (components of II H, closely linked with I and J)? How will it explain the complete isolation of 32 from the rest of

Group III, or of 69–70, 75, and 113–114 from the segments of Group II?

Here we come to a test; and the hypothesis continues to work consistently, for all of these serious dislocations, save that of 113–114, can be traced to a single 'event,' the mingling of a slightly disarranged Group II with a slightly disarranged Group III.

This event is, of course, an inference; but Q's sonnet order, a given, objective order no one can change, requires the inference once we assume—in order to test for consequences—that restored groups II and III were once intact in manuscript. If they were, then Q not only prescribes their mingling but prescribes its highly specific results. And these results provide the test. Do they indicate a haphazard, 'irrational' mixture of elements from groups II and III? If so, any relation between the two restored groups and Q (their presumed disarrangement) is put in doubt. Or, do the results of mingling prescribed by Q indicate a simple, plausible coming together of groups II and III? If so, the objective relation between Q and the two restored groups may show a pattern hard to explain as accidental or fortuitous.

Here is the pattern shown. In the Q sonnet order, 71–74, the first poem of III, directly follows 69–70, a fragment of II H; and 82–86, the last poem of III, immediately precedes 87–96, elements of II G and H. Besides, 32 of III joins 33–42, elements of II I and J. Finally 75 of II E falls between 74 of III A and 76 of III C. Hence in Q there are four points of contact between the two groups, two of them involving the beginning and end sonnets of Group III, and all but one involving consecutive poems at the end of Group II: the terminal poems, G H I J, which become the apparent 'area of mingling.'

What does this mean? We can easily imagine Q showing no contact points at all between two restored groups (there are none between groups III and IV), or showing a disorderly dozen with no common factor such as a restricted area of mingling. Instead Q shows our two 'ostensible' groups II and III mingling with a simple consistency one would expect only from actual groups in actual manuscripts. Although this consistency is provocative enough in itself, we might explore it further with two questions. Will minimum disarrangement in groups II and III allow them to mingle at points of contact arbitrarily prescribed by Q? And when they join at these points, to what extent are radically or eccentrically dislocated fragments (those resisting the 'segment' pattern) brought into a scheme of orderly, rational disarrangement? Table B (pages 260–261) answers the questions.

First, the minimal disarrangement. The two groups must merge so as to bring 69–70 and 75 of II into close or actual contact with 71–74 76 of III, and to bring 32 of III into close or actual contact with 33–42 of II. Table B illustrates the simplest, most direct way of fulfilling these conditions with minimal prior disarrangement in II and III. As the table shows ('Intrusion of Group III,' left column), Group III has but one dislocation, a dropping of 32 to the bottom of the group manuscript, which thus remains intact although slightly disarranged. This enables III to combine with II at the Q points of contact, 70–71 and 32–33. And these two necessary points have been established not only with minimal disarrangement of III (just described) but with quite simple disarrangement of Group II. First assume Group II as intact. Then note the position of sonnets 87–96 near the bottom of the second column ('Group II . . . Before Intrusion of Group III'). To account for this displacement, assume that a sheaf of manuscript leaves containing II G and H, intact save for 49 of G and 69–70 of H, simply dropped down below 33–42, slightly disarranged elements of I and J. In short, the bulk of G H and the whole of I J are but transposed. This means, of course, that two fragments seriously displaced in Q, 49 (of G) and 69–70 (of H), simply remained in their original places—that the movement of other G H elements to a position below I J merely left them behind. Note their position in the column as fragments following 57–58—in the original order, F G H.

Aside from the simple dislocation of G H elements (87–96) and the slight disarrangement of I J (33–42), the only displacement in Group II as Table B shows it is that of 75, one of the anomalies. It drops down but five sonnets from its original location (between

48 and 56 of E) to a position between 49 and 69–70. Hence in later simple disarrangement (coming after the intrusion of III forms the new series: 75, 69–70, 71–74 ff.), it may drop down below 74.

Now, the second question—simple, rational disarrangement accounting for apparently irrational dislocation. Each of the radically separated elements, listed on pages 256–257 as unaccounted for by segment formation, is marked by an asterisk in the table. And the table, interestingly enough, brings all but one of them (II A, 113–114) into relationships that either explain or will explain their strange positions in the Q order. They have not been rigged into these relationships. They just assume them in a simple disarrangement and mingling of two restored groups under a strict condition Q demands: that the mingling produce definite points of contact. When we disarrange the restored groups to allow for contact at three of these points, we find the disarrangement minimal: confined in III to poem B, in II to consecutive poems G H I J, plus one fragment of E. And finally—as a windfall—when we reconstruct this minimal disarrangement and allow the two groups to combine at points of contact in Q, we find four puzzling fragments of the restored order now fitting into the hypothesis and well on their way to Q's disposition.

For with the mingling of groups II and III as shown in Table B, our hypothesis now explains how 49 could become so radically separated from 87–90, its companion sonnets of II G; how 69–70 of II H could be widely parted from 91–96 and attached to 71–74, an element of III; how 75 of II E could appear within Group III; how 32 of III B could merge with 33–42, elements of II I and J. Assume the minor disarrangement of II and III prior to Group III's intrusion; assume this intrusion between two contact points prescribed by Q (70–71, 32–33); then, later simple disarrangement confined to the resulting sequences (the 'simple internal disarrangement' shown by Table B, right-hand page) will explain some of the most difficult portions of the Q order. And except for prior displacement allowing Group III's intrusion to set up two ultimate Q sequences (69 ff. and 32–42), the simple disarrange-

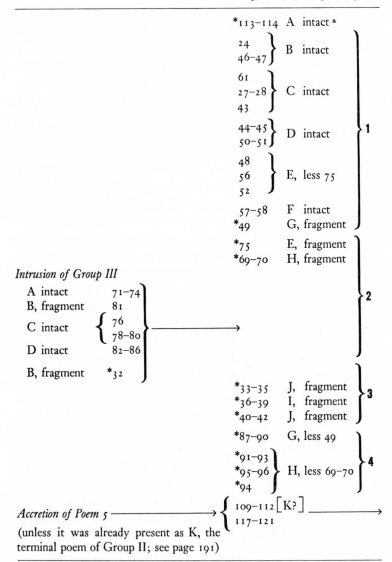

Group II and Poem 5 (II K?)
Before Intrusion of Group III

*113–114 A intact [a]

24
46–47 } B intact

61
27–28 } C intact
43

44–45
50–51 } D intact

48
56 } E, less 75
52

57–58 F intact
*49 G, fragment

} 1

*75 E, fragment
*69–70 H, fragment

Intrusion of Group III

A intact   71–74
B, fragment   81
C intact   { 76
              78–80
D intact   82–86

B, fragment   *32

} 2

*33–35 J, fragment
*36–39 I, fragment } 3
*40–42 J, fragment

*87–90 G, less 49

*91–93
*95–96 } H, less 69–70 } 4
*94

Accretion of Poem 5 ⟶ { 109–112 [K?] ⟶
                          117–121
(unless it was already present as K, the
terminal poem of Group II; see page 191)

---

[a] All elements radically dislocated in Q (see page 256) are indicated
by asterisks.

TABLE B: THE MINGLING OF GROUPS II AND III

Resulting Composite MS Except for Final Movement of 113–114 and 32–42

*113–114

	24	
	27–28	
With simple internal disarrangement, series 1 (at left) becomes............	} All sonnets in Q order
	43–52	
	56–58	
	61	

| With simple internal disarrangement, series 2 (at left) becomes............ | 69–76 } All sonnets in Q order |
| | 78–86 |

| Note accretion of 32 by series 3 (at left) which becomes............. | 32–42 | All sonnets in Q order |

| With simple internal disarrangement, series 4 (at left) becomes........... | 87–96 | All sonnets in Q order |

| | 109–112 } All sonnets in Q order |
| | 117–121 |

ment of groups II and III could have occurred at any time, whether before Group III's intrusion, after it, or—as is likely— partly before and partly after.[2]

The hypothesis seems to be doing well, but here we come to a decisive step. The resulting sonnet order at the right of Table B follows the ultimate order in Q with two exceptions, one the position of sonnets 113–114 and the other a separation of 78–86 and 87–96 by 32–42. Mingling of groups II and III explains the anomalous attachment of 32, an element of III, to 33–42, elements of II. Yet, to account for the final dislocation in Q of these now attached elements, that is, for the ultimate sonnet order, we must assume a block movement of 32–42 to a position before 43–52—plus the intrusion of Poem 3 (29–31) after 27–28. As a glance at Table B (last column) will show, this is necessary to account for unbroken sequences that became Q 27–52 and 78–96. But if this added assumption is gratuitous, if such a block move- ment of 32–42 has nothing to support it save a truism—that the restored sonnet order must finally become the Q order—then our hypothesis is in trouble. Thus far it has avoided such tautol- ogy—or so I hope.

In previous stages the hypothesis has shown cumulatively, a meaningful connection between the restored sonnet order— established on 'subjective' or qualitative grounds—and its pre- sumed disarrangement, the 1609 sonnet order—established, of course, objectively. A brief summary of steps in verification will show the nature of this connection. In verification, the restored order and Q reciprocate, that is, each responds significantly to any condition prescribed by the other, and the responses are progressive. First, qualitative evidence prescribes a unified group of poems. Q then responds by showing them badly fragmented but still rationally distributed, found in meaningful concen- trations, the segments. Yet a few group fragments—the anomalies—appear outside this pattern.

Now, when Q's sonnet order shows a disarranged group di- vided into segments, the restored sonnet order responds by ac- counting rationally for segment content: to form a sequence that can split into segments as Q actually splits it, no restored group needs more than simple, minimal disarrangement. But the objective Q order has prescribed more than just a segmentation of restored groups: it has implied segmentation by set means with set results. If the groups are presumed authentic, their alternating segments in Q must stem from a mingling of group manuscripts. This prescription is not disquieting until we note that Q's numerical order requires the mingling to produce set 'points of contact.' Fortunately, the restored sonnet order responds by showing—again—that very simple disarrangement in two mingling groups, II and III, will provide such contact points, that the points converge, in fact, within four consecutive poems at the end of Group II. And here the unexpected appears: this group mingling, not at places chosen for 'adjustment' but at Q's arbitrary points of contact, now will account simply for all but one of the radical displacements, the fragments unexplained by the normal segment pattern.

At the same time (to recall the difficulty) this result leaves sonnets bearing numbers 32–42 squarely between 69–86 and 87–96 (Table B, again). Obviously, Q now requires further disarrangement of this sequence by block movement. Will the alternating verification, just described, continue? Will independent evidence now support the required block movement of 32–42, or are we forced into tautology, into a lame statement that the sonnets Q ultimately numbered 32–42 'must' somehow have found their way to that position in Q's order?

To be effective, verification here ought to support not one but two conclusions, and—again—support them independently. First, it should provide signs that the block of sonnets, 32–42, actually was, at one stage of disarrangement, in the position shown by Table B—that it is not there as a result of manipulation in, of all things, an attempt at verification. Second, verification should give us independent signs that the block of sonnets moved later to its present position before 43–52—that it was not there from the beginning.

Support for the first conclusion, that 32–42 was once in the midst of 69–96, can be drawn from relations actually shown by Table B, but they need explaining. Recalling earlier examples of verification, examples of progressive, consistent interaction between the amended sonnet order and Q's order, we start here with two restored units: Group III entire and the last part of II—poems G, H, I, J. Both units are remarkable for internal coherence, but neither bears any clear relation to the other.

These two units are independently restored on multiple grounds, and the 1609 text then prescribes what one must assume as their disarrangement. Now, the question as before: does the 1609 text respond 'rationally?' It does; for although the two units as restored are unrelated, Q combines certain fragments from both in one disarranged sequence, and then in a second disarranged sequence, combines fragments missing in the first. In Q's sequence 69–96, appear 71–86 representing all of Group III but 32; also in the 69–96 sequence appear 69–70 of II H, 87–90 of II G, and 91–96, the rest of II H.

Hence Q's response to the restoration of III and II G H is that they mingled, came together, to form the disarranged but quite rational series 69–96. But in that case, what happened to II I J, linked originally with II G H, and to 32, the missing fragment of III? Q's answer here is completely consistent with the first answer: these additional elements of the two units were also involved in the mingling. In another, a far removed part of the 1609 text, we find—with nothing else—fragments of the two restored units missing in the 69–96 sequence: 32, the key sonnet of Group III, followed by 33–42, elements of II I J, the continuation of G H. So here again, and independently, Q implies the very accident it implied in 69–96, a mingling of the two restored elements in the course of their disarrangement.

Thus, after internal evidence restores III and II G H I J, the Q sonnet order responds with outright consistency of 'accidentals': the two restored units are unconnected, yet disarranged elements from both fill each of two widely separated runs of the 1609 text. Within these two runs every element of the two units is accounted for, save 49 of II G. (And on 49, see page 258.) This is a rational, consistent pattern, the kind one expects from authentic sequences undergoing disarrangement. Q's simple implication is that if fragments of the two disparate units consistently appear together, no matter where found, then the two units as a whole must at one time have come together. So we have good signs that our first conclusion is valid—that the sonnets now numbered 32–42 were at one stage of disarrangement in a mingled state with the sonnets now numbered 69–96. And such is their position in the last column of Table B.

But Q, objective in its demands, now requires our second conclusion: that 32–42 separated from the mingled sequence shown in Table B, and moved to its present position in the 1609 miscellany. Here, in the now familiar verification process, Q poses an ultimate condition for the restored order to meet. And if the restored order is to meet this condition without a begging of the question, it must do so with evidence separate from that establishing Group III and II G H I J, and also independent of earlier steps in their verification. Aside from our experience with favorable interaction between Q and the amended order, we have no reason to expect this support, but from the course verification has taken, its nature—should it appear—ought to be predictable. If 32–42 did move as a block of sonnets to its present location, there could be signs there of its intrusion. Clearly if 32 and 33–42 came together in a mingling of two groups (Table B), and, if later, they intruded (with 29–31, an independent poem) between 27–28 and 43 ff., then 27–28 and 43 ff.—unless they are also intrusions—must once have been joined in a closed series. Hence, if there are clear signs of that formerly closed series, and if they are independent of previous steps in verification, we are virtually in the clear; we reach the point in a puzzle where loose pieces begin falling into place.

Reference to the "Text and Commentary," pages 77–78, will show links between 27–28 (the middle sonnets of II C) and 43 (II C's end sonnet) not often equalled in a restored poem. The links extend, moreover, to a coherent relation between 27–28 43 of II C and 44–45, the first two sonnets of the next poem (II D). And the main condition is satisfied: evidence for these ties is separate from evidence used in prior steps verifying III and II G H I J. Apparently, sonnets 27–28 and 43 ff. were once together; thus they were parted by intruding sonnets, among which were 32–42, a sequence that began as 33–42 in a simple disarrangement of two adjacent Group II poems, became fully formed with the addition of 32 in a mingling of Group II with Group III (shown in Table B), and finally landed far from home.

A last check of Table B for remainders shows every radically displaced element of groups II and III accounted for in its Q order, save 113–114 (II A), a fragment dislocated even more severely than 32 of III B. Still, the position Q gives it is rational. Assume that either before or after the intrusion of Group III, as shown in Table B, it dropped from the top to the bottom of manuscript leaves containing Group II. This displacement, normal enough in disarranged manuscripts, gives the fragment a position after sonnets that became 91–96 (see their location in Table B), and so puts it well on its way to isolation in Q. Here, to anticipate a query, I must add that restoration has not placed the fragment 113–114 at the top of Group II so that it might show up at the bottom in a disarrangement typical of loose-leaf manuscripts. It belongs at the top. It has close affinity with II B (page 69), of which 24 is the opening sonnet; and 24 appears as the first, or 'top' sonnet in Q's presentation of Group II fragments, a presentation that retains, vestigially, much of the restored, or original order (pages 66, 69). Q thus gives objective support to the position of 113–114 in restored Group II, a position allowing it to approach its final isolation by simple top-to-bottom displacement.

In lodging at the end of the manuscript, 113–114 joins 109–112 117–121, sonnets either attached to Group II's manuscript by accretion of Poem 5, or already present in Group II as poem K which, if it belonged to Group II, must have been the terminal poem (see Table B and pages 190 ff.). This contact made, 113–114 can reach its ultimate position by simple disarrangement. Here again we have reciprocal verification. After the restored order puts 113–114 at the top of Group II's manuscript and Q drops it to the bottom, Q now requires that the fragment come between

109–112 and 117–121. The restored order verifies this—again on independent grounds—by clearly implying the intrusion. See pages 187 ff. for the multiple evidence that 109–112 and 117–121 (fragments of Poem 5) were once joined in a closed series. Hence the case here for intrusion, the last step in verification, is exactly parallel to the end process in accounting for Q's displacement of 32–42.

With this disposition of 113–114, following that of 29–31 and 32–42, the 'resulting composite manuscript' ending Table B has all of its disarranged elements in the 1609 order. It becomes a manuscript whose sonnets represent three blocks of the 1609 edition: (24, 27–52, 56–58, 61)—(69–76, 78–96)—(109–114, 117–121). To this extent, then, the restored sonnet order has disarranged itself by continually verifiable steps into the sequence found in Q. So far as Groups II and III are concerned, not only are the segments representing them in Q fully formed (as shown previously in Table A), but a mingling of the two groups in the manner prescribed by Q (Table B) explains the position of each radically dispersed element, including the anomalies—32, 69–70, 75, 113–114—which appear outside any regular segment.

Whether the disarrangement hypothesis will continue to serve well remains to be seen. We now have to assume a mingling of Group IV, in manuscript, with the composite manuscript containing elements of groups II and III. And the factors behind this step parallel those behind the mingling of II and III. First, the extensive case for restoration points to Group IV as an original unit. Q then corroborates this by showing Group IV badly disarranged, yet having a rational pattern of segments. In turn, the restored order explains this pattern by showing that Group IV in its presumed original state needs only simple disarrangement to produce a sonnet order divisible into the segments (page 245). And in its turn, the Q order now requires us to assume an entry of Group IV elements (the three segments and one anomaly) into the composite manuscript of disarranged groups II and III. Table C, on the following page, illustrates this.

TABLE C: MINGLING OF ELEMENTS FROM GROUP IV
WITH THE COMPOSITE MS PREVIOUSLY DERIVED

Entry of Elements from Group IV	Previously Derived Composite MS (from Table B and pages 262 ff.)		Resulting Composite MS		Ultimate Sonnet Order of the MS Behind Q (18–121)[a]
Segment 18–19			18–19		
21–23 →	24	forms	21–24	With intrusion of Poem 1 (20) and Poem 2 (25–26), this sequence becomes..............	Q 18–52
	27–52		27–52		
	56–58		56–58		
	61		61		
Segment 53–55			53–55	With simple disarrangement of now adjacent elements, this sequence becomes..........	Q 53–61
59–60			59–60		
62–68 →	69–76	forms	62–76	With intrusion of Poem 4 (77), this sequence becomes..........	Q 62–108
Segment 97–108	78–96		78–108		
'Anomaly' 115–116 →			115–116,	With simple disarrangement of now adjacent elements, this sequence becomes..........	Q 109–121
	109–114		109–114		
	117–121		117–121		

[a] Intermingling of restored groups appears in Q only between 18 and 121.

The three segments of Group IV (first column) mingle with the composite manuscript of II and III (second column) at points of contact or near-contact prescribed by sonnet numbers in the 1609 order. In Table C, for the sake of clarity, I show the segments of IV with all elements finally in Q order, although, as mentioned before, disarrangement purely within segments, once they are formed, could have occurred at any time up to printing (pages 245–246).

Since the 'resulting composite manuscript' (Table C, third column) requires only simple disarrangement and minor intrusions to form Q's ultimate sonnet order (Table C, last column), our hypothesis accounting for disarrangement of all mingled groups holds together—if it satisfies a now familiar condition: in prescribing entry of Group IV elements into the composite elements of Group II, Group III, and two independent poems (Table C, second column), do we avoid tautology? Can we verify intrusion of the Group IV elements, or must we just invoke it, beg the question, in order to come up with the 1609 numerical order?

First, the sonnet order in the second column of Table C is not a question-begging arrangement. It is the series we have just considered, the one formed by Group II, Group III, and other elements under strict requirements of verification. Initially established on qualitative grounds, these groups and poems have assumed Q's order by minimal internal disarrangement, and by mingling normally in one simple process to account not only for orderly segments but for radically isolated fragments. In repeated instances, each based on independent evidence, the 1609 sonnet order and the restored sonnet order have interacted in a manner hard to explain save by viewing the one as an actual disarrangement of the other.

Into gaps of the order thus formed in Table C, column two, the segments of Group IV now fit. And if tautology has likewise had no part in forming these segments, the result should have meaning. Here, beyond noting that internal disarrangement of Group IV has met strict conditions governing plausibility (pages 243 ff.),

I need only refer to the question raised when its segments first appeared in discussion (pages 246 ff.): restoration of this group is finally independent of any concern for where its pieces may fall in the 1609 sonnet order. So, if the pieces happen to form segments that happen to fit open spaces of the mingled series in Table C, the result is not tautology. Instead, it amounts to one more example of the restored series forming the 1609 order as its many separate elements respond consistently to one another, and to Q's many conditions.

Three final matters need brief comment. First, Q requires that Group IV's only anomaly, 115–116, lodge between 114 and 117. In Table C this final displacement involves two moves: the entry of 115–116 with Group IV's third segment (97–108) puts the fragment in contact with 109–114, a mixed sequence previously accounted for (page 266); and simple disarrangement does the rest. This double move may seem contrived, gratuitous, but the restored order, as before, underwrites it. The fragment 115–116 is not tacked onto 97–108 so it may enter at the 'right' place; it belongs with the entering combination. See the grounds (pages 180 ff.) for restoring IV F, a poem in which 115–116, the concluding 'stanzas,' pointedly follow 107–108. The entry of 115–116 with 97–108 does not presuppose even simple disarrangement, for the order 107–108 115–116 is the presumed original order.

Typically—by now perhaps inevitably—separate verification appears for the next move, Q's requirement that 115–116 take its final position before 117–121 (reference to Table C continues). If the restored order remains consistent, it should confirm an intrusion at this point. Signs of one are unmistakable, signs already described in accounting for the final position of 113–114. The familiar case for 109–112 117–121 as a coherent poem readily implies intrusion of the two fragments dividing it. One of these, of course, is 115–116.

Another final condition set by Q is the disarrangement of 56–58, 61, 53–55, and 59–60 into the ultimate sequence 53–61 (Table C, third and fourth columns). Since these fragments are elements in segment one of Group II and segment two of Group

IV (Table A, page 255), and since the segments have already come together at a verified stage of disarrangement, one might rest here by saying that close contact between the fragments allows their simple disarrangement. Just the same, it is worth noting that the contact is neither contrived nor unexplained. It comes as one more example of a delightful logic the segment pattern offers, for when we find (Table A, again) that a segment of Group II joins a segment of Group IV we do not find merely that 56–58, 61 appear within one of these segments, and 53–55, 59–60 within the other; instead 56–58, 61 come at the end of the first segment and 53–55, 59–60 come at the beginning of the second. At this contact point, the 'overlapping,' a presumed mingling by fragments of one segment with fragments of another, occurs. And at what point would mingling be more likely? No rigging, no arrangement for future convenience, lies behind this result; in fact, the evidence for restoration would have been far more congenial had it led to nonoverlapping segments: Group II's segment ending with, say, 56 and Group IV's running continuously from 57.

Now we come to the minor intrusions shown in Table C (third column, right). That of Poem 2 (25–26) between elements of Group II could have occurred at any stage of the manuscript history. That it did occur, that it is not an assumption, is made likely by several independent signs. Sonnet 24 links closely with 46–47 to form II B; sonnets 27–28 join closely with 43, forming II C which leads into 44–45, the first two sonnets of II D. Thus sonnets 24 and 27–28 are cognate with one another as elements of Group II, and link intensively with sonnets in Q's 43–47 sequence, which implies that both 24 and 27–28 were isolated from sonnets in the '40' series by the entry of miscellaneous elements. Two of these elements are 29–31 and 32–42, already verified as intrusions (page 265), and the intrusion of 25–26 finishes the picture. Here, as frequently elsewhere, verification is compounded.

Finally, in Table C, the accretion of 20 and 77. Such minor and obvious intrusions may need no explanation. But it so happens that the presence of 20 and 77 at division points between signatures of the 1609 edition can account very nicely for their anomalous position in the Q order (pages 284–286). If so, evidence from the printed text will verify qualitative evidence pointing to 20 and 77 as insertions. Such evidence, relating to the time of publication, indicates intrusion at a terminal point in manuscript history. And the stage of disarrangement shown by Table C is terminal.

By this time, although the success of verification may be in dispute, the general course it is meant to take may be repetitively clear (tactics will work against tact in this kind of demonstration). Still, I want to remark finally, and briefly, on the premise or 'first principle' behind verification.

To assume the restored sonnet order, or any part of it, as originally intact (that is, 'real' or 'actual'), that we may check it against Q for plausible disarrangement, does not beg the question so long as Q's response may be unsatisfactory. And (prior to verification) that possibility always exists so long as a concern for plausible disarrangement has not initially controlled restoration. In this respect, Q's order, the presumed disarrangement, has controlled the restored order in but one way: where Q is plainly coherent I have not disturbed its sequence.

Otherwise I have made many changes, each one based on independent evidence. Hence, when the restored text is assumed intact in order to test for consistency of disarrangement, there is no single, inclusive assumption but, instead, as many separate assumptions as there are restored poems and groups—almost as many, in fact, as there are separately restored *parts* of poems and groups. So the test for disarrangement becomes one of consistency between any single restoration (including all independent bits of evidence in its favor) and, potentially, any or all other restorations. When Q, for example, presents two fragments (113–114, 115–116) from separately restored sequences at a place in its order where they happen to split a third restored sequence (109–112 117–121), then four elements that might not have shown this close relationship—the three restored sequences and Q—all point in a consistent direction. The three restored sequences (II A B, IV F, and Poem 5) indicate separately that their individual fragments are disarranged; Q verifies this by presenting two of the fragments as a double intrusion between two others that, in the restored order, belong together. Redundancy plays no part here: so far as primary evidence is concerned, none of the three restorations is contingent on another; none depends for initial (qualitative) validity on Q's rational disposition of its fragments. (If Q's disposition is mentioned in supporting commentary it represents verification, not primary evidence for restoration.) Far from being a star exhibit, the example just given is typical, although it illustrates but one kind of verification furnished by agreement between independent elements. And there are several kinds which appear repeatedly.

Verification can, of course, play tricks. I recall once being asked a disturbing question. Is it actually significant that Q presents fragments of the restored order in a sequence that seems to imply 'rational' disarrangement? *Given* these fragments—singles, twos, threes and larger units—would not *any* disarrangement of them in Q appear rational? Now this may be true—with serious limitations. There are forty-nine fragments of the emended sonnet order in Q 18–126, the area of segmentation and group mingling. If their restored sequence is disarranged thoroughly, repeatedly, and wholly at random (by lottery), some 'verifying' combinations (see pages 232 ff.) may be expected. Segmentation of fragments from groups II and IV will also occur. Yet the segments tend to be many and short, or, if longer, to be broken continually by minor intrusions. Fragments from Group III, the one so essential in Table B (page 260), never seem to avoid extreme disorder. The number of anomalies representing all three groups becomes excessive. This result, scarcely encouraging as 'verification,' appears in experimentation limited to forty-nine fragments. But there has been a fallacy, so far, in this assumed number. Actually, an intact fragment in Q having five or more sonnets is likely to be several potential fragments—several manuscript leaves which have remained together in Q's disarrangement, but could have separated. An intact 'four' may well represent two manuscript leaves, and even a three may be divisible. If we allow two separable leaves for each of the fours, and three such leaves for the fives and the one six (see pages 286–294), we must add twelve fragments to the forty-nine previously assumed. If forty-nine fragments, disarranged repeatedly at random, produce less than orderly distribution of the three groups, disorder should increase when we put twelve more into the lottery.

And there is still something forgotten. In experimental random disarrangements we may encounter an occasional 'verifying' combination. And for two of the three groups we may produce segmentation (of very uncertain quality)—whether with forty-nine fragments or with sixty-one. But can we now account for the chance segments by simple, plausible disarrangement of restored groups (cf. pages 243 ff.)? And can we account for the anomalies —now multiplied extensively—by a simple process of group mingling that explains all but one in a single required 'move' (cf. pages 256 ff.)? These last steps are, of course, essential to any verification through segmentation; without them, the process loses meaning.

Hence the really pertinent query is not whether any disarrangement of fragments from the emended order will have, by definition, *some* kind of rational sequence, but whether it will have a sequence as highly rational as the one Q actually provides. The answer is that it will not—certainly not 'by definition.' Further conditions, moreover, strengthen this answer. The next section will introduce a new aspect of verification, the consistency of manuscript forms implied by fragmentation in Q. From the nature of implied manuscripts described there, we can estimate that fragments subject to disarrangement in Q 18–126 numbered not forty-nine or sixty-one, but around seventy. If this estimate can be trusted, the chances of random disarrangement showing a rational pattern like the one Q exhibits become more remote than before. Thus, although the concluding section will present a wholly independent step in verification, it relates directly to the question just considered: the number of fragments subject to disarrangement, and its possible bearing on 'accidental patterns.' Verification remains many-sided, interactive, and cumulative; none of its aspects can be weighed apart from any other.

VERIFICATION BY IMPLIED MANUSCRIPT FORMS

Most rearrangers overlook this matter. On one basis or another they decide that Q has disturbed an original sequence and then, unaware of strange implications, go about repairing the damage. The strange implications they overlook have to do with physical properties of the manuscript behind Thorpe's edition, physical properties necessary to allow separation of an original sequence into its fragments as they appear in the 1609 series. Some rearrangers arrive at an original order that could have divided into Q's order only if most sonnets had been inscribed individually on separate manuscript leaves (thus permitting almost indiscriminate mixture), or only if the number of sonnets on a manuscript leaf had varied eccentrically (thus permitting disarrangement in 'blocks' of highly irregular content). An occasional restorer of the text, perhaps sensing these difficulties, invents the copyist or compositor who mischievously scrambled the contents of a manuscript from which he worked. But this will not do either, for although copyists or compositors have done their work madly, their aberrations are usually explainable; generally they are mad but north-northwest, and with method.

However difficult its solution, the problem is easy to state. If a rearrangement of the Sonnets implies disarrangement in Q that only an implausible manuscript, or the implausible copying of a manuscript, could provide, the rearrangement becomes implausible even though other evidence favoring it may be strong. But if a restored sequence based initially on good evidence implies the kind of disarrangement a normally designed manuscript could readily undergo, then it passes a critical test. Passing the test cannot, as a single factor, validate an emended series, but failure to pass it ought to raise wholesome doubt.

Does the restored sonnet order meet this requirement? At one time I thought the internal evidence might yield a sequence whose disarrangement in Q would appear in fragments either of two consecutive sonnets or some multiple of two: a restored order in which, for example, a pair of adjacent poems, would run (according to Q numbers) 48–49 87–90, and 91–94 69–70 95–96 36–39. Had internal evidence supported the two poems (in final analysis, it did not), their disarrangement in Thorpe's text would thus have appeared as a fragment of two (48–49), a fragment of eight (87–90 91–94), and remaining fragments of two, two, and four. And, had other restored poems or sequences shown this content of twos and multiples of two, the pattern would have implied that Q derives from a loose-leaf manuscript in which the Sonnets, original combinations intact, had been copied out two to a leaf and then disarranged by leaves, with some leaves, of course. remaining together in the right order. Moreover, had occasional transposition appeared (such as Q's 143 144 for the 144 143 of restored poem V B), all the better for the theory; the transpositions would have implied that each manuscript leaf contained one sonnet recto, another verso, and that some leaves of two were simply turned over. For a time I also weighed the chances of a restored sonnet order disarranged in Q by fours.

Although on the face of it too good to be true, the possibility of an entire copied sequence disarranged by twos or fours was worth considering. But the internal evidence, which one can learn to respect, will not frame this fearful symmetry. Still, such a notion seldom dies easily. I tried modifications of it, such as assuming initial and minor disarrangement within separate groups, then a copying of the whole into leaves of two sonnets each, and then final disarrangement of the copy by leaves. But the trouble is that if we assume disarranged original manuscripts followed by an extended copy in turn disarranged, we invoke not probability but possibility. The difficulty is not that such a manuscript history becomes implausible but simply that when reconstructed, it becomes neither probable nor improbable. If the restored sonnet order and the Q order representing its disarrangement can be related in terms of a simple manuscript hypothesis, a degree of verification will appear; but if they can be related only by a string of hypotheses—one plausible disarrangement followed by another—verification will have to come from another quarter.

Besides, any theory of disarrangement specifying a lengthy homogeneous manuscript is improbable from the start. If, for example, seventy-seven leaves each inscribed with two sonnets is one of its conditions, then another condition is the likelihood of either the sonnets or leaves being faithfully numbered (witness the manuscript of Fulke Greville's *Caelica*).[3] Hence the improbability of serious disarrangement after completion of the manuscript. One can say, of course, that a publisher like Thorpe would not have bothered to put even a numbered loose-leaf manuscript in order before using it as copy, but I am unable to say this with any conviction, and if I were, it would scarcely change the nature of a shaky assumption.

For several reasons, then, Q's apparent disarrangement of the restored order fails to imply a copying of short original manuscripts into an extended manuscript (or manuscripts) with uniform leaf content. Hence, one must try to explain disarrangement in terms of separate original or intermediate manuscripts— perhaps one for each original poem—with a strong chance that their number and variety will show no consistent or simple form. Yet, in one way the approach will be more realistic. In all likelihood, the Sonnets passed from poet to recipient not as long sequences but piecemeal: a poem at a time, a few poems at a time, or possibly in an instance or two, a completed group at a time (see the table of restoration, pages 40–41, for these divisions). Thus, initially at least, the Sonnets would have remained in a series of miscellaneous manuscripts, and at this stage no systematic numbering, likely in a comprehensive manuscript, has to be reckoned with as a bar to disarrangement. But if these manuscripts are to explain disarrangement of the restored order into Q's order, their reconstruction must show a relation between sonnets and leaves allowing for fragmentation of the kind Q shows. So here again is the crux: if the restored poems, varied as they are, point to such a sonnet-leaf relation, and if it turns out to be simple and consistent—the kind normally found in manuscripts written by the same hand—our restoration will have survived an objective test, one more than likely to show up a plausible but bad guess by implying implausible or impossible variations of manuscript form.

Consistency in a series of manuscripts does not require that all have the same leaf content. Such uniformity, in fact, is unlikely in manuscripts differing with respect to time and occasion. But consistency does require that the manuscript forms be few in number, that each form appear with some frequency, and, above all, that any single manuscript adhere to a dominant form. If necessary, we may assume that Shakespeare inscribed some poems (short ones) entire on a single manuscript leaf, some (also short) one sonnet to a leaf on several leaves, and others two, three, or four to a leaf. But we may not assume that he turned out manuscripts in which, for example, the first three sonnets of a single poem appeared on one leaf, the fourth sonnet by itself on another leaf, the fifth and sixth on a further leaf—and so on. There are poets who will do this sort of thing, but if, to account for disarrangement, a restored sonnet order requires eccentric manuscript foliation, it puts itself in serious doubt. Again, possibility is not probability.

Now to the problems of this edition. If we assume as a general rule that Shakespeare's sonnet-poems first appeared in individual manuscripts, no poem that Q preserves will require explanation in this part of the discussion. If a poem survives intact we merely infer a separate manuscript that, whatever its nature and whatever its history, held together. Reference to the emended sonnet order on pages 40–41 shows sixteen poems as intact in Q, whether displaced or not: A and B of Group I (the entire group); A, F, and I of Group II; A of Group III; B, D, and E of Group IV; C and F of Group V; and five of the six independent poems (all but Poem 5). In the restored sequence, poem D of Group III (82–86) is intact in Q, but since it follows III C closely and may well belong with C in a single composition (page 142), I do not include it here. Instead, for purposes of testing, I join the two as III 'C-D' (76, 78–80, 82–86), which when viewed as one poem is not intact.

Including III 'C-D,' just mentioned, eighteen restored poems suffer fragmentation in Q. But if the fragments imply a 'rational'

or homogeneous original manuscript—as they do in seven of the
eighteen fragmented poems—we have no difficulty. Thus poem D
of Group II appears in two equal remnants of two sonnets each,
and J of the same group as two equal remnants of three. Equal
division in disarrangement suggests uniform foliation. Poem E of
Group II is disarranged into four fragments of one sonnet each,
which implies a homogeneous manuscript of four leaves, each
containing a sonnet. And each of the following poems is disarranged into two such 'singles': B of Group III; A, E, and G of
Group V.

From here on, in eleven poems, we find apparent irregularity:
in II B, C, G, H; III 'C-D'; IV A, C, F; V B, D; and Poem 5. But
in a major instance, the irrational manuscript form readily trans-
lates itself into order. Poem B of Group V runs 144, 143, 135–136,
131–134. Literally, its disarrangement in Q appears as four fragments: a single sonnet, another single, a pair, and a run of four. If,
in explaining the disarrangement, we infer manuscript leaves
equivalent in content to the Q fragments, we have a highly
improbable document composed eccentrically of one sonnet on
the first leaf, one on the second, two on the third, and four on the
last. But the disorder is only apparent; we can account for the
disarrangement in Q by assuming a perfectly regular manuscript,
one of four leaves, each inscribed with one sonnet recto, another
verso. The foliation by sonnets (in terms of their Q numbers,
acquired later) becomes 144 recto, 143 verso/135, 136/131, 132/
133, 134. So, in Q the fragmentation of this poem shows a pattern
of two, two, four which implies a manuscript with two sonnets to
a leaf. Thus in disarrangement (Q), the last three leaves remain
together, although the second (135–136) takes a position following the fourth; the first leaf not only mingles with an alien
manuscript but is turned over (now reading verso, recto), so that
in the manuscript behind Q the poem's second sonnet (appearing
first) becomes Q 143 and the first sonnet follows it as 144. Hence,
far from raising difficulty, the presumed disarrangement of V B
strongly suggests a manuscript form not only regular but known
to have been used in Shakespeare's time.[4] The two Q fragments of

two sonnets each (135–136 and 143–144) point to a sonnet content of two to a leaf; one of these fragments, reversing the poem's
order (originally 144, 143), points to leaves inscribed recto and
verso; and the single fragment of four sonnets (131–134) is
perfectly consistent with these implications.

With slight variations, functionally explainable, a two-to-a-leaf
arrangement in manuscript will explain other seeming anomalies.
It can readily account for the independent Poem 5, presented by
Q as a fragment of four (109–112) and a fragment of five
(117–121). If we assume sonnets distributed two to each leaf,
splitting of the manuscript in disarrangement would have occurred at the division point between leaves two and three, that is,
between what are now sonnets 112 and 117. The last part of the
manuscript, represented by Q's fragment of five, would have
contained four sonnets (117–120), two to a leaf on leaves three
and four, and the final sonnet (121) on a leaf by itself—
presumably inscribed on the recto side, leaving the verso side blank.
(This necessary disposition of 121 on an end-leaf would likewise
have occurred had the first eight sonnets of Poem 5 appeared four
to a leaf—two recto, two verso.)

Thus in a manuscript having two sonnets to a leaf, the final
sonnet of an odd-numbered series will naturally appear on a leaf
by itself, and the assumption that it did so in the instance of Poem
5 implies no irregularity. With some restored poems, however,
not the last but the first sonnet becomes the variant. In terms of Q
numbers, poem IV F runs 106 59–60 107–108 115–116, thus
appearing in Q as four fragments. Fragments two through four
plainly imply a manuscript form of two sonnets to the leaf, but
we have the variant single 106 alone on a single leaf. And this leaf
must be the first, since internal evidence places 106 at the beginning of the poem.

Poem V D implies the same arrangement. With a fragmentation
of one, two, six, it runs in terms of Q numbers: 137, 141–142,
147–152. Unless we assume implausibly that the last fragment
represents a manuscript leaf carrying six sonnets, we must divide
its content among several leaves. The second fragment, 141–142,

points to a basis of division which, again, appears to be two sonnets to the leaf. If so, the fragment 147–152 represents the last three leaves, still in their original order. But 137 stands alone; like 106 of IV F, it is a beginning sonnet, and like 106 it must appear on a leaf by itself.

Now we come to poem H of Group II. Since it runs 91–93 69–70 95–96 94, we must assume a manuscript that could undergo a split, in sonnets, of three, two, two, one. Again, clear-cut fragments of two, 69–70 and 95–96, suggest leaves of two sonnets each, and again (as in Poem 5) we have the last sonnet, plausibly enough, on a leaf by itself. But we also have a three-sonnet fragment, 91–93, beginning the poem. If this means a first leaf containing three sonnets, the manuscript becomes irregular: the sonnet content by leaves will be three, two, two, one. Yet if we take our cue from 69–70 and 95–96, and thus infer a two-sonnet leaf represented by 92–93, then the opening sonnet, 91, will be left on a leaf by itself. The manuscript foliation becomes 91/92–93/69–70/95–96/94, a basic two-to-a-leaf pattern with the first sonnet on a separate leaf (as in IV F and V D) and the last sonnet also on a separate leaf (as in Poem 5).

The disposition just made of II H has involved conjecture from a Q fragment of three sonnets (91–93) that the beginning sonnet appeared alone on a first leaf. Poem A of Group IV, however, implies the manuscript form given II H, and does so with no need for conjecture about the first sonnet. Running 62 22–23 102–104, this poem requires separate foliation for 62; and with a two-to-a-leaf distribution suggested by 22–23, the complete manuscript arrangement becomes 62/22–23/102–103/104. So here again is a dominant two-to-a-leaf pattern with both the beginning and the end sonnets as variants.

We have already noted that a last sonnet on a leaf by itself is to be expected in a two-to-a-leaf arrangement if the number of sonnets in a poem happens to be uneven. But what of a beginning sonnet alone on a separate leaf, the variant we must infer if we accept a dominant two-to-a-leaf arrangement for II H, IV A, IV F, and V D? Does this amount to eccentric and hence improbable foliation? Not if, like the end-sonnet variation, it has a functional explanation. And it does: a blank recto side for the first leaf of a manuscript protects the contents by placing the opening sonnet 'inside,' and furnishes an outside space usable for inscription or for 'addressing' if transmission is involved. The manuscript forms a packet. Further, if more than one poem is included in the packet, a blank recto side for leaf one of the first poem becomes the cover, as just described, and a blank recto side for the first leaf of any following poem serves as a divider between poems.

    Well and good; but if the usage is functional we should expect restored poems to suggest it frequently. Here, the evidence is too consistent to be taken lightly. Of the six 'irregular' poems whose disarrangement we have considered, four (II H, IV A, IV F, and V D) have implied a manuscript with a single sonnet on the initial leaf. Of the five irregular poems not yet considered, three point to such a manuscript. For these, whatever foliation we allow to subsequent sonnets, we must assign the first sonnet to a separate leaf:

II B   24/46–47
II C   61/27–28/43
II G   49/87–88/89–90

    As tabulated here, these poems appear in a two-to-a-leaf man-uscript arrangement, except for the now familiar variants of an opening sonnet or a 'leftover' end sonnet on a leaf by itself. But unlike others reducible to this arrangement, the three poems just listed are short; hence their manuscript form might have been one sonnet to a leaf throughout. Even so, the 'packet' arrange-ment—the first sonnet inscribed verso, leaving the recto side blank as a cover or divider—would remain functional. In fact, for four of the restored poems whose inferred manuscript form *must* be one-to-a-leaf (page 279), the packet hypothesis seems espe-cially appropriate. Each of these poems is composed of two one-sonnet fragments. Using III B as an example, we can suppose the arrangement: blank recto, 32 verso/81 recto, blank verso. Here is the neatest of packets, two leaves with a sonnet on each of the inside facing pages, and the two blank outside pages providing cover or divider, front and back.

Of the restored poems with irregular fragmentation in Q, two—III 'C-D' (see page 278) and IV C—remain for discussion. From the standpoint of evidence used in restoration, IV C is more interesting, perhaps, than any of the others; and the group formed around it is fundamental in reflecting standards and procedures governing this edition.

If we have been on the right course, IV C as a longer poem of eleven sonnet stanzas ought to imply the basic two-to-a-leaf manuscript pattern implied or suggested by other extended poems: II H, IV A, IV F, V B, V D, and Poem 5. As the internal evidence restores it, IV C runs 100–101 63–68 19 21 105—which gives it a fragmentation pattern in Q of two, six, one, one, one. The first fragment suggests a two-to-a-leaf arrangement, and the second (six sonnets intact) is amenable to that form. But the pattern breaks down with the last three Q fragments. Obviously, a manuscript of seven leaves, each of the first four containing two sonnets, and the last three leaves each carrying one sonnet, is eccentric.

And, quite clearly, we cannot give this hypothetical manuscript a dominant two-to-a-leaf form by regarding the first sonnet as a variant. Sonnet 100 on a leaf by itself only adds to the confusion, which—incidentally but significantly—ought to quiet any suspicion that the variant leaf form for an opening sonnet can be used at will to supply orderly manuscripts for poems having disorderly implications. IV C promises trouble.

True, we can imagine this eleven-sonnet poem in an eleven-leaf manuscript with a sonnet on each leaf. But if we do, all previous distinctions become pointless: why not imagine one-sonnet-to-a-leaf manuscripts for all the restored poems? So far, the only ones implying such an arrangement have been short—poems of two sonnets, save for II E which has four; and this is not only appropriate but encouraging, for an extended one-to-a-leaf manuscript is bulky, wasteful, implausible.

The eccentric manuscript indicated by the fragments of IV C in Q is just the kind of anomaly a restored sonnet order might have supplied frequently. Yet we meet the difficulty here for the first time. Three 'singles' in a row (19, 21, 105), which the primary evidence requires, cause the trouble. And the frustration has its comedy, for were the three sonnets but numbered 19, 20, 105, then IV C could be the capstone of our two-to-a-leaf hypothesis for longer poems: a fragment of two (100–101) representing the first leaf, a fragment of six (63–68) representing leaves two through four, a fragment of two (19–20 in place of 19, 21) representing leaf five, and a leftover single (105) representing the last leaf. But the Q numbers, alas, happen to run 19, 21. What conclusions follow? One, of course, might be that nothing is so unconvincing as an hypothesis that 'almost' holds. But in the context of other elements, the near-miss may be more provocative than a hit. Sonnet 20, one of Q's notable oddities, is also one of the more likely intrusions, and if it intrudes it does so, of course, between 19 and 21. Hence the chance that 19 and 21 were once adjacent in manuscript and together on a single leaf.

Now I hope no one will think I doubt Shakespeare's authorship of 20 or its propriety among the Sonnets. I merely question its position in Q's order. In the first place, it appears in a series, 18–28, packed with miscellaneous and divergent fragments. But more important here is the nature of 20. In Shakespeare's collection there are better sonnets, but none takes the stage as this one does, this inquiry into "doting" Nature's blunder in equipping the young man with a penis. Sonnet 20 belongs at large in the Sonnets—of course it does—but it does not belong between 19 and 21 (see page 166 for their connection), or in the midst of any purposeful sequence. It is unique and, of all the Sonnets, is the one most likely to have circulated widely, and independently.

In Q the anomalous position of 20 between 19 and 21 finds a direct parallel in the appearance of 77, another self-sufficient single, between 76 and 78–80. Interpolations of this kind are hypothetically explainable in any sonnet sequence: random mingling of separate manuscripts, casual insertion by a scribe in the process of copying—any such accident or incident can account for what we find. But with 20 and 77 there are signs of interpolation in the printing house. In Q we encounter 20 as the first complete sonnet to appear in signature C. Signature B ends with the first eight lines of 19, C begins with 19's last six, and then comes 20. Now, imagine the printer in possession of a separate manuscript leaf containing this extraordinary sonnet. For obvious reasons Thorpe will want it included, and if this involves insertion, 20 is apt to intervene between two consecutive sonnets of a primary manuscript being used for copy. In the printing of Q a likely place for insertion of miscellaneous items would have been the beginning or end of a signature, a division point in the typesetting process favoring attention to odds and ends. This would have been the case whether insertion had been left to the compositor or whether his copy, with any insertions, had been prepared for him, possibly cast-off for printing by formes.[5] In the setting of Q, the first eight lines of sonnet 19 were used to complete signature B: hence its last six lines were carried over to begin the first page of C. Then the compositor (or the preparer of copy) was free to insert 20. If he did so, he then turned back to his primary copy[6] for the sonnet that immediately followed 19, and rendered it as 21. Under these circumstances we can readily suppose that 19 and 21, contiguous in manuscript, were inscribed on the same leaf.

As noted before, an interpolation of 20 during printing is not the only means by which 19 and 21, originally on the same manuscript leaf, could have been separated by one sonnet in the ultimate 1609 series; and I should not have described the hypothetical printing process were it not that we meet identical signs of it in the intrusion of 77. Like 20, 77 is plainly a sonnet unto itself, and no one can doubt that it interrupts the close relation between 76 and 78–80, components of III C or the opening sonnets of III C-D if the two poems were one. In Q the fragments of III C-D (76 78–80 82–86) run one-three-five and imply, of course, an irregular sonnet content for the separable leaves of a manuscript. Yet, as in the crux of IV C, a single sonnet (77, the obvious intrusion) causes the difficulty, for without interruption by 77 the fragmentation of III C-D would be four-five. Now again, as in the case of 20 and IV C, suppose 77 in a separate manuscript and assume printing-house arrangements for inserting it into the Q series. Just as 20 appears at the division point between two signatures, so does 77. Here, in beginning signature F, the compositor has no sonnet to complete before inserting 77; in fact, the setting of 76 has left the last page of signature E two lines short. So the compositor used the first two lines of 77 to end the last page of E and the remaining twelve lines to begin the first page of F. Hence, if he set 77 from separate copy, he then returned to primary copy and set as 78 the sonnet that followed 76 in manuscript.

Sonnet 20, unique in theme and tone, and sonnet 77, unique in purpose, are the only two of the first 126 having no close or cogent relation with any other sonnet. They stand so obviously apart that their intrusion, at some time or other, into the larger sequence is virtually certain. Is it mere coincidence that they both appear at separation points between signatures in the 1609 edition? Perhaps so, but whether or not this is coincidence, and thus whether or not 20 and 77 are printers' insertions, the two sonnets remain so distinctive as isolated 'singles' that their placement respectively between 19 and 21 and between 76 and 78 is more than suspect. Hence when we find that 19 and 21 function aptly together in IV C and that 76 and 80 join neatly in III C, we may suppose with good reason that the 'almost consecutive' sonnets were once actually consecutive.

In this view of the matter, III C-D of the restored series—with 76 and 78 as consecutive sonnets—now suggests the familiar manuscript arrangement, two to a leaf with an end variant: 76, 78/79–80/82–83/84–85/86. And with 19 and 21 regarded as once consecutive, the manuscript now implied by IV C takes on the same rational foliation: 100–101/63–64/65–66/67–68/19, 21/105. Simply accept 77 and 20 as intrusions, and the two anomalous poems fit a dominant two-to-a-leaf pattern suggested or implied by the fragments in Q of six other extended poems.

We now know that, whether severely disarranged or not, the restored poems appear in Q according to a pattern that seems to mean something. Summary, a table, and some interpretation can sharpen this meaning.

As Q presents them, sixteen of the poems are intact: A, B of Group I; A, F, I of II; A of III; B, D, E of IV; C, F of V; and all of the independent poems save Poem 5. Although several of these are detached from their groups or in disarranged poem order, none shows internal disarrangement. To explain their disposition in the 1609 text, we need only assume individual manuscripts that, whatever their form, remained intact. It is important, of course, to understand that nothing suggests any fundamental difference in form between these manuscripts and those implied by poems fragmented in Q.

Eighteen restored poems, we must presume, have suffered internal disarrangement; that is, each appears in Q as two or more fragments. To account plausibly for this disarrangement the fragments must imply separable manuscript components (leaves) on which sonnets were inscribed according to some orderly scheme of distribution. What do we find?

Poem E of Group II appears in Q as four 'singles' (fragments of one sonnet each); poems B of III and A, E, G of V appear each as two singles. Hence these five poems imply a consistent manuscript form of one sonnet to a leaf. And appropriately they are short; in manuscripts of longer poems, leaves containing a single sonnet would have been both awkward and wasteful.

Among the remaining thirteen poems disarranged in Q we encounter fragments of two, or fragments having multiples of two, often enough to entertain the hypothesis of a two-to-a-leaf manuscript form with a pair of functional and therefore permissible variants: the first sonnet may be on a leaf by itself and, if the series ends unevenly, the last or odd sonnet will be on a leaf by itself.

If this manuscript hypothesis is to explain disarrangement of the thirteen remaining poems, three conditions must be met.

1. By clear warrant of the primary evidence, evidence establishing connection and order in these poems, all of their fragments in Q having but one sonnet must either begin or end a poem. Since the two-to-a-leaf hypothesis permits functional variants of one sonnet to a leaf only at the beginning and end of a poem's implied manuscript, the basis for condition 1 is obvious.

2. By clear warrant of the primary evidence behind these poems, not only their Q fragments having one sonnet, but *all* of their fragments having an odd number of sonnets (three or five) must either begin or end a poem. Condition 2 follows from condition 1. In a two-to-a-leaf manuscript hypothesis with variant leaves limited, as described, to those having one sonnet, any intact Q fragment [7] of three sonnets must be interpreted as two originally adjacent leaves: one bearing two sonnets, the other bearing one; and any intact Q fragment of five sonnets must be regarded as three originally adjacent leaves: two leaves having two sonnets each, and a leaf having one sonnet. And since, in either case, the leaf bearing one sonnet must begin or end a poem (condition 1), the entire fragment of three or five must begin or end a poem. If it begins the poem, its first sonnet must be presumed on a leaf by itself: for example, 91/92–93, the fragment of three beginning II H. If the fragment ends the poem, its last sonnet must be presumed on a leaf by itself: for example, 117–118/119–120/121, the fragment of five ending Poem 5.

3. Although redundant (implied by 1 and 2), condition 3 will help to set matters straight. Since the hypothesis we are testing specifies a two-to-a-leaf manuscript with variants only at the beginning or end, no Q fragment of one, three, or five may appear in the 'interior' of a restored poem (when the poem has three fragments or more). Every Q fragment placed in such an interior position must contain two sonnets or a multiple of two. (But this is not to say that all fragments of two or a multiple of two must have an interior position; the manuscript hypothesis allows for a two-to-a-leaf arrangement throughout a poem—the initial or terminal one-to-a-leaf variants are 'optional,' although frequent.)

A requirement that Q fragments of the thirteen disarranged poems meet such conditions is a severe one. If these restored poems are wholly or mainly fortuitous, if they never existed and hence were never subject to norms of manuscript usage, there is very little chance of such demands being fulfilled by their twenty-one fragments of one, three, or five—any of which may turn up in the wrong position. Unless, of course, I have been partial to restorations that anticipate the manuscript hypothesis. Of that, more in due time.

In the following table are the thirteen fragmented poems to be tested for agreement with the conditions just outlined. Opposite each is its fragmentation pattern in Q. Since fragments of one sonnet, three, or five—each representing one presumed single—are central to the test (conditions 1 and 2), I emphasize their positions by italics.

FRAGMENTATION IN Q OF THIRTEEN RESTORED POEMS [a]

Poems		Fragmentation Pattern in Q
II B	24 46–47	*One*, Two
II C	61 27–28 43	*One*, Two, *One*
II D	44–45 50–51	Two, Two
II G	49 87–90	*One*, Four
II H	91–93 69–70 95–96 94	*Three*, Two, Two, *One*
II J	33–35 40–42	*Three*, *Three*
III C–D	76 78–80 82–86 [b]	*One*, *Three*, *Five*
IV A	62 22–23 102–104	*One*, Two, *Three*
IV C	100–101 63–68 19 21 105	Two, Six, *One*, *One*, *One*
IV F	106 59–60 107–108 115–116	*One*, Two, Two, Two
Poem 5	109–112 117–121	Four, *Five*
V B	144 143 135–136 131–134	*One*, *One*, Two, Four
V D	137 141–142 147–152	*One*, Two, Six

[a] Poems having single-sonnet fragments only are not included here.
[b] For the combining of III C and D here, see page 278.

One may object that five of these poems (II B, D, G, J, and Poem 5) cannot test the manuscript hypothesis since each has but two fragments and, consequently, no interior fragment which as a single, three, or five could violate the conditions. But the objection would miss the point. It is true, for example, that II J and Poem 5, as the evidence restores them, have no interior fragments that could violate the hypothesis. Yet this is a direct result of the

Q sonnet order being what it is and not what it might have been.
Suppose some very slight differences: what if sonnet 33 had
appeared in Q as 40, 40 as 33, 108 as 111, and 111 as 108? Then II
J, exactly as internal evidence restores it, would run 40 34–35 33
41–42 (a fragmentation of one, two, one, two—compare II J in
the table); Poem 5 would run 109–110 108 112 117–121 (two,
one, one, five); and IV F would run 106 59–60 107 111 115–116
(one, two, one, one, two). All three restored poems would imply
eccentric manuscripts and deny not only a two-to-a-leaf hypothesis but any hypothesis (save one to a leaf) requiring consistent
foliation for single poems. If these and many other differences of
sonnet order are recognized as conditions Q might have imposed—and they must be—the hypothesis is being tested. The
actual emergence of any poem such as II J without interior
fragments, which if present could prove eccentric, is part of its
verification.

Another possible objection is that disarrangement of the first
four poems in the table can be explained as the fragmentation of a
one-to-a-leaf manuscript. The poems are short; such a manuscript
would have been suitable. And disarrangement of II J can be
explained as the separation of two manuscript leaves, each containing three sonnets. But these objections, too, would miss the
point. Whether or not a poem in the table can imply an alternative manuscript form, we may test to see whether it is amenable
to a basic, an inclusive form (two to a leaf) so frequently suggested by other poems. Hence the accompanying table contains
all fragmented poems save the five short ones (page 287) explainable *only* in terms of a one-to-a-leaf manuscript. The latter form
their own class and provide their own consistency within that
class.

Now, what appears? In the thirteen restored poems of the table
are fourteen fragments of one sonnet, five fragments of three, and
two fragments of five. And to satisfy conditions of the manuscript hypothesis (page 287), all such fragments must appear at
the beginning or end of their respective poems. According to the
table, seventeen of the twenty-one do so. Four do not: the frag-

ment of three, 78–80 of III C-D, the singles 19 and 21 of IV C, and the single 143 of V B. But 143 comes directly after 144, the first sonnet of V B, to form a fragment of two in reverse order, a simple transposition explainable as a turned-over leaf containing two sonnets—one recto, the other verso (see above, page 279). The three remaining aberrations—78–80, 19, and 21—register the interesting 'near-misses' already discussed at some length (pages 283–286): prior to the intrusion of 77, sonnets 78–80 would have combined with 76 as an original sequence of four; prior to the intrusion of 20, sonnets 19 and 21 would have formed an original sequence of two.

Hence, of the four aberrant fragments, one becomes 'regular' by simple transposition and three conform when two single-sonnet intrusions are removed. If 144 and 143 are transposed to form a 'two,' if 76 and 78–80 are joined in a 'four,' if 19 and 21 are brought together in a 'two,' then the fragmentation pattern of V B becomes two-two-four, that of III C-D becomes four-five, and that of IV C becomes two-six-two-one. Compare these patterns with patterns in the table.

With this, all poems in the table now conform with the manuscript hypothesis. The table will show nine fragments of one (19, 21, 76, 143, 144 eliminated), four fragments of three (78–80 eliminated), and two fragments of five. All nine fragments of one—representing, according to the hypothesis, a single sonnet on a first leaf or last leaf—now either begin or end their poems. Two fragments of three—each representing a first leaf with one sonnet and a second with two—begin their poems (II H and II J). Two remaining fragments of three—each representing a next-to-last leaf with two sonnets, and a last leaf with one—end their poems (II J and IV A). Both fragments of five—each representing two leaves with two sonnets, followed by a last leaf with one—end their poems (III C D and Poem 5).

The fifteen fragments of two in the table (now including 19 joined with 21 and the transposed 144, 143) are remarkably well distributed among the poems, thus implying a basic two-to-a-leaf arrangement. To this end they are supplemented by four frag-

ments of four (now including 76, 78–80) and two fragments of
six—all multiples of two. The basic two-to-a-leaf form, implied
by the twos, requires that all 'interior' fragments be twos or
multiples of two. They are; ten interior fragments now appear:
nine twos and a six. (Their interior position is, of course, already
implied by the exterior position of other fragments, those of one,
three, and five.)

Were the poems in the table imaginary—fortuitous but mistaken restorations never, of course, committed to manuscripts
with consistent foliation—the chances of their presenting such
consistency among their diverse fragments in Q would be slight.
Or, to put it another way: if fragmentation of the restored poems
in Q is imaginary, if the fragments were actually composed *as*
fragments (loosely, often incoherently strung together in 'sonneteer's style')—if they merely seem to rearrange themselves cogently into poems and groups—then it is odd that thirty-six
random singles, twos, threes, and the rest happen to come together in an imaginary order that, nevertheless, implies throughout a set of consistently leaved manuscripts.

Now that tangents and cross-purposes are understood, it is
possible to define the matter quiet briefly in terms of singles,
remnants of the restored sonnet order appearing in Q as fragments of one sonnet. Again, if 77 and 20 are intrusions affecting
III C D and IV C, and if Q 143–144 is a transposition affecting V
B, the thirteen disarranged poems just examined present nine
singles. The five other disarranged poems, those composed entirely of singles (page 287), furnish twelve more, bringing the
number to twenty-one. These are 'literal'; if we add six singles
that the manuscript hypothesis requires us to infer, one for each
fragment of three or five (page 288), we have a total of twenty-
seven.

With respect to orderly or disorderly manuscript forms implied by fragmentation of the restored poems in Q , it is clear by
now that singles are the fragments from which serious difficulty,
anarchy in fact, could be expected.[8] Yet, in spite of their large
number and their wide dispersal in Q, singles appearing in the

restored sonnet order finally cause no trouble. Twelve of the twenty-seven form five appropriately brief poems (four having but two sonnets each), in which no Q fragments other than singles appear. They thus imply a consistent manuscript form of one sonnet to a leaf, and a restriction of that form to short compositions. The fifteen remaining singles appear in restored poems with other fragments (twos and multiples of two) that imply or suggest a basic manuscript arrangement of two sonnets to a leaf. And every one of the fifteen singles turns out to be the first sonnet of a poem or the last, thus invariably implying the functional variant in a two-to-a-leaf arrangement—a single sonnet on the beginning or end leaf.

But this remarkable consistency of pattern invites two opposed explanations. Either the restored poems imply a consistent manuscript usage because they once actually existed in manuscripts of consistent form; or they imply a consistent manuscript usage because, anticipating difficulty, I have favored restoration that implies the 'right' sort of manuscript, restoration in which the singles behave themselves.

Although I shall ask skeptical readers to judge the second and less glorious alternative for themselves, I think it merits, by way of warning, an autobiographical detail or two. Actually, I resisted for some time the placement of singles in restored poems (except at the end of an odd-numbered series) because I hoped that a dominantly two-to-a-leaf manuscript behind Q was in the making. But the singles kept coming, and one either respects the internal evidence—allows it to govern—or one does not. But I cannot pretend that I failed to see a pattern forming once I began to place singles where they insisted on being placed. Consequently, the results should be checked carefully for a wishful begging of the question. Evidence placing singles at the beginning or end of restored poems must be compelling and may not, of course, depend in any way upon assumptions of the manuscript hypothesis.

Any reader interested in this evidence may test it by reference to the "Text and Commentary," using as a checklist the table on page 289. I trust he will find it sufficient and decisive. Excellent evidence independently establishes 24, 33, 91, and 137 as beginning sonnets of their respective poems, and 42, 43, 86, 94, 104, 105, and 121 as end sonnets of theirs. And in II C, if 43 is the end sonnet, 61 must begin the poem because it cannot come between 27 and 28 or impede the resolution of 27–28 by 43. In II G, 49 would be an anticlimax after 90, and 87–90 is an intact unit; hence the order clearly should be 49, 87–90. In IV A, 22 must follow 62 and 23 precede 102–104; hence 62 must be the opening sonnet. In IV F, 59 could precede 106, but the sequence 106, 59 is equally good and it allows 60 to lead into 107–108, while keeping intact the Q order 59–60.

This exhausts the list of fifteen 'critical' singles remaining in poems of the table (page 289) after the adjustments involving III C-D, IV C, and V B (page 291). A testing of primary evidence behind these placements will at least explain why I was forced to put singles in positions incompatible with an originally 'pure' two-to-a-leaf hypothesis. And if this has led to another set of coherent manuscript implications, it has done so because the 'pieces,' the singles, arrange themselves.

Whatever the extent of verification as we have considered it, the process is still incomplete. Until those who know and value the Sonnets offer their response, no attempt at restoration can be more than tentative, more than a clear suggestion that finished, well-rounded poems by Shakespeare remain undiscovered and unread. This, of course, is another way of saying that verification of a restored text is finally a matter not of individual but of collective judgment. As a contribution to this ultimate judgment I have set down my personal response to the Sonnets, partly founded, as any personal response must be, on a long tradition of interpretation both good and bad. At the same time, in an effort to add something more than another personal experience, I have introduced the rather formidable 'apparatus' of verification, believing that a collective judgment upon Shakespeare's sonnet order is possible only if many sensitive readings lead to publicly understandable interpretation, which we then can test, in part, by something other than our preferences.

Such a restricted approach to the Sonnets in no way defines the range and depth of responsible criticism. It is addressed rather to findings of authenticity, and to critics who prefer an authentic whole poem to a nonpoem, or a garbled poem, as an object to be valued. If, in time, certain poems and groups of this edition are judged authentic, the 'critical implications,' the extent of artistry to be found and enjoyed in the Sonnets, will, I think, increase substantially. To enlarge at present on these possibilities of criticism would be out of order and, of course, absurd. It should be enough, in closing, to venture that interpretation of any restored poem might well attend to structure, to the relations of part to whole that Q's fragmentation of poems has obscured or destroyed. And if 'structure' is understood to mean here what it means in terms of *Othello,* a restored text of the Sonnets may exemplify in new but characteristic ways the essential Shakespeare.

 # Notes

1. Hyder Rollins, ed., *A New Variorum Edition of Shakespeare. The Sonnets* (Philadelphia and London, 1944), II, 83.

2. A. L. Rowse, *Shakespeare's Sonnets* (London, 1964).

3. R. P. Blackmur, "A Poetics for Infatuation," in *The Riddle of Shakespeare's Sonnets* (New York, 1962), pp. 131–132. Italics are Blackmur's.

4. Tucker Brooke, *Shakespeare's Sonnets* (New Haven, 1936).

5. Subsequent to the *Variorum*, little comment suggesting rearrangement has appeared. Dover Wilson is an exception to the almost complete reticence among editors. He remains willing to face the question of Q's faulty sonnet order and contributes pertinent information or suggestions in notes on various sonnets. I have found Wilson's interest in my own earlier work (on 127–154) both heartening and informative. See J. Dover Wilson, ed., *The Sonnets* (Cambridge, 1966).

6. Where duplication occurs it rarely involves more than a few sonnets. The context of other sonnets in which these few are placed, and the principle on which rearrangement is based, are main points of difference between one rearranger and another, whether or not they agree on isolated details.

NOTES TO CHAPTER I

1. Compare Rollins' position with the conventional but inconsistent one taken recently by Hilton Landry (*Interpretations in Shakespeare's Sonnets* [Berkeley and Los Angeles, 1963]). Rollins had little or no faith in the possibility of restoring the sonnet order, but he likewise had little confidence in the 1609 order except, of course, where its sequence is self-justifying. Landry, on the other hand, in a 'double standard' judgment typical of critics who support the 1609 text, ends by denying his own premise.

Landry's often valuable commentary on association between sonnets requires him to affirm a correct order in Q only when the relationship he is discussing actually depends on strict continuity. Yet, assuming that any questioning whatever of Q's order is a threat to security, he finally concludes (page 130) not that his evidence supports the 1609 order at certain points (many of them obvious), but that it shows the sequence in Q to be "generally and essentially right." Earlier, however (pages 3–4), while granting that Q has no external authority, Landry claims that internal evidence can never support a rearrangement (on the usual ground that it supports too many). But if this is true, what becomes of his ultimate statement? If internal evidence cannot justify a rearrangement, how can it justify the 1609 order against the suspicion, wholesomely entertained even by Rollins, of *dis*-arrangement? This, of course, does not show that rearrangement is possible; it simply implies that Landry should not (and need not) have 'justified' the Q text as "generally and essentially right." One guesses his tacit reasoning here—that the dubious 1609 text is, after all, the only printed edition of Shakespeare's time. But that argument, aside from naïvely dodging the question, would deny his earlier statement that Q has no external authority.

Landry also impulsively decides (with Nejgebauer; see page 6 of my "Introduction") that all rearrangements assume the Sonnets to be a homogeneous composition, whereas they actually are a miscellany of separate poems and groups (Landry, page 4). Of course they are such a miscellany, but what then of the essential issue? Are some of the miscellaneous poems and groups disarranged in Q?

2. That is, differing in sonnet content; difference in sonnet order or organization of poems within the group might not be an essential difference.

NOTES TO CHAPTER II

1. C. Knox Pooler, ed., *The Sonnets, The Arden Shakespeare* (London, 1931).

2. Or 'deepest thought'; see W. G. Ingram and Theodore Redpath, *Shakespeare's Sonnets* (New York, 1965), p. 160. Or 'hearts' desire'; see Edward Hubler, *Shakespeare's Songs and Poems* (New York, 1959), p. 76.

3. No matter what order of typesetting is assumed, whether seriatim by pages or by formes (see G. W. Williams, "Setting by

Formes in Quarto Printing," *Studies in Bibliography*, II [1958], 39–53) it is most unlikely that in setting sig. G1 the compositor set the first seven lines of that page (sonnet 96.6–12); then erroneously turned to a much earlier point in the copy (corresponding to sig. C4v in Q) to set the couplet of sonnet 36 as 96.13–14; and finally returned to the correct point in the copy to resume setting the next following sonnet (97)—all this without being aware of his error, or (if aware) without correcting it. But even if there were evidence that a printer's error might readily have occurred, we should still have to explain how a mistakenly repeated couplet could make not ordinary but perfect sense in both sonnets which contain it. In checking these matters, a reader is sure to be interested when he sees that the last nine lines of 36 stand at the top of C4v and the last nine lines of 96 correspondingly at the top of G1. Further examination will show, however, that this line division, or a close approximation of it, occurs in Q at the top of every fifth page. Uniform length of sonnets with close uniformity in number of lines per page is, of course, the explanation.

4. The 1609 sequence 100–105 is, in fact, so badly confused that the separation of 102–104 from 100–101 and 105 becomes necessary. See the discussion in note 5, immediately following, concerning Q's misplacement of sonnets comprising restored poem IV C.

5. Since the case for bringing together the sonnets placed in IV C is extensive, I avoid confusion by separating it from the case, also extensive, pointing to their faulty order in Q. Accordingly, all evidence that Q has misplaced certain sonnets of IV C will be found in this note.

All five of the sonnets now joined with the 63–68 series are centers of difficulty in the 1609 text. We may consider them in the order of Q's arrangement.

Sonnets 19 and 21. Shakespeare's series 1–17 can scarcely be questioned. Sonnets 1–14, many of them clearly linked, urge the friend to marry and defeat Time by perpetuating himself. Sonnet 15 then introduces another note: as Time "takes from you, I engraft you new," i.e., perpetuate you in my verse. But sonnet 16 neatly subordinates this to the earlier theme: "wherefore do you

not a mightier way Make war upon this bloody tyrant Time?"
The mightier way, of course, is the initial way of marriage and
procreation; in bestowing immortality, Shakespeare's "pupil pen"
cannot hope to match the fathering of children. Sonnet 17 amplifies this to the limit and then ends on the original theme: who will
believe the poet's verse years hence if it is filled with the friend's
"high deserts"? Even if the friend's grace could be described, the
amazed "age to come" would say, "This poet lies."

> So should my papers, yellowed with their age,
> Be scorned, like old men of less truth than tongue,
> And your true rights be termed a poet's rage
> And stretchèd meter of an antique song:
>   But were some child of yours alive that time,
>   You should live twice, in it and in my rhyme.

Thus, in the absence of fair descendants, poems can never confer
immortality. And the whimsical point is clear—the fair descendants will confer it whether the poems are there or not (see also
16.9–14). Now, however, just after the point has been made so
well, anticlimax spoils it. If we accept Thorpe's arrangement we
must believe that Shakespeare followed 17 with 18 ("Shall I
compare thee to a summer's day?"), a very good sonnet but, in its
sudden promise of immortality in verse alone—as if that magic
had not just been questioned—a pointless negation of 17. The
negation is not paradox or witty reversing of the field; it is
fatuous. Non sequitur, both of poetry and logic, has begun with
18 after the strict development of 1–17, and we now encounter 19
and 21, two of the sonnets I wish to remove from Thorpe's order.
The first of these repeats the unqualified promise of eternity in
verse made by 18 and thus adds to confusion already begun,
which is then doubled by the notorious tour de force of 20 (the
friend's penis). Chaos is indeed come again. Next we have 21, the
second sonnet I propose to displace, one which Brooke, however
(page 253 of his edition), accepts as "a kind of apologetic postscript" appropriate enough "after the daring informality of 20."
An apologetic postscript might well follow a sonnet like 20, but it
is hard to read 21 as such a statement. It merely rejects sonnet
conceits in favor of the true love which generates true writing,

and its only apparent connection with 20 lies in its disapproval of painted beauty, a common idea in the Sonnets which, incidentally, appears also in the 63–68 sequence with which I link 21. I agree with Pooler and others who consider 21 displaced.

The close, progressive order shown by 1–17, clearly a standard established at the outset, is not restored until 26, or perhaps 27. Sonnets 18–25 present a jumble which begins by dislodging the capstone (15–17) to Shakespeare's first series. Significantly, 19 and 21 are in the midst of the confusion.

Sonnets 100–101 and 105. If these are kept in Thorpe's order, Shakespeare again arrives at maximum anticlimax in a minimum of space. 100 and 101 are plainly meant to introduce a sonnet series by declaring its theme; this they do elaborately, and they present, moreover, the only formal invocation of the Muse to be found in the Sonnets. So, if they were seriously composed, succeeding sonnets should carry out their intent. But if the 1609 text is valid, no Muse was ever invoked to less purpose. Sonnet 100 charges her with forgetfulness and urges her to give the friend fame "faster than Time wastes life"; 101 then warns the truant Muse to make no excuse for muteness—to desist above all from the hackneyed plea that the friend's grace is beyond all praise and adorning: "Because he needs no praise wilt thou be dumb? Excuse not silence so; for 't lies in thee To make him much outlive a gilded tomb." "Then do thy office, Muse . . ." If we are to credit the 1609 arrangement, this august office is now performed in four oddly grouped sonnets, the first two of which upset the office itself. Sonnet 102 declares that the poet, like Philomel, will not sing in late summer. Other birds are singing and, because sweets are thus grown common, he may hold his tongue. This is not the excuse for silence which Shakespeare has just denied to the Muse in 101, but it is quite like it. Sonnet 103, however, expressly offers that forbidden pretext: "Alack, what poverty my Muse brings forth"; the poet is dumb because the friend's countenance "overgoes" his invention, and to attempt a description of it were "sinful," a gross, needless impiety. So the high duty of the Muse (100) is now sinful, and the forbidden excuse for failure in it (101) has become virtue itself.

Immediately we suspect playfulness, a diverting possibility which must be scouted before we can say that the sonnet order is doubtful. Does Shakespeare strenuously warn his Muse that awe must not be mute, and then fall ironically into awed muteness? If this mischief were actually in the text, only pedantry could point to breached logic. But there is no real comic reversal; as in 17–21, the transition lands in fatuity. Sonnet 101: my friend himself needs no praise, but through my Muse posterity must hear of him; silence is thus inexcusable; do thy office, Muse! I teach thee how. . . . Then 102: I am silent, like Philomel in "riper days"; when other birds are singing, "I would not dull you" with common song. Philomel, unlike the Muse, has not been told that gracious silence is not transmissible to posterity. A good sonnet by itself, 102 succeeds the urgent 101 with something less than cogency, either of logic or irony. More than inconsistency appears; there seems to be a vacant unawareness of 100–101. Sonnet 103 lapses in the same way, for after 101's ringing statement that posterity alone is to be served by poems about the friend, it declares that the friend can be served better with a looking glass. Far from ironically contradicting 100–101, sonnets 102 and 103 move to awkwardly inapposite ideas which might characterize a haphazard sonnet sequence but are altogether 'wrong' in a series begun by the energetic invocation of 100–101, with its strict forecast of subject.

Finally, we have the superb 105, which occurs in Thorpe's sonnet order as a puzzling summation: the poet's praise is not idolatry because the worshiped friend embodies a trinity of virtues, a theme "which wondrous scope affords." By what development has the paralysis of expression described in 102 and 103 led to the continuing and wondrous scope of utterance avowed in 105? One may be fond of meaningful contraries, but 105 scarcely ends a series of them. Nor does it seem to function with ensuing sonnets.

I suggest that 105 was intended to follow something more to the point than sonnets at sixes and sevens with its peroration. I also suggest that 100–101 were meant to invoke Shakespeare's Muse not to truncated irrelevance but to the large subject they prescribe. If, for reasons offered earlier, these two sonnets are allowed to begin our group of eleven, and if 105 is allowed to conclude it, Shakespeare's adjuration, "Then do thy office, Muse," will perhaps have been heeded.

The next question is whether 63–68 can be set off, as IV C requires, from preceding and following sonnets in Q. The only good test of this is a close reading of 59–74. Although common-places on the Former Age, Time's scythe, and preserving verse appear in 59 and 60, the next two sonnets on broken sleep and self-love offer nothing, except the "tanned antiquity" of 62, which might preface 63–68. Four succeeding sonnets, 69–72, deal with a guilt in the friend and a shame in the poet quite out of keeping with 63–68. The test we are applying at the moment asks only whether sonnets relocated immediately before and after 63–68 break any genuine link between that group and sonnets which precede and follow it in Q. I can find no close link which could be broken, but Tucker Brooke and T. W. Baldwin have suggested several.

Brooke's rearrangement renumbers certain sonnets; but in what follows here, Q numbering replaces any he may have substituted. He held with some other editors (page 41 of his edition) that 62 with its reference to Shakespeare's "tanned antiquity" leads to 63: "Against my love shall be as I am now," i.e., "crushed and o'erworn" by Time. For this problem of connection, see the commentary on restored poem IV A, page 147.

Brooke's further connection (pages 41–42) of 66–68 with 69–70, after which he places 94–96, is as doubtful as any grouping can be in the absence of multiple evidence such as we have been using. In addition, Brooke appears to assume that sonnet 67 ("Ah wherefore with infection should he live . . . ?") points to the friend as sharing the world's infection; hence his relation of it to 69 and subsequent sonnets on the friend's lapse into evil. I understand 67 to mean that the friend's goodness is incongruous with an impiety "graced" by his presence. If this is the correct reading, Brooke's sequence here becomes very questionable.

Before considering Professor Baldwin's linkage of 63 ff. with preceding sonnets, we may glance at two of his observations which affect the general problem. (All references here are to his book, *On the Literary Genetics of Shakespeare's Poems and Sonnets* [1950].) He establishes Ovid as a source for much of the 63–68 sequence and for three of the five sonnets I add to it (see his index references to the sonnets involved). Baldwin also dates many of these sonnets, and his chronology is on the whole compatible with my belief that the sonnets form a group. The date given sonnet 19 is one exception (pages 217–220). It is likely, however, that Professor Baldwin's deductions of date from the relation of sonnets to other works of Shakespeare are sometimes more specific than the evidence warrants—if only because Shakespeare, like most writers, could repeat ideas at fairly wide intervals and in the repetition either expand or condense his original material. The reader must judge this for himself.

In any event Baldwin's theory that sonnets 55–64 were composed in chronological order (because some of them reflect the order of certain passages in Ovid) cannot be extended as proof that 63–68 connect with the preceding Q series. That 63 and 64 may show a continuation of the source for some previous sonnets in no way keeps the two from belonging to a separate composition, or for that matter, even links them closely in time of writing with 55 ff. Shakespeare could, and did, use successive bits in a compendious source for different purposes, and at widely different times.

Finally, with reference to a purely cognate relation between 55, 59–60, 62, and 63–68 (the only necessary relation implied by Brooke and Baldwin), note that these sonnets remain here in context, that of restored Group IV.

6. In an essay "Sonnets 127–154," *Shakespeare 1564–1964* (Brown University Studies, 1964), I suggest substantially this optimum order. As explained, I now think it best to accept Q's order in a doubtful case. In any event, the issue is not critical, since the same sonnets are combined in a group by either rearrangement.

NOTES TO CHAPTER III

1. In verifying this estimate with the restored order as shown on pages 40–41, note that an intact sequence preserved in Q occasionally represents more than one restored poem. Thus, 1–17 preserves I A and B entire; 43–45 preserves the last sonnet of II C and the first two of II D; 87–93 preserves the last four sonnets of II G and the first three of II H; and 97–101 preserves IV B intact, followed by the first two sonnets of IV C. This means, for present purposes, that since 91–93 (see II H, above) is involved in

the 'second class' of verification, so is 87–90; that since 100–101 is likewise involved, so is 97–99.

In counting the number of restored sequences preserved intact by Q I have included 144 143 among them—as an intact but transposed pair. Later discussion will explain this.

2. In other words, nothing in this reconstruction of disarrangement attempts the impossible—a prescription of time order for dislocations that neither lead to others nor result from others. For example (with reference to Table B, page 260), the disarrangement of 52 and 56 (of II E) could have occurred at any time; the initial displacement of 32 (of III B) allowing it to merge with 33–35 (of II J) is most plausibly (but not necessarily) assumed as prior to a mingling of groups II and III; but the final disarrangement of 32–42 (pages 262 ff.) must be inferred as subsequent to the group mingling that brings 32 and 33–42 together.

3. See Geoffrey Bullough, ed., *Poems and Dramas of Fulke Greville* (New York, 1945), I, 27–29, and photocopies opposite pages 32 and 112. In the *Caelica* manuscript not only the sonnets but the pages are numbered.

4. In the *Caelica* manuscript the distribution of sonnets on leaves is not uniform because of the varying length of Greville's 'sonnets,' some running to 30 lines or more. But the scribe normally begins a new page with each new sonnet. See Bullough, I, 266.

Besides the *Caelica* manuscript, two editions and two manuscripts of Constable's sonnets supply information on the usage implied by V B. For the Constable material, I am indebted to Joan Grundy's, *The Poems of Henry Constable* (Liverpool, 1960).

In Harleian MS. 7553, Constable's seventeen "Spiritual Sonnets" appear on ff. 32–40, two to a leaf, recto-verso, with apparent exception of the final sonnet on an end leaf by itself. There is no numbering, although the sonnets have titles which appear to be in ink different from that used in the text (Grundy, pages 101–102, 183). Except for presence of the titles, the manuscript is exactly in the form of our hypothetical manuscript for V B.

Three different arrangements of twenty-one Constable sonnets (unrelated to the "Spiritual Sonnets" of Harleian MS. 7553) offer an interesting problem which can be solved, I think, only by assuming an earlier manuscript source of the kind I infer for much of the Shakespeare series. In content, the Harington manuscript, the 1592 *Diana*, and the first twenty-one sonnets of the 1594 *Diana* are substantially the same except for the sonnet order (Grundy, pages 87–89, 255–256). The sonnets from 1 to 10 in the Harington sequence are the sonnets that 1592 presents as 1, 3, 5, 7, 11, 13, 15, 17, 19, 21 (Harington omits number 9 of the 1592 order). The sonnets from 11 to 21 in Harington are those appearing in 1592 as 2, 4, 6, 8, 10, 12, 14, 16, 18, 22, 20. The 1594 sequence is similar to the Harington; in terms of the 1592 sonnets, it runs 1, 3, 5, 7, 9, 11, 13, 15, 17, and a substitution for 19; then follows 8, 2, 4, 10, 12, 14, 16, 18, 20, 22, 6. Thus, so far as the twenty-one sonnets are concerned, the Harington manuscript and the 1592 and 1594 editions apparently stem from the same source. Kenneth Muir (*NQ*, CXCIX [1954], 424–425) explains the strangely separate grouping, in Harington and 1594, of the 1592 odds and evens by assuming an original manuscript with the sonnets arranged in two parallel columns. The copyist responsible for 1592 read this text crosswise, and in transcribing it proceeded from each sonnet in the left column to the opposite one in the right column. The Harington copyist worked down the left column, finished it, and then transcribed the right column. (Mr. Muir's account allows for deviations which cannot be discussed here.) Thus, in sonnet content Harington's 1, 2, 3, 4 . . . duplicate 1592's 1, 3, 5, 7 . . . ; Harington's 11, 12, 13, 14 . . . reproduce 1592's 2, 4, 6, 8 . . .

One difficulty with Mr. Muir's theory is that it requires either an original manuscript page of some three or four feet in length—one that could contain columns having eleven sonnets—or else a copyist (for Harington) who for two or more consecutive pages could follow the left column only, and then double back to transcribe the right column from the same pages. I offer a different explanation: an original manuscript in eleven loose leaves with the sonnets, in the 1592 order, running two to the leaf, recto-verso. This, of course, is the kind of manuscript I have inferred for V B and other restored poems. The 1592 copyist accurately followed its order from page to page, but the Harington scribe worked from leaf to leaf, first copying all the recto sonnets (odd numbers in the 1592 order). As he finished each sonnet he discarded the original manuscript leaf recto side up, thus completing a pile with 11^r on top. Then he turned the pile over and addressed himself in the same way to the verso sides (2, 4, 6, etc.—even numbers in the 1592 arrangement). In this process, the Harington copyist skipped the ninth sonnet (5^v) and transcribed his last two sonnets in reverse order. If the 1594 copyist or compositor worked from the same original manuscript, he followed a similar course, although he produced a rearrangement, accidentally and otherwise, as he moved through the verso sequence (note the differences between Harington and 1594 in their rendition of the 1592 even numbers, and see Muir and Grundy for evidence of editorial rearrangement in 1594).

This explanation of a memorable confusion implies, of course, that 1592 correctly reproduces the original manuscript order, while Harington and 1594 do not. Why should the latter two contain the same error? If the original manuscript had numbered leaves, the numbers (from 1 to 11) would have been on the recto sides only and could have implied not the leaf order but the sonnet order. Hence a rendering by Harington and 1594 of the recto sonnets first. It is worth noting that, except for the Harington copyist's missing the sonnet on 5^v, both his arrangement and 1594 reproduce the assumed recto order but depart accidentally or intentionally from the verso order, the one that would have been without leaf numbers.

Miss Grundy concedes that the Harington sonnet order is clearly superior to that of 1592 only "in one small point" (page 89). Further, it is plain that none of the three Constable texts— Harington, 1592, or 1594—approximates the order of these sonnets in the authoritative Todd manuscript. Thus my explanation would imply not that the 1592 scribe or compositor produced the right sonnet order, but that he copied accurately from the text placed before him.

The nature of Harleian MS. 7553 (Constable's "Spiritual Sonnets") and my explanation, if valid, of sequential variants in three other Constable texts suggest that the manuscript form attributed to V B was not unusual. A practice of inscribing sonnets two to a leaf, recto-verso, is borne out by the Harleian manuscript, and an assumed original manuscript of the same kind accounts for the *Diana* confusion without complication. An assumption that can do this and can also explain sequential difficulties in Shakespeare's text may prove useful.

5. See G. W. Williams, "Setting by Formes in Quarto Printing," *Studies in Bibliography*, 11 (1958). The compositor begins with the first page of a signature whether the setting is seriatim by pages or by formes with cast-off copy—if the outer forme precedes the inner.

6. Unless, of course, 19 and 21 were also insertions (not in primary copy) at this point.

7. An intact Q fragment is any part of a restored poem isolated in Q, the isolated part having its sonnets in proper order. Thus, 33–35 of II J is an intact fragment; 94–96 is not—because in the restored sequence the order is 95–96 94.

8. If this is not otherwise apparent, note again the drastic consequences produced by only four sonnets, 33, 40, 108, 111, had they appeared in Q not as they do, but as isolated singles (page 290).

❧ GENERAL INDEX

THE NATURE of this book has required, in Chapters I and III, a great deal of classification, tabulation, and systematic cross reference. And in Chapter II the emended sonnet order appears in tabular form with commentary adjoining each of its divisions and subdivisions. Almost any essential element of the text or item of discussion can be found readily by consulting the Contents (page ix) and by proceeding from there to the desired chapter, section, or part of a section. Thus, since a fully detailed index would be largely redundant, the index below calls attention to tables and lists that serve as location guides, indicates central items not specifically mentioned in the tables and lists, and registers the names of persons cited in discussion.

There are two aids for the finding of individual sonnets and primary commentary addressed to them (which is always adjacent to the text): the table on page x and the Index of First Lines on page 313. The emended sonnet order in condensed tabular form appears on pages 40–41.

Redpath, Theodore, 197, 298 n. 2
Rollins, Hyder, 1, 8–9, 24, 29
Rowse, A. L., 297 n. 2
'Run-on,' defined, 12

Segments: disarrangement of restored groups into, 237–272;
table of, 255; anomalies in pattern of, 253–267, 270; mingling
of manuscripts responsible for,
256–272 *passim*
Spelling and punctuation of sonnets in this edition, 4
'Syntactical link,' defined, 12

Thorpe, Thomas, 1, 2, 7, 15, 276,
277, 285, 301

'Unattached sonnets' in Q, table
of, 22

Verification: forms of, *see* Contents, ix; evidence of not limited to chapter so titled, 231;
problem of tautology in, 246–
250, 269–274, 293–294; ultimate
nature of, 262–265, 272–274,
294–295. *See also* 'Multiple factor test,' Groups

Williams, G. W., 298 n. 3, 308 n.
5
Wilson, John Dover, 297 n. 5
Wolff, M. J., 6

❧ Index Of First Lines